NEW HOME SALES MANAGEMENT

How To Build and Lead A Winning Team

Bonnie Alfriend

AND

Richard Tiller

Printed in the U.S.A. by Alfriend And Associates, Incorporated
2984 Cormorant Road, Pebble Beach, CA 93953
ISBN: 0-9639500-1-0

ACKNOWLEDGMENTS

I have watched the success and failure of hundreds of people. Clearly it is the character possessed by a person that is the most distinguishing trait which makes for success. With this thought in mind I would like to acknowledge with gratitude the many who have influenced my career through their noble and brilliant leadership. In particular my humble appreciation goes to Dave Stone, and to Bob Schultz, President, New Home Specialist Companies — my mentors extraordinaire. Dave Stone, who was there from the start, I personally credit for giving me the inspiration to channel my energies in the right direction. Bob Schultz, my dear friend and colleague, has so graciously shared his time and expertise to groom me into further service for our great industry. Thank you from the bottom of my heart.

And to my family who always nourishes my life with their unconditional love.

— Bonnie

I want to express my appreciation to the hundreds of salespeople and managers across the country who have enriched the past five years of my life in one-on-one training and consulting. Thank you for allowing me to share your ideas with others, helping them to improve their careers through your experiences and successes.

— Richard

DEDICATIONS

This book is dedicated to Kyle and Kim, who make me proud to be called Mom. You bring me the greatest joy I have ever known.

— Bonnie

This book is also dedicated to my wife, Chris, and to our children, Laura and Christopher. You have been the most wonderful blessing I can imagine.

— Richard

Contents

PART ONE

MANAGEMENT

"WHAT HAVE I BECOME?"

Imagine that it is a few minutes before 6:00 in the evening on a Sunday in August. Your assignment is to sell out your company's toughest community. The quota is two sales per month; you have been selling three. You are the company's number one troubleshooter; that is why they gave you this community. Some days you would settle for being only the second best salesperson. Life might be easier and you would probably make more money. At times it's tough to watch those big numbers being posted at the easier communities while your boss keeps saying, "We're counting on you. You're the only one who can make this job turn a profit."

Your last customer left an hour ago, and now you are preparing your paperwork for the Monday morning sales meeting. The phone rings. It's your boss, the vice president of sales and marketing.

"Linda," he says, "I need to see you prior to tomorrow's group meeting. Can you be in my office at 8:00?"

"Sure, Bill, what's up?"

"I can't tell you now," the boss answers. "I'll see you at eight."

"OK, I'll be there," you answer, trying to sound composed and upbeat. The truth is, panic just consumed you. If it were something good, he would have told you. It must be something bad. How bad? And why? You haven't been setting the world on fire, but your numbers have been decent, and you have exceeded company quotas. What kind of trouble could you be in?

Politics! It's got to be politics. Sure, there are some people on the sales team who are jealous of you. But what harm could they have done? Has somebody started a rumor? Would Bill actually fall for that type of maneuvering? You've earned his trust. You've paid your dues. You deserve better.

The paranoia persists. You just can't shake it, even though logic tells you there's no basis for it. A slow community can do that to you. Quickly, ever so quickly, your confidence is eroded.

Your sales have been okay, but with only eight customers a week, what can Bill expect? And look at all the homeowner problems dating back to before you even arrived on site. For the most part, you've been able to keep yourself motivated. Things sure are a lot better now than when you first took over. You've come up with some great ideas, solved many problems, and doubled the closing ratio, allowing your builder to increase prices. What more can they expect? Yet tonight you're depressed. Why couldn't Bill have told you what the problem was? Sometimes this job can be so lonely!

The next morning you get to Bill's office at 7:55. "Come on in," he says. "Have a seat."

He seems fine, but still you need to test the water. "How are you this morning, Bill?"

"I'm doing fine, Linda. Although I must admit, I'm a little tired, which is what I wanted to talk to you about."

"*You're* a little tired?" you want to say. "Thanks to you, I barely slept two hours." But instead you ask, "Is there anything I can do to help?"

"Well, Linda, as a matter of fact, there is. We have six communities up and running, and by the end of the year we'll have eight. It's getting to be more than one person can handle. I need a sales director, and I'd like it to be you, if you're interested."

Unbelievable! You knew a sales director would be needed, and you've certainly earned the position, but it never occurred to you that today would be the day. After six years in the business, and all the times you went that extra mile for the company, it's finally paying off. It's really happening!

"I'd like to discuss the details of the job with you," Bill continues, "and, if it sounds like what you want, I'd like to make the announcement during our meeting."

After briefly discussing the job description, you accept. With a feeling of excitement and a tremendous sense of satisfaction, you head for the meeting. Suddenly, on the way to the conference room, one question overwhelms you: "WHAT HAVE I BECOME?"

* * *

Before we move on to answering this enormous question, let us first take a look at three areas of Bill's presentation to Linda regarding the position of sales director. They will give you a preliminary insight into the awesome responsibility of managing people.

First, his phone call should have been more sensitive. He could have at least included a few words like, "I'd rather tell you in person than over the phone. Don't worry, you'll like what you hear. Enjoy your evening."

Second, if Bill was ready to offer the position to Linda today, it should not have come as a complete surprise. The job of sales director takes preparation and training. A decision to offer (or accept) such a position requires several honest conversations over a period of time, and a great deal of soul-searching by both the manager and the candidate. Too often the job of sales director is pursued (or given) for the wrong reasons, as we will discuss later in this chapter.

Third, if for some reason it was not possible to go through a preparation process, then half an hour is not enough time between the offer and the announcement. The candidate needs time to make sure all of his or her questions are answered and the transition process is mapped out. In the situation cited above, Linda was moving from her position as a peer and colleague with the sales team to a position as their supervisor. She needs time not only to absorb the transition herself, but also to receive counseling on how to handle reactions from the team. This is not a change to be handled lightly.

* * *

Now back to the question, "What have I become?" The following is a summary of "the right stuff" for new home sales management. It will help you create a vision of yourself as a sales director. It is very important to create this vision and then keep it intact. This does not mean the image cannot change. It can always improve, but it should never deteriorate or grow dim. The clearer your vision of yourself as a sales director is, the better your chances of fulfilling that vision. Napoleon Hill once said, "Man will become what man thinks about most of the time." Focus on the image of yourself in the role of a productive, effective sales director. The mental picture will have a profound effect on your actions.

If you have not already created this vision, begin by using the following attributes as your outline. Then fill in the details and the colors with your own unique strengths, personality, character and values.

A LEADER, BOSS AND MANAGER

Why do we list these three roles as a single item? After all, they are so very different. We have combined them here in order to emphasize the fact that they work together. It is fashionable to say that "a manager should be a leader, not a boss." While the intent of this statement is enlightened benevolence, it has its pitfalls. The functions of manager, leader and boss are three sides of the same triangle. A manager organizes and directs the team. A leader creates and conveys the team's vision. He or she then motivates and supports the team in its pursuit of that vision. A boss uses authority wisely to defend the team's high standards, and keeps the pursuit of the vision a priority. The boss keeps things fair.

In Linda's case, she has moved from a position of "peer" to a position of "boss" in an instant. This can be a very complex, delicate transition. It can produce more anxiety than any other challenge a sales director will ever face. In Chapter Two we will explore the concept of leadership in detail, and how to complete the transition from peer to boss successfully. We will also discuss ways to combine the roles of "leader," "boss" and "manager" to become an effective sales director.

A PLANNER

A sales director is a careful planner. As a salesperson, your primary concern was planning your own job. Now you are now planning for an entire team. Your new challenge contains many more elements than the old one. Your team provides you with a variety of skills and personalities to manage and support. Other pieces of your puzzle include department goals, product design, pricing, marketing strategy, opening new communities, generating and sustaining momentum at these communities, and, perhaps most important of all, communication.

You are creating a broad vision. At the same time, you are responsible for managing an infinite number of details. You are now focused on people, paper and profits.

An Administrator

Until you become a sales director, it is hard to imagine how much of that position is administrative. While the job description of a sales director can vary significantly from one company to the next, organizational ability is always critical. The excuse that "salespeople usually don't focus on paperwork" won't hold water any more. You should learn as much about your company's paperwork system as possible in your first two weeks as sales director. If you hate paperwork, you will have to change in order to become a successful sales director. There's no way around it.

Time management also becomes more complex, so we will devote Chapter 6 to that topic. Many people have asked what percentage of time should be devoted to people vs. paper. Our belief is that in order to keep your department running effectively over the long term, you should divide your time equally between the two: 50% to administrative tasks and 50% to your greatest asset — your sales team.

A Support System

Your most important function as a sales director is supporting your sales team. Your success in this area determines the level of confidence your salespeople will give you as their leader, boss and manager. Your ability to provide a support system will make or break your credibility. Your credibility, in turn, will make or break your success.

If you are not yet a sales director, but are considering it as a possible goal, ask yourself this soul-searching question: "WHY DO I REALLY WANT TO BE A MANAGER?" Remember that your goal should be to have the job which is most personally rewarding, not just the one with the best-sounding title. Many sales directors wind up realizing that on-site sales offered them greater personal satisfaction than management. They return to sales with renewed enthusiasm and a deeper sense of purpose.

Unfortunately, many salespeople pursue the job of sales director for one of the following reasons:

• They want the title.
• They want the power. (The power of the sales director position is often an illusion.)

- They want weekends off. (Sales management is *not* a Monday-through-Friday, 9-to-5 job.)
- They are tired of dealing with the public.
- They view it as a stepping stone to an executive position.
- They believe it will be more financially rewarding than sales. (In fact, top sales professionals frequently earn more than sales directors.)

As fringe benefits, all of the above are legitimate. The title does have an element of prestige attached to it. Decision making does occur at a higher level. You will have opportunities to pursue weekend activities more as a sales director than you can as a salesperson. You will not usually have to face the public every day. You may even become a vice president. However, it is important to view these luxuries only as fringe benefits of the sales director position, not as reasons to pursue it. *The best reason to pursue a career in management is the genuine desire to provide the best possible support system for your sales team.* Contributing to the development of quality salespeople must be your number one motivation. Offering this support includes a commitment to developing a broad range of management skills. There are seven support skills which are crucial to your success as a sales director.

1. A STABILIZER

An effective sales director is a source of stability in a tumultuous profession. In our story of Linda and Bill, we saw one way that the loneliness and stress of new home sales can take its toll. In a job with so much uncertainty (at times even seeming "unfair"), salespeople must sometimes hope that their boss can be the anchor which will keep them from being "lost at sea." To provide the kind of stabilizing support which gives a sales team the feelings of hope to keep going, sales directors must demonstrate four virtues:

- OPTIMISM — not blind, reckless optimism, but a sincere belief that tomorrow offers the *potential* to be better than today.
- CONFIDENCE — the sales director's belief that his or her expertise, and the expertise of the team, will contribute to a "better tomorrow."
- DECISIVENESS — a willingness to make those decisions necessary to meet challenges and keep the team moving forward.
- CONSISTENCY — creating a sense of security that the next decision will

be compatible with the last one. In the homebuilding industry, a manager's failure to demonstrate consistency can often destroy the morale of the sales team. Consistency not only increases the sales team's confidence, it also helps train them to use *your* thought processes to make their own decisions.

2. A PROBLEM SOLVER

We said earlier that a sales director's credibility grows out of his or her ability to provide an effective support system to the team. Nowhere is this support more visible than in problem solving. Using the four virtues of a stabilizer, a sales director must be able to provide solutions to sales challenges with optimism, confidence, decisiveness and consistency. The manager must also train salespeople to develop these same four virtues in order to increase their own problem-solving ability.

3. A TRAINER

The ability to train is a valuable asset for a sales director. However, many successful sales directors do not have this ability themselves. While they may not be gifted trainers, they are able to fulfill their commitment to training by *taking responsibility* for providing a comprehensive, continuous training program for veterans as well as rookies. Hiring only veterans does not relieve the sales director of the responsibility to provide consistent training for every member of the team. The best way to create loyalty, motivate and retain salespeople is by providing them the tools and knowledge for success.

This obligation is such an important part of sales management that we will devote three chapters (Seven, Eight and Nine) to helping you offer the best training support possible.

4. A COACH

This is one type of training for which a sales director should take *personal* responsibility. No training program is really complete without personal coaching to help salespeople sharpen their skills and maintain their competitive edge. Even top producers need continuous coaching, just as star athletes do. Each salesperson can have more than one coach, but you must be included among them.

Fulfilling this responsibility will benefit you as well as your salespeople. Coaching will make you more aware of their challenges and will give you a better understanding of what is happening on the front lines. It will also enhance your own position of leadership by demonstrating your personal commitment to the success of each of your salespeople.

5. A MENTOR

A mentor is different than a trainer or a coach, although all three responsibilities overlap. Like coaching, mentoring is a personal commitment. However, mentoring is broader in scope. A mentor is sometimes a trainer and sometimes a coach, but is also a *counselor*, even occasionally a *confidant*. Funk and Wagnalls dictionary defines mentor as "a wise and trusted teacher or guide."

While you must find the time for personal coaching of each salesperson on your team, it will not always be possible for you to provide personal mentoring to everyone. Nevertheless, every salesperson should have a mentor, even if it is not you. Salespeople often are fine mentors for their colleagues. If you create a formalized mentoring program using salespeople as mentors, just be careful who you choose. We will discuss mentoring in detail in Chapter Eight.

While there may not be enough hours in the week for you to bear the mentoring responsibility alone, it is important for your salespeople to know that you are at least available to serve as "a wise and trusted teacher or guide" if they turn to you with a mentoring need.

6. A MOTIVATOR

This, too, is a critical responsibility for a sales director, and it also warrants three chapters (Ten through Twelve). New home sales can be exhilarating or discouraging, energizing or exhausting. While salespeople can often motivate themselves, motivation is still one of your most important contributions. Contests and incentives can provide temporary stimulation. True motivation is much more profound. It involves belief in one's self and in one's mission. It demands a quality support system which provides appreciation and recognition as well as direction and encouragement. Occasionally, motivation requires discipline. For this reason, the final element of a support system requires you to become a disciplinarian.

7. A DISCIPLINARIAN

Since "disciplinarian" may have an unpleasant ring to it, we assure you that we don't mean "dictator" or "power-hungry egomaniac." We mean taking responsibility for creating or maintaining your team's high standards. Like inconsistency, a failure to enforce discipline can devastate the morale of a sales team. While some people may not like discipline to be administered to them, the team still looks to you for justice. They want their own good actions to be rewarded, and they want to know that the bad actions of others will bring consequences. It is incumbent upon sales managers to set and enforce standards of performance. The foundation for discipline is already in the minds of your salespeople. All you have to do is administer it fairly to everyone.

SUMMARY

When you accept the position of sales director, this is *what you have become*:

1) Leader, Boss and Manager
2) Planner
3) Administrator
4) Support System
   • Stabilizer
   • Problem Solver
   • Trainer
   • Coach
   • Mentor
   • Motivator
   • Disciplinarian

Sales management is a wonderfully rewarding career, as long as you approach it as a career. As a stepping stone or an escape it can bring tremendous disappointment.

This book was written for you if you:
- are already a sales director,
- want to be a sales director, or
- currently supervise one or more sales directors.

We will explain the skills and mentality that make a top flight sales director. The information in this book is based on the successes and failures of many who have gone before.

The life of a sales manager is an adventure unlike any other. It offers an enriching variety of challenges, and an opportunity to enhance the quality of life of many people whose lives you will touch in different ways.

We will begin our adventure by visiting the exciting world of leadership.

HOW TO BECOME AN
EFFECTIVE LEADER

In the year 333 B.C., Alexander the Great of Macedon faced King Darius of Persia at the Battle of Issus. While Alexander's army was numbered at about 35,000 men, Darius' force was over 200,000. A brilliant strategist and a great leader, Alexander fought shoulder to shoulder with his troops to achieve a remarkable victory against overwhelming odds. Alexander's confidence, courage and determination were contagious. Each member of his "team" trusted in the skill and commitment of their leader.

Darius' army, on the other hand, degenerated into demoralized chaos with word that their leader, despite his enormous advantage, had fled the scene. As Alexander thrashed the enemy alongside his troops, Darius literally headed for the hills, and his troops soon followed. What an incredible difference a leader can make!

WHAT MAKES A LEADER?

In Chapter One we described a sales director as a LEADER, a BOSS and a MANAGER. We said that a LEADER "creates and conveys the team's vision" and then "motivates and supports the team in its pursuit of that vision." Leaders cannot depend solely on authority to get results. Instead they must use their *influence* to get people to commit themselves to action, and then to follow through on their actions until the final result is achieved. A BOSS "uses authority wisely to defend the team's high standards, and keeps the pursuit of the vision a high priority. The boss keeps things fair." A MANAGER "organizes and directs the team."

So much for definitions. The challenge is, "How do I make all of this happen in real life? I only became a manager yesterday. Who am I today, and who should I be tomorrow? How can I combine all three of these identities to become a successful, respected sales director as quickly as possible?"

Here is how your three different identities work together. The instant you become a sales manager:

- A BOSS is what you *are*. This is a plain fact that needs only a corporate chart to prove. Your goal as a boss is to be fair and wise.
- The job of MANAGER is what you *do*. Your goal is to do it competently, intelligently and effectively.
- A LEADER is what you will *become*, once you *earn the right*. Your goal now is to develop a *leadership demeanor* so that your team will acknowledge you as a person worth following.

Being a successful "boss" and "manager" are day-to-day challenges, and will be discussed throughout this book. For the moment, let's take a closer look at how a newly-hired sales director becomes a leader. To begin, we will address two closely related questions which most sales directors ask (and should ask) as soon as they assume their new responsibilities:

- "What can I do to make my sales team *accept* me as their leader?"
- "How will my team *judge* whether or not I am a successful manager?"

Both of these questions relate to the same basic issue: "How do I prove myself?"

When all of the leadership rhetoric and management philosophy are stripped away, sales directors are judged by their people primarily on their ability to *get things done*. While there is certainly a lot more to successful management, showing that you can get things done is the fastest and most effective way to establish a position of leadership in a residential sales department. Salespeople need a leader who can solve problems.

A sales director's most important function and most valuable contribution is to *provide an effective support system for the sales team*. This is the team's primary need. Just as in sales, the most effective way to develop a position of credibility and strength is to *fulfill your "customer's" needs*. In sales, customers will surrender control and follow the lead of a salesperson if, and only if, the salesperson is fulfulling their needs. This principle works the same in sales management. The one difference is that *the sales director's "customer" is the salesperson*. While the sales director is the *boss*, the salesperson is the *customer*. This is a delicate balance to be sure.

Just as in sales, in order to fulfill your customer's needs you must first determine what those needs are. If you are moving directly from sales into management within the same company (or division), you have a head start because you already know many of the team's needs. You can begin assuming leadership by taking five steps to "identify and fulfill your customers' needs."

1) Make a list of all the good support benefits you felt that management provided for you as a salesperson.
2) Make another list of the types of management support you feel you needed but did not get.
3) Have a discussion with each of your salespeople individually to discover what kinds of management support *they* believe are most important. An important benefit of these one-on-one discussions is that they enable you to convey your perspective and to hear those of your salespeople. Once these discussions are completed, you may choose to discuss some of the issues with the group as a whole at your next sales meeting.
4) Combine your three "needs" lists and eliminate any items you believe are inappropriate or impossible to fulfill. It is important to give a thorough explanation for those items you delete to show you have considered all input. The manager who believes that explanations are unnecessary will fail as a leader.
5) With the items on your finalized list, commit to a specific plan for providing each of these management support benefits to your sales team. Taking this approach in the beginning will go a long way in establishing you as a sincere, credible leader.

Once you begin to develop your position of leadership by creating a support system, how do you continue building leadership? Here are seven priorities which demand your focus throughout your management career.

7 PRIORITIES FOR SUCCESSFUL LEADERSHIP

The first priority takes the idea of a support system a step farther.

1) BE SUPPORTIVE

"Being supportive" takes more long-term effort than "creating a support system." The creation of the system involves thinking, planning and writing. "Being supportive" means *doing* — bringing your *commitment* to life through *action*.

2) BE CONSISTENT

A manager's level of consistency has a tremendous effect on a sales team's level of morale, and consequently its level of motivation. While management frequently requires spontaneity and creativity, a sales manager must be consistent in dealing with salespeople and sales policy. Salespeople who are frustrated frequently cite management inconsistency as the primary source of their feeling. They express their frustration in ways like this:

"We never know if we're doing the right thing or not."
"The rules keep changing from day to day."
"I'll wait until the boss is in a good mood to present this offer."
"If it had been someone else instead of me, the answer would have been yes."
"What good is having a policy when you never know if it's going to be enforced?"

Salespeople need to know:

• The minimum standard of excellence expected of them.
• The extent of their decision-making authority.
• Which solutions to a particular problem are acceptable and which are not.
• Their boss is rational, intelligent, consistent and fair, and will not give in to squeaky wheels and political pressures.

This does not mean all salespeople must be treated exactly the same way. Salespeople who act more responsibly are often rewarded with more responsibility. It is the principles and the reasoning process behind the way salespeople are treated which must remain consistent.

This also does not mean you must avoid change. You can implement change whenever you believe it is necessary. Just explain the change honestly and openly to everyone who is affected, and make sure that you put it in writing.

Consistency does not mean keeping everything status quo forever. It means being fair, and having a pattern of behavior and decision making which can be understood and relied upon by your salespeople.

3) ENSURE COMMUNICATION

This is a big one! Huge, in fact! The homebuilding industry is plagued by communication problems. Not all of these problems can be addressed by a sales director, but some of them can. Examples of such problems can appear in communication between:

• Management and sales (the main office and the field).
• Sales and production.
• Sales and lenders.
• Sales and customer service.
• Sales and customers.

The sales director frequently winds up at the center of each of these five communication paths. The problem in communication breakdown is not only a lack of communication skills, but also a lack of *desire* to communicate.

Does this mean that you, the sales director, should take responsibility for each of these different avenues of communication? You may have to. Why? Because you may be the one person who is most aware, most motivated and best equipped to improve the communication system. Your livelihood and the livelihood of your team depend on it. It is your sales team who ultimately bears the burden of misunderstood and undelivered promises.

What can you do, as the *leader* of a sales department, to ensure better communication?

- Make a list of all areas where you know communication needs to be improved, and write down a plan of what steps you personally can take to improve it.
- Take personal initiative in any communication which involves you directly. Don't wait for co-workers to communicate with you. Take the lead in the communication responsibilities.
- Encourage others to follow your lead. Tell them you need and expect to be kept informed, just as you have done for them. Thank them when they do provide the communication you need.
- Follow up to see that your communication initiatives are paying off, and be as persistent as necessary to see that communication problems are being addressed by all parties involved.
- Teach your salespeople the need for them to take similar initiatives so that problems can be avoided before they become sales hazards.
- Teach salespeople to convey correct expectations to customers. A good salesperson can sell just as successfully by conveying correct expectations as incorrect ones.

Taking the *initiative* in the communication process of the company is very important. Equally important is the personal communication between you and each of your salespeople. You were an excellent communicator as a salesperson. Those same communication skills will bring you success as a sales manager.

Listening
Listening is also as important in sales management as it was in sales. Make sure you know what the salesperson is saying so that you will understand his or her needs. If you are not sure, ask more questions.

As in sales, follow up listening with feedback. Let the salesperson know what you think and what you will do. Do not avoid giving feedback just to avoid a confrontation. If there must be a confrontation, it is best for it to be face-to-face, honest and private. A confrontation can be gentle and still be direct. The goals in these types of confrontations are to increase understanding on both sides, protect mutual respect, and achieve a resolution.

Explanation

When you share a decision or plan, follow it up with an explanation to whatever extent is necessary. Your salespeople do not have to agree with you, but they do need to understand you and respect the action you have taken. Try to explain your thought process as clearly as possible in an attempt to persuade them, knowing that even when they are not persuaded they are at least informed.

4) Be Decisive

We said earlier that your success as a sales director will be judged largely on your ability to *get things done*. As a manager you will be expected to *provide answers*. In situations where you are unable to *give* an answer, you must be able to *get* an answer. And they must be *honest* answers. Salespeople suffer tremendous frustration at the hands of indecisive managers. It can be demoralizing to find out that the answer one received turned out to have a different meaning than what they originally understood. There must be no hedging and no tricks when it comes to providing answers to salespeople. Your responsibility is to communicate what they *need* to know, not just what they want to know. If your answer is not what your salespeople want to hear, you must face the situation head-on with as clear an explanation as you can provide.

There is a big difference between being "decisive" and being "impulsive." Being decisive means offering sound, firm decisions, and standing behind those decisions with consistency (assuming that the decision was a correct one). Your goal as a decisive manager is to *resolve issues*, and not leave them hanging. You are providing an environment where your salespeople know where they stand, and can pursue their own objectives with confidence.

The goal is to be decisive without being impulsive. Funk and Wagnalls dictionary defines "impulsive" as "actuated by impulse rather than by reflection." It defines an "impulse" as "a sudden, unreasoned inclination to action, often induced by an emotion, etc." The reason that this distinction is so important in management is that our society frequently rewards impulsiveness with such accolades as "swashbuckling," "courageous," "action-oriented," and, unfortunately, "decisive." In new home sales management, an enormous amount of damage can be caused by "impulsive" leadership disguised as "decisiveness."

You can be decisive and still be cautious. Being decisive does not mean that you must make every decision instantly. When you are unable to provide your salespeople with an important answer right away, explain your situation and tell them when you will be able to provide an answer. Then do whatever it takes to provide that answer by the deadline you promised. If you honor your commitment, then you have still acted decisively. Your credibility is at stake here, and in management your credibility is the foundation of your success.

If you do not believe that a prompt answer is necessary or possible, tell your salespeople up front. Don't tell them you will get them an answer, and then blame someone else for your failure. Be respectful of the time of other managers, and weigh the true importance of the issue before imposing. Just as your credibility with salespeople is essential, so is your credibility with others in your company. If you become known as "the one who cried wolf," it will eventually undermine your position, as well as the success of your entire department.

There will be times when you will feel overwhelmed. Things seem out of control. There are too many issues. You are exhausted. These are the times when decisiveness can be especially difficult. When you are feeling overwhelmed, it is very important to do everything in your power not to let it show. Stay aware of the consequences that can result when your sales team believes that your job is too much for you. This is another way your credibility can be damaged, and with it the morale of your team. During these discouraging times, your ability to provide answers is as important as ever. The success of your team depends on it.

5) Be a Problem Solver.

Many salespeople do not perceive that they need a boss. What they need is someone in a position of higher authority who can help them solve their toughest challenges.

One of your goals as a manager is to help your salespeople to remain *clearheaded*. The more clearheaded they are, the more *focused* and effective they will be in the field. You can help them to be clearheaded and focused by helping them to solve problems and keep their problems in perspective.

Problem solving is one of the key ingredients of a support system. Your ability to provide assistance in solving sales challenges will enhance your position as a leader.

6) Set a Tone

Setting a tone covers perhaps the broadest territory of the seven priorities for successful leadership, and can also be the hardest to pin down. We could have used the phrases "create an environment" or "set a standard." All are variations on the same theme, and all are intended here by the term "set a tone." We chose our words because we want them to include the "mood" or "feeling" of a sales department.

Suppose an applicant for a sales position asked you, "What's it like to be a part of your team?" You would respond by describing the "tone" of your sales department, including its character, standards, style and feeling. The tone of the department should come from its leader.

As a leader, what kind of tone do you want to set for your sales department? Here are ten characteristics the tone of your department should include.

• A High Standard of Ethics

A commitment to *total honesty* and to *always doing the right thing* provides the cornerstone of a well-run sales department. This is where greatness begins, and where the quality of a leader makes such an important difference. A sales department (or any other group) in which people are looking for shortcuts at someone else's expense, and are shading the truth in the name of expediency, cannot sustain long-term success. One gratifying aspect of our business is that a high standard of ethics really can contribute to a company's success. Nowhere is this more true than in a sales department, and no one can offer a stronger influence than the leader.

• Fairness

Where you find a high standard of ethics, you will usually find fairness. Outstanding performance may earn extra privileges, but the *standards* of the department remain consistent for everyone. Where a tone of fairness exists within a department, it can more easily extend outward to other co-workers and to customers. Fairness means serving the best interests of everyone in a way that promotes a high standard of ethics.

Sometimes fairness requires *toughness*, such as insisting that a salesperson say "no" to a customer, or administering discipline to a salesperson who is frequently late.

Combining fairness with a high standard of ethics produces trust, an important fuel for the engine of a sales team, or a company as a whole.

• *Caring and Sensitivity*

Sales is not just about numbers. It is about the people who produce the numbers. The way to set a tone *of* caring is *by* caring. Combining strong ethics and fairness with personal sensitivity will give your sales team greater confidence. Demonstrating that you personally care about your salespeople, the other departments and your customers will make it easier for everyone else to pursue that ideal.

True caring includes taking time to understand the needs of your team as a whole and each of its individuals. It takes a lot of listening and a lot of patience. But it all pays off when people recognize that a tone of caring and sensitivity characterizes your department.

• *A Positive Outlook*

A successful leader provides *hope* to those who follow. He does not pretend that there's never a cloud in the sky. But he knows where to find shelter before the storm hits, and that the sun will come out again once the storm has passed.

A strong leader does not appear headed for defeat, even when the odds look bad. He stays focused on the objective and how to achieve it. Alexander won at Issus because he provided hope to his outnumbered army at the same time that Darius was taking hope away from his superior force. If Alexander ever lost his positive outlook at Issus, he never let it show.

• *Supportiveness*

We have already talked about supportiveness as a priority for successful leadership. Here we are seeing it as a priority for a successful sales team. By being supportive of the team as a whole and of each of its individuals, a leader can set a tone of supportiveness which becomes a part of the team's "culture." As you create a support system for your salespeople, you are also creating an environment in which your team is more supportive of one another, and of other departments within your company. Through the consistent commitment to better communication which we discussed earlier, you set a tone of cooperation for your team to build upon.

• *Respect*

One of the most frequent complaints we hear from salespeople is that "management does not seem to have any respect for us. They treat the sales department like second-class citizens. Even our own manager treats us that way." We have to be honest about the fact that this is a widespread problem in our industry. Fortunately there are also many companies who do treat salespeople with the respect they have earned by virtue of their value to the company and the many trials they endure on the front lines.

Treating salespeople with respect is a daily activity, not an annual pledge. It involves seeking their input, listening to it and weighing it carefully. It includes attentiveness to *meeting* needs as well as *hearing* them. It requires *open-mindedness*, and willingness to see *their* challenges through *their* eyes and, if necessary, to walk in *their* shoes by helping out in the field. Sales managers should never reach the point where they consider selling to be secondary to the success of the company. That is an insult to customers as well as salespeople.

Successful salespeople work just as much for respect as for a paycheck. The sad thing is that some managers forget this so soon after they move from sales into management. Keep the salesperson's dignity at the top of your support priorities.

• *Appreciation*

Appreciation goes hand-in-hand with respect. Companies who unwittingly demoralize their employees by taking a "no-news-is-good-news" approach to employee recognition are headed for big trouble. "If we're not punishing you, then assume that your work is acceptable." Silence is not a very successful form of motivation. To ignore another is to diminish their value as a human being. Recognition for achievements contributes more to an employee's long-term success than punishment for errors. While both may be necessary, take advantage of every opportunity to provide recognition for positive achievements. The achievement is the behavior you are trying to get them to duplicate. *If you want to create a pattern of behavior, reward the behavior when it occurs at random.*

We will discuss motivation in Chapter Ten. In "setting a tone," it is important to remember that the more you appreciate your salespeople, the more they will appreciate you.

The nature of appreciation is that once it gets started, it grows by itself. Appreciation, recognition and praise are easy concepts for people to get enthusiastic about. Adopt a motto of "striving daily to find each member of your team doing something good, and then be sure to tell them."

• *Responsibility*

One of a leader's greatest triumphs is to establish an environment in which every member of the team takes responsibility. Your willingness to take responsibility sets the standard. You then have the right to expect the same from your team.

Your expectations for their level of responsibility must be clearly stated. The standard must then be consistently enforced.

• *Initiative*

Along with setting a tone of responsibility comes encouraging your salespeople to grow by taking extra initiative. While this does not mean going beyond the rules, it does mean going beyond the minimum. The path to success includes a willingness to undertake tasks that others "don't have time for," or that "aren't in their job description." When your salespeople can see you going the extra mile to help them, you have earned the right to ask them to occasionally do the same for you, or another salesperson, or a customer or the company. "Setting a tone" goes beyond "setting a standard." You are encouraging your team to meet and raise your standard of excellence, and then rewarding their efforts through appreciation and recognition.

Initiative is the beginning of growth.

• *Problem solving*

As a leader, you provide a support system which includes being a problem solver. In setting a tone, you encourage each member of your team to be a problem solver, too. Once you have set a tone for problem solving through your leadership style, you can then require your sales-people to *propose a solution whenever they bring you a problem.* As a leader you offer problem-solving expertise and support, but that does not mean allowing yourself to become a dumping ground for sales problems. Once the salesperson thinks through the problem completely and proposes a solution, you have the option of either accepting the solution or using it as a starting point for a solution-focused discussion. Your problem-solving leadership style sets a tone for a problem-solving sales team.

We have discussed ten ways you can use your position of leadership to set a tone for your sales team. Now let's move on to our final leadership priority.

7) Lead by Example

As a leader, you are also a *role model.* Successful leadership does not permit double standards. At the Battle of Issus Alexander fought shoulder to shoulder with his men. He put his life on the line every time he rode into battle with them. He lived the life which he demanded of his men. He played by the rules he established.

Each of the objectives we discussed for setting a tone provides an opportunity to lead by example.

For example, sales directors who refuse to work weekends quickly lose their credibility, and with it their ability to lead effectively. As a leader, you personally represent the standards of your team.

Making The Transition From Peer to Leader

Balance Your Loyalties

Yesterday you were part of the team. Today you're the manager. This is not always an easy transition, for the manager or the rest of the team.

The good news is that by following the priorities we have been discussing in this chapter, the transition can be smoother and faster.

The first thing to remember is that you are still part of the team. The roles of leader, boss and manager are the roles of a team player. You support the team and protect its standard. The quality of your support will determine the credibility of your leadership.

One challenge you will face is balancing your loyalties to the sales team and the management team. Our intention here is not to draw a line between these two teams. On the contrary, they should both consider themselves part of the same larger team. However, since their assignments are different, and will sometimes appear in conflict, your role as a member of both teams is critical. You are the vital link between the sales and management teams.

Your loyalty to the sales team exists within the context of your loyalty to the management team. Your loyalty to the management team does, in fact, come first. If you undermine or ridicule the management team (or the building team), you will ultimately undermine your own position as leader.

You should defend what you believe is right. If you believe that management is wrong, make your case as clearly and well-documented as you can. At the same time, you must still support the existing management strategy as long as it is morally and ethically legitimate. If you still believe that your strategy is the better one, then keep trying to persuade management to give it a chance, and be prepared to take responsibility for its success or failure. In the process, be careful not to create the image to your sales force of a management team in disarray. A sales department's productivity is determined partly by its level of morale.

This priority of loyalties may be very natural for you. It is likely that one of the reasons you were promoted is because you correctly reconciled your priorities as a salesperson. Even in situations of conflict, you continued to support your management team while you took advantage of opportunities to improve the system.

TRANSITIONS TAKE TIME

One of the myths of sales management is that new managers should seek to replace the old team with their own new team. The theory is that a team which has been hired directly by the new manager will be more loyal and more motivated. While there are times when this will turn out to be true, it should rarely be pursued as a goal. Replacing much or all of a sales team may be necessary if problems of morale, attitude or incompetence have become so enormous that the situation cannot be turned around. However, managers should not systematically set out to "turn over" a team that has been successful just because they believe it will make their own job easier. Committing to the priorities discussed in this chapter will enable you to make the transition from peer to manager successfully without having to drive good people away.

Do not expect a smooth transition overnight. You may be blessed with one, and that is ideal. However, you may, through no fault of your own, find yourself in a situation where a successful transition will take some time. Set the goal of succeeding with the team you have (assuming that they had been performing well before). Then give yourself six months to develop a strong leadership position. Your efforts to provide a better support system may not pay off the first week. But each week will pass more quickly, and one day you will say to yourself, "I've made it." For managers who commit to the priorities we have been discussing, that day frequently comes sooner than they thought it would.

What about the salespeople who don't accept you? If you stick to your support system priorities and gain the endorsement of most of your team, then you have earned the right to call your transition successful in spite of the few who may not go along.

There can be a variety of reasons why you may not win over the entire team. Some salespeople may believe they should have gotten your job. Perhaps one or more simply don't like you. Or they may like you, but do not want you to be their manager. Some people don't want anyone to be their boss, because they have a problem with all forms of authority.

With these types of employees, just treat them fairly. Keep your standard consistent. Do not treat them better with the hope of appeasing them or worse with the hope of driving them away. Both of these tactics can wind up causing you bigger problems than your original one. By treating these people fairly and going on about your business of providing quality leadership and support, you will usually wind up with one of three results:

1) They will come around, and eventually become loyal, productive team players. This actually does happen more frequently and quickly than you might anticipate.
2) They will quit. If this happens after you have done your best to treat

them with respect, you must not carry a burden of guilt. The fact is that some salespeople may leave within a year of your management transition. Sometimes this can be healthy, with you, the salesperson and the remaining team all benefitting from the departure.

3) The salesperson never does come around, and also never leaves. He or she continues on as a disgruntled employee who is still productive, but who casts a dark cloud over the rest of your team. This is, of course, the most difficult of the three scenarios, and will be covered in Chapters Four and Five. For this overview, let us simply make the point that the way to meet this challenge is to have more influence over the sales team than the disgruntled employee does. Once again, your sincere commitment to providing a support system is the most effective way to develop and protect your influence.

CREATE A "VISION AND ACTION PLAN"

When we set out to write a chapter on leadership, one of our goals was not to overglorify or overglamorize it. We do not want to depict leadership as sitting in an ivory tower with incense swirling about, philosophizing and building castles in the sky. Leadership is a very down-to-earth concept. It takes place here and now, one day at a time. Yet it also requires a sense of vision. While leaders must live in the present, they direct their followers toward the future. Leadership is not an abstract ideal. It must succeed within the context of tough realities. Yet leaders must direct their followers toward their ideals. A leader is a realist as well as an idealist.

Leaders get things done. They act as well as envision. As we said earlier, you will be judged as a success or failure largely on your ability to get things done. So a leader combines the ability to *envision* with the ability to *accomplish*.

How do you get started in the direction of pulling vision and accomplishment together and then bringing them to life?

Start out by creating a vision of yourself as a leader. Begin by considering this question:

1) WHY DO YOU WANT TO BE A LEADER?

Be sure to write down your answer. This will help you to organize your thoughts, commit to them and review them over time, revising them as necessary.

Next write down your answer to this question:

2) What kind of a leader do you want to be?

In answering this question, answer two other questions which are closely related:

2a) What kind of leader would you like to have?"

Thinking through this question provides a good starting point for determining what kind of a leader you want to become.

2b) "How do you want to be perceived as a leader?"

Perception is very important in leadership. This can become difficult during those times when, as a leader, you must stand alone. If you know you are right, you must be courageous and stand by your position, even though giving in would seem to make you more popular for the moment. Your goal is "to do the right thing," and this is an important principle for strong, effective, credible leadership. Selling out a position of "rightness" in order to take the path of least resistance is the way of the coward, and the momentary popularity ultimately disappears behind the dark cloud of disrespect.

On the other hand, the leader who says, "I don't care what anybody thinks because I'm the boss," is equally doomed to failure. This is not courage. It is selfish arrogance — one of the most contemptible ways that the power of leadership can be perverted. Selfish arrogance in leadership can quickly degenerate even further into abusiveness, dishonesty, incompetence and corruption.

Sometimes a manager will say, "My salespeople just don't get it. They don't understand where I'm coming from." A manager cannot settle for this situation. If the manager has a communication problem, then communication must move up on that manager's list of priorities.

The team's perception of a leader is usually a pretty fair characterization. When a leader is not concerned with the team's perception, it usually turns out to be just what it appears — contempt for the team. In leadership, it is *right* to care how you are perceived if you are earnestly trying to provide a support system for your team, meet their needs and make them more successful.

Here is the next question to think through in developing your vision of leadership:

3) "WHAT KIND OF TEAM DO YOU WANT TO HAVE?"

Once you have developed a vision of yourself as leader, it is time to create a vision of your *successful* sales team. What makes them successful? How do they sustain their success? How do they stay motivated? How do they continue to improve? What is the "feeling" or the "tone" of your sales department?

Envision the successful team as a whole. Then envision each of its members as individual successes.

Leadership includes *action* as well as *vision*. Once you have finished writing out visions of yourself and your team, write out an action plan for how you will bring your vision to life. Your *Vision and Action Plan* will then be composed of four parts:

1) WHAT WILL YOU (AND YOUR DEPARTMENT) BE LIKE?

This is the vision we have already discussed.

2) WHAT STEPS WILL YOU TAKE TO BRING YOUR PLAN TO LIFE?

What will you do to get yourself and your team moving toward your vision? One of the steps will be communicating your vision, or at least those parts of it which are relevant to motivating your team. Another step will be creating a plan to recognize and reward success.

3) HOW WILL YOU COMPLETE THESE STEPS?

You may be able to combine questions 2 and 3. We separated them here to make the point that "how you will do it" is just as important as "what you will do." For example, you may know that you will have to communicate certain ideas to your salespeople; but will you do it in a group meeting or one-on-one? In either event, what will you say? How will you put your plan for recognizing success into action?

4) WHEN WILL YOU COMPLETE THESE STEPS?

Many plans never reach fruition simply because there was no timetable. A plan without a timetable is still only a fantasy. When will you accomplish each of these steps? When will your vision be fulfilled? Setting a date for fulfilling your vision may seem impossible, but it is still necessary in order to assure you that your vision is really achievable. If it is not, then reshape it until it is. Your vision must be *realistic* and *achievable*. A vision of perfection is difficult for most people to stay focused on as a top priority.

Becoming a leader is one of those marvelous opportunities we occasionally have to *recreate ourselves*. It is important to make the most of these rare opportunities. Completing all four parts of your "vision and action plan" will take a lot of time, but it is the kind of work which will reward you with the greatest payoff in becoming a successful leader.

If you are currently a salesperson who is hoping to become a sales director, begin working on your vision and action plan now. It will help you get a head start in developing a *leadership thought process*. If you are already a manager, it is never too late to develop a "vision and action plan." The potential for growth in leadership never runs out.

SUMMARY

Becoming a leader is one of the most important challenges you will face as a sales director. If you have been promoted to this position, it is likely that you have already shown leadership ability. Now leadership becomes a full-time job.

Leadership is a heroic task requiring sacrifice, courage and commitment. It achieves greatness, but more importantly, it helps others to achieve greatness. A leader creates and conveys the team's vision, and then motivates and supports the team in its pursuit of that vision.

A sales director's most important leadership duty is to provide an effective support system for the sales team. To be a successful leader who provides an effective support system, focus on seven leadership priorities:

1) Be supportive.
2) Be consistent.
3) Ensure communication.
4) Be decisive.
5) Be a problem solver.
6) Set a tone for your sales department.
    a) A high standard of ethics
    b) Fairness
    c) Caring and sensitivity
    d) A positive outlook
    e) Supportiveness
    f) Respect
    g) Appreciation
    h) Responsibility
    i) Initiative
    j) Problem solving
7) Lead by example.

The transition from peer to leader takes time. The quality of support you provide will determine the credibility of your leadership. Providing a good support system will help you achieve a successful transition more quickly. Replacing the existing team with a new one should not be seen as the short cut to a successful transition.

A successful leader not only creates and conveys a vision, but also takes whatever action is necessary to bring that vision to life. To stay focused on achieving your vision, create a **VISION AND ACTION PLAN** which answers these four questions:

1) What will you (and your department) be like?
2) What steps will you take to bring your plan to life?
3) How will you complete these steps?
4) When will you complete these steps?

This chapter has explored priorities for making a successful transition from "team member" to "team leader." It has been composed largely of ideas and principles. Effective leadership involves putting *ideas* into *action*, and must therefore include a certain amount of *risk-taking*. As leaders, we put ourselves at risk, like Alexander, who put himself at risk every time he led his troops into battle. While we may have a desk at the corporate office, our most important work is in the trenches, facing *real* problems head on. Sales directors are "field generals," not "office generals."

In the remaining chapters we will explore the many leadership opportunities you will face as a sales manager, and the ways you can bring to life the ideas we have discussed in this chapter.

Let's move on from how to take over a sales team and achieve a position of successful leadership to look at the steps you will be taking in order to *create* and *build* a successful sales team.

BUILDING A TEAM

Your plan of action for successfully making the transition from peer to leader is now complete. It may take some time for your plan to achieve all of its goals, but time is on your side. You do not have to be a perfect leader the first day. No one expects you to be. Achieving excellence is a journey which will continue throughout your career as a sales director. As long as you are committed to the kind of leadership that provides a support system and meets the needs of your salespeople, they will allow you time for your leadership to mature.

As we said in the last chapter, the change may be difficult for some of your salespeople, especially if you are promoted from within their ranks. There may be people who, for whatever reason, feel uncomfortable and decide to leave. You will have to replace them. There may be additional needs for new salespeople. You may have to fill the position you left when you were promoted. Perhaps you have been hired by a new company (or transferred to a new division) where you will be creating a sales team from scratch. Whether immediately or in the future, you will eventually find yourself faced with the task of hiring salespeople. Recruiting is an ongoing responsibility.

The many hats you wear as a sales manager take a variety of skills which will be explored throughout this book. Among the most important is the ability to interview, select and recruit salespeople with the drive and potential to become the best in the business.

RECRUITING SALESPEOPLE

The key to a successful recruiting program is a *proactive* approach. Do not wait until a position is open to begin looking for someone to fill it. Keep your recruiting network going all the time, whether you have immediate needs or not. Continuous recruiting is important for several reasons.

The best salespeople may need time to leave their current position before joining your team. While they may have expressed an interest in your company, it may not be prudent for them to leave a successful situation. First-rate salespeople can sometimes take months to join your team.

Money can be an issue. With a large backlog of commissions due over the next few months, they may need to bring cases to settlement before they can leave.

Once they make the decision to leave, they may be considering offers from other companies as well as yours.

They may want to work for your company, but are waiting for the community which best suits their desires and skills.

They may need to get their real estate license.

You can establish contacts with top salespeople who tell you, "Call me the next time you have an opening." If you have five prospective salespeople in this situation, it increases the likelihood that one of them will actually become available at the right time for you.

Having several good candidates with whom you have built rapport puts you in a stronger position to set your terms and get a prompt decision. When an opening arises suddenly, you do not want to be desperately chasing one good candidate. This puts control in the hands of the salesperson. A desperate recruiter can make disastrous mistakes.

A consistent, proactive recruiting program can help you develop a stronger position with your existing team. When members of your sales force know that there are successful salespeople who want to join your team, those who are troublesome or unproductive know they can be easily replaced. They will often be motivated to focus on improving their behavior or performance.

Keep a list of salespeople who have impressed you and could help build your team in the future, especially if they have taken the initiative to express an interest in your company. You can tell them, "I don't have anything available right now, but I would like to keep in touch. If an opportunity opens up that could work well for you, I'll give you a call." With your top candidates you may want to stay in touch with them regularly just to keep up to date with their situation. We recommend an initial interview with prospective candidates to qualify that indeed they meet your expectations.

How do you develop this recruiting network? There are three primary ways to seek out prospective salespeople: advertising, people you already know, and referrals. Each has its pros and cons.

ADVERTISING

This is the "Help Wanted" ads you would run in newspapers, industry publications, or other places where prospective candidates might be looking.

PROS

Ads will usually provide you with the widest range of candidates, including successful people you may not know, or whom you may not have realized were looking for a new company. Having a larger selection of candidates can also provide you with greater control in setting the timing and terms of your job offer.

We are accustomed to seeing ads where a specific position is available and needs to be filled immediately. A "proactive" recruiting program which chooses advertising as one of its strategies would occasionally feature more generic ads that describe your company and your desire for top people interested in joining a winning team.

CONS

The advertising method can cause you to spend a great deal of time reviewing and responding to applicants of a lesser caliber than you were hoping for. Developing sound telephone techniques for interviewing will narrow down the field — a time management must.

The ideal candidate may not be reading the ads, although they could become available if they were aware of your opening. Sometimes the best people are not looking for a job.

There can be a significant cost in running consistent, generic recruiting

ads that are large enough to promote your company and explain the
desired qualifications of candidates.

PEOPLE YOU KNOW

These are prospective candidates whom you know well enough, either
personally or by reputation, to pursue before you have seen their resume
or interviewed them formally.

PROS

You can start out with a greater feeling of confidence that they will be
successful team members. You can also feel more confident that they will
be *loyal* team members.

CONS

You may actually find yourself in a weaker position if they attempt to
use their friendship or reputation as a bargaining tool.

Being pursued is flattering. They could be making you jump through
hoops only to turn you down later.

They can still fool you once they become part of your team. It is important
not to assume too much about the kind of salesperson they will be, even if
you think you know them. Don't skip any steps in the recruiting process. You
may even want to have a second person in the company interview them.

You run the risk of demoralizing the rest of your team if they believe
you are filling all new positions with personal friends or "hand-picked
favorites." Impartiality and total fairness are critical when you hire
friends or people you have actively pursued. They might believe they are
entitled to preferred status on your team because you pursued them on
account of their successful past record.

While some managers believe that pursuing successful salespeople they
already know is the most intelligent and least risky way to build a team,
others disagree. Those in disagreement prefer to hire only people who have
taken the initiative to come to them. Both methods have proven successful.

REFERRALS

Although this source of candidates is different from the last one ("people you know"), the pros & cons tend to be similar. The obvious benefit of these candidates is that they already have a credible reference. If you are concerned about protecting your own position of strength, you can always ask the referral source to have the candidate call you. This way you can test their interest and initiative, and avoid the problems which are sometimes associated with chasing the candidate. Often, your best source of referrals is your own sales team. Train them to be on the look-out for folks they would like on their team.

WHAT KIND OF PEOPLE DO YOU WANT FOR YOUR TEAM?

We have talked in previous chapters about the importance of creating *visions* and *standards*. What is your vision of the kind of salespeople you want to hire, and what minimum standard will you be expecting them to live up to? What kind of demeanor, temperament, selling style, values and skills do you seek as you build your team?

Here are some examples of traits you may want to consider for your vision. They are taken from Chapter One of Richard Tiller's book, <u>Success in New Home Sales.</u>

- Personal warmth
- A non-threatening demeanor
- Compassion
- Patience
- Ability to sell both product and service
- Honesty
- A genuine sense of fairness
- Confidence
- Perseverance
- Competence and diligence in paperwork
- Ability and willingness to understand your company's systems
- Knowledge of construction
- Knowledge of financing
- Knowledge of your market and your competition
- Intelligence
- Willingness and ability to solve problems

- Sense of humor
- High level of energy
- Willingness to make sacrifices

From this list you can make whatever additions or changes you believe will complete your vision of an ideal salesperson. Again, your purpose in creating this vision is to set the standard by which you will judge whether candidates qualify for your team. Since it is often hard to find a person who lives up to these standards by running one classified ad, the consistent, proactive approach to recruiting that we described earlier will make it easier to fulfill your vision.

Some of these criteria require training which they will receive after you have hired them. You must make your best decision during the evaluation process as to whether your training will enable them to achieve the knowledge and skill level you are seeking.

Many companies that do have a comprehensive sales training program recruit candidates from fields other than residential sales. Successful new home salespeople have come from the following careers:

- Teaching
- Retail sales (especially high-ticket items)
- Middle management
- Computer sales
- Small business managers
- Rental agents/property managers
- Financial planners
- Loan officers
- Nurses and care givers
- Flight attendants

WHAT WILL YOU WANT THEM TO DO?

In addition to determining the kind of people you want for your team, you must have a clear idea of exactly what you want them to do. Many companies have written contracts and/or job descriptions for salespeople in order to assure fairness, uphold standards and reduce misunderstandings. Some smaller, privately-held companies prefer not to put this information in writing. They believe they must retain the flexibility to change their policies without worrying that written documents could backfire on them.

Whichever approach you prefer, you must have a clear understanding of what responsibilities and level of performance you will require. It is equally important that each of your team members have the same understanding of these expectations. Many salespeople express the concern that they really do not know what is expected of them. With any new hire this information must be conveyed — *and agreed to* — before employment begins.

HOW WILL PROSPECTIVE SALES CANDIDATES ACQUIRE THE SKILLS THEY NEED?

Some companies offer very little training, preferring to hire only salespeople who have already acquired the necessary skills and knowledge during previous experience. Be careful with this approach. Sometimes management can become so complacent with training that necessary product knowledge is not accurately conveyed. Sales skills become rusty or outdated through lack of consistent coaching. Salespeople become cynical and demoralized over the lack of management support.

Even when the company policy is to hire only experienced salespeople, it is still essential for management to provide continuous training that will keep knowledge current, skills sharp and morale high.

At the opposite end of the spectrum are companies who prefer to hire inexperienced people and train them from scratch. The risk with this approach is that the training program must be top-notch. This requires a significant commitment of time and money. Once again, both approaches have proven successful when management has made the commitment to cover the necessary bases.

A third approach is to hire a combination of rookies and veterans. In this situation your formal training programs support all of the salespeople. Beyond that, veterans supply training and mentoring to rookies, while the newcomers help to keep the veterans fresh. For this approach to succeed everyone involved must believe there is a benefit for them. You must also monitor the program to make sure everyone is fulfilling their responsibility.

Be sure you know in advance what kind of person and what level of skill you are looking for, and then be sure to provide the kind of support system that will enable your people to succeed. Failing to match your support system with your vision puts you at greater risk of failure.

HOW TO CONDUCT AN INTERVIEW

As you set about the process of building your sales team, you have paved the way for the interviewing phase by completing the following steps:

- You have developed a continuous recruiting process to give you a better opportunity to select qualified candidates.
- You have created a vision of your ideal sales candidate so that you know what kind of person you are looking for.
- You have decided on the level of experience and skill you are seeking, knowing that you and your co-workers can make the commitment necessary to bring that skill level up to the standard which you have set.
- You have established a clear set of responsibilities and expectations so that you and your new salesperson will have the same understanding of what duties and performance level will be required.
- Through resumes, referrals and personal contacts you have developed a list of candidates you believe could meet your expectations.

Now you must develop an interviewing process that will enable you to select the best candidate. Initially you will get to know the candidates, their goals, desires and interests. During the interview you will need to convey your company's mission statement and philosophy. Naturally you will also want to explain the benefits of working for your company. Your years of selling experience will be useful once again. You must also develop a set of questions that will allow you to make the following decisions about each candidate:

1) Are they the kind of *person* I am looking for? Do they have the *character* and *values* that will help me build a successful team?
2) Do they have the appropriate skill level and aptitude (even if they nev-

er actually sold new homes before)? *Can* they do the job?

3) Do they have the right attitude and level of commitment? *Will* they do the job?

4) Are they the right person for my team? Will they make a *contribution* beyond simply earning money for themselves? Are they *team players* as well as independent producers?

To help you answer these four general questions, we will discuss nineteen specific questions you can ask during an interview. You would never ask all of these questions during the same interview, nor is this intended to be a complete list of questions. Our purpose for choosing these questions is to discuss some of the options that are available for successful interviewing.

We are deliberately avoiding the legal aspect of interviewing in this chapter, as we will be avoiding legal issues in the chapter on discipline. The reason is that we feel these principles should be taught *within* individual companies, and not in a management book such as this one. While the legal implications of hiring are most frequently associated with race, religion, sex and age, the list of potential liabilities is much longer. Danger areas can include marital status, child care, future family plans, physical condition, personal finances, criminal record, type of military discharge and personal appearance. To someone inexperienced in such matters, some of these principles can seem subtle and confusing. They are best explained face-to-face, by an expert, with plenty of time for examples and questions. We urge every company to provide in-house expert training (or to hire an outside expert, if necessary) to present this information clearly and completely to every manager with the authority to hire, discipline or dismiss.

As you are asking your interview questions, bear in mind a few basic guidelines.

Don't dominate the conversation. Let the applicant do most of the talking. At the same time, encourage the applicant to ask as many questions as they need in order to help them make a decision.

Ask "open" questions (which require complete explanatory answers that allow you insight into the candidate's mind) not "closed" ones (which require shorter answers — often "yes" or "no").

Be careful not to word your questions in a way that steers the candidate toward the answer you desire. An example of a "steering" question would be: "I know that tradition says, 'Buyer beware,' but do you believe a salesperson has an ethical responsibility to go beyond the minimum in providing accurate information to the consumer?"

Our final guideline may be controversial, and some sales managers will disagree with us. It is our opinion that the interview is *not* the place to require candidates to demonstrate their selling expertise. If they have gotten as far as the interview and you still don't know whether they can sell, then have them shopped, or schedule a separate selling exercise in a different environment.

Use the interview as an opportunity to get to know your candidates and to let them get to know you. The interview is your opportunity to learn what they're all about — their background, ideas, priorities, motivations, strengths and weaknesses.

With these thoughts in mind, let's look at the specific kinds of questions that will help you conduct productive interviews, so that you can determine the best people for your team.

1) "WHAT IS IT ABOUT OUR COMPANY THAT INTERESTS YOU?"

As with each of the questions that follow, the goal with this first one is to get your applicants to open up and tell about themselves with as little steering from you as possible. With this question you can begin to get an idea of how they will fit into your team. How much do they know about you? Why are they there? Do they simply want a job — any job — or do they specifically want to work for *your* company (or perhaps even for *you*)? Have they already envisioned themselves as part of your team? Are they looking for a career opportunity? What is it they are hoping to get, and what are they hoping to contribute?

With any of our nineteen questions, the applicant's answer can lead to a whole new series of questions or a unique exchange of ideas. Don't feel that you have to stick with your agenda. Just be sure that by the time the interview is over you have achieved all of your objectives.

2) "WHAT IS IT ABOUT THIS JOB THAT INTERESTS YOU?"

They may answer this question in the course of answering the first one. Your objective with this question is a little different, however. In the last question you wanted to determine if there were any ways they considered your company uniquely suited to them. If they did not, that can still be okay, depending on the answers to your other questions.

This is another question you ask in order to learn about the candidate, but not to make a value judgment. Suppose they say, "I just want to be a salesperson. I don't have any desire to be a manager." Do not assume that they are complacent. They may have found their calling, and truly desire to be the best salesperson who ever lived. You can respond to their answer by saying, "That's great. We need people who appreciate selling for what it is. What is the next accomplishment you would like to achieve in your selling career?" Once they answer that question, you can then ask, "How do you plan to get there?"

9) "WHAT IS YOUR PHILOSOPHY OF SELLING?"

This should never be used as a "knockout question." You are hiring salespeople, not philosophers. For many outstanding salespeople selling is more instinctive than thought-provoking. Still, the question can give you an idea of what kind of thought process they have developed. Their answer may be simple and direct: "I believe that selling is teaching customers why my homes are best and then asking them to buy." Another response could be, "Showing customers how my homes will fulfill their needs and improve their lives better than any of the other alternatives." Whether or not you believe that either of these two statements is the final word on selling, at least they both demonstrate a selling mentality. A response such as, "Selling is making friends," could cause concern and requires more questioning.

10) "WHAT IS IT ABOUT YOU THAT HAS MADE YOU SUCCESSFUL IN THE PAST?"

With this question you should encourage your candidates to take all the time they need and give as many examples as they want. One of the most important objectives in an interview is to provide opportunities for applicants to brag. Allowing them to discuss their greatness gives you the opportunity to watch them shine.

With all of your other management responsibilities, you cannot afford to spend an unlimited amount of time on every interview. However, remember that the interview is the most important part of the selection process. You will be doing yourself a disservice by scheduling eight or ten consecutive interviews at half-hour intervals. If your time is limited, it is better to select fewer candidates to reach the interview stage, and then try to select from that smaller group. An initial telephone interview can be helpful here.

If you complete these interviews and still feel the need to keep looking, then by all means do so. A bad hire can be a costly error, as well as a ball and chain around your ankle for a long time.

Give yourself at least an hour for each interview. You can always bring an interview to a close more quickly, but you need time to spend with candidates who look promising.

A second interview for your leading candidates is often appropriate, especially when you need the approval of a supervisor in order to complete a hire. However, the first interview should be complete enough to provide you with a sense of whether the candidate is appropriate.

11) "CAN YOU GIVE ME A FEW EXAMPLES OF THINGS YOU'VE DONE IN THE PAST THAT YOU FELT WERE OUTSTANDING?"

You may occasionally have a candidate who responds to that question by asking, "Do you mean just in sales, or in anything at all?" Tell them, "Anything at all," and let the conversation take its own course for awhile. You want to get to know the "person" as well as the "salesperson." They will "both" be a part of your team. You do want to make sure they eventually give you examples of outstanding sales accomplishments, so you may need to ask the question once more in a strictly sales-related context before you move on.

Here are three more questions where you can allow candidates to pursue whatever direction they desire, and then draw them back into a discussion of new home sales as a wrapup. Continue to give salespeople the time they need to demonstrate their unique excellence.

12) "TELL ME ABOUT THE BEST SALE YOU EVER MADE, AND WHAT YOU DID THAT WAS SPECIAL."

13) "WHAT DO YOU THINK HAS BEEN YOUR MOST SIGNIFICANT ACCOMPLISHMENT IN YOUR CAREER SO FAR?"

14) "WHAT IS YOUR FAVORITE JOB THAT YOU'VE EVER HAD? WHAT MADE IT YOUR FAVORITE?"

The next question gives your candidates an opportunity to talk about themselves as individuals, allowing you to gain a more well-rounded understanding of them.

15) "TELL ME ABOUT YOURSELF — ANYTHING YOU'D LIKE."

Then sit back and listen, asking questions at whatever point you want the candidate to elaborate. What do they think is important in their life? Where have they been, and where are they going? What kind of people are they? What kind of salespeople could they be with the proper training and support?

With this type of question, you must be careful not to use any personal information in a discriminatory way — not even by accident. The courts are not sympathetic to "accidental" discrimination.

16) "WHAT AREAS ARE YOU WORKING ON TO IMPROVE?"

Two traditional interview questions are:
a) "What is your greatest strength?"
b) "What is your greatest weakness?"

You can create a more relaxed atmosphere in your interviews if you can avoid the typical wording of such essential questions as these. A number of the previous questions have been designed to allow your candidates to talk about their strengths. Questions about weaknesses are frequently unproductive, because you can receive answers like, "People tell me I care too much," or, "I'm a workoholic." Questions about weaknesses are less important than those regarding strengths. Still it's worth a try to see if they can articulate their attitude toward self-improvement. That is the goal of this question.

In the course of answering the questions discussed so far, candidates may have found several opportunities to talk specifically about closing skills. Their goal throughout the interview should be to help you create a vision of them as a successful salesperson. However, if you find that more specific questions about their skills and techniques are required, then you can ask questions like this one:

17) "HOW WOULD YOU DESCRIBE YOURSELF AS A CLOSER? WHAT DO YOU DO TO MAKE THE CLOSE HAPPEN?"

If they are able to articulate a closing process that progresses through the sale to the point where they can ask for the agreement, it shows they have a clear strategy and thought process toward selling. You can then ask them to give examples of exact words they might use to ask for the sale.

On the other hand, if their answer to your original question is, "I don't know, it depends on the customer," then you would need to ask more specific questions. In an interview for a sales position, you cannot allow the candidate to hedge on questions that involve how they sell. You do not have to role play or ask them to "sell me this paperweight" (you are not hiring them to sell you a paperweight), but they need to be able to convince you that they can be a successful part of your team.

Once you are convinced that they could be the person you are looking for to help you build a successful team, you have two more pieces of business to complete.

18) YOU EXPLAIN TO THE CANDIDATE THE COMPLETE JOB DESCRIPTION AND YOUR EXPECTATIONS FOR PERFORMANCE. THEN ASK IF THERE IS ANYTHING ABOUT THIS INFORMATION THAT CONCERNS HIM OR HER.

You can head off a lot of employee problems by including this stage of the hiring process in the initial interview. Some managers want so much to please their candidates that they soft-peddle the down side of the sales position. Your top priority is to build a first-rate team, not please the candidates. Candidates will be pleased enough that you gave them the whole truth. That is part of the *tone* you are trying to set for your team anyway. If you believe there are issues which could impact an applicant's well-being soon after they join your team, you should tell them before they accept the position. You owe it to them to let them know the challenges they will face, and you owe it to yourself to see if they are ready and able to accept those challenges.

Promises about the future should also be avoided. Assurances of outstanding income, a better community down the road, or a good chance of promotion into management should not be used as carrots to attract the right person for your team. Overly optimistic expectations and unfulfilled promises can destroy morale.

By getting them to agree that they accept your job description and expectations at the interview, you can quote these words back to them if a problem arises later on.

Even when these issues are discussed at the initial interview, they should be reviewed again at the time of the hire. If the actual hire is accomplished over the phone, then a face-to-face meeting on or before the first day of work is the time to review the interview discussion.

19) ASK FOR REFERENCES.

Some managers overlook this final step, believing that "candidates can't use their current employer, and that's the only opinion that really counts," or "they will only give names of people they know will sing their praises."

It doesn't matter. Call whatever names they give you. Let the people sing your candidate's praises. That is important information. You can then follow up with one of several questions:

"How would you rate him on a scale of 1 to 10?"

If the answer is 9 or less then you can ask, "What is it that would make him a 10?" This is an upbeat way of asking about weaknesses. Another way to ask this would be:

"If I hire her, is there anything you could recommend that I do to help her be even better?"

If you have a concern that the references you are calling have all been too well-rehearsed, then try getting a "reference from a reference." As you are concluding your call with the person whose name the candidate gave, ask them:

"I need just one more person that I can call. Is there anyone you could recommend?"

You may occasionally be hindered by the fact that some companies do not give out any information on former employees other than job title and dates of employment.

As you go through the process of recruiting, remember to be discreet. You must protect your applicants. It is shocking how often managers find out from their competitors that their salespeople have inquired about another job.

Shopping the market is perfectly normal in our industry. It does not necessarily mean that a salesperson is unhappy or that their performance may be at risk. Some salespeople need to look around from time to time just to remind themselves how fortunate they are. Others seriously consider leaving, but wind up deciding to stay with a greater sense of commitment than they ever had before. Their reputations should not be tarnished by this exploration.

SUMMARY

Selecting the right people for your sales team will help you succeed in management much more easily. To be sure that you continually have access to a network of top salespeople who might join your team if the opportunity arises, you will need to develop a consistent, proactive recruiting strategy. Keep networking for new people all the time, whether you have immediate openings or not.

The three most widely used recruiting methods in the homebuilding industry are:

1) Advertising.
2) Recruiting people you know.
3) Contacting referrals.

Before you begin your interviewing process, make sure you have decided:

1) What kind of person you are seeking.
2) What level of skill and experience you are seeking.
3) The job description.
4) Your expectations for performance.
5) What information you want to provide for the candidate at the interview.
6) What information you want to obtain from the candidate, and what questions you will ask in order to get it.

The interview should normally be the primary factor in your hiring decision, unless you personally know the candidate so well that the interview serves only to discuss details. Resumes, reputations, outside testing services and referrals are all important. It is *your* team, however, and you are the one who needs to be sold on them face to face, just as they need to be sold on you. The interview is where the *total person* begins to emerge. It is also where your *relationship* with team members begins to build, and with it their loyalty to you.

It is important to respond as promptly as possible to every application. If you know that you are not going to hire an applicant, let them know so that they can get on with their lives, even if your volume of applications requires you to use a form letter. See your personnel department or legal staff for the proper wording as to the reason for the rejection. It is usually not necessary to be specific; but be cautious. Failing to respond is not only disrespectful to the applicant, but could hurt your reputation as an employer.

When new salespeople arrive for their first day of work, you need to provide them with a complete orientation program to get them started off right. This orientation is the first critical part of your support system. When we get to our section on training, Chapter Seven will explain how to put together an orientation program. In the meantime, our next chapter in the management section will discuss ways to apply the principles of management and leadership to conducting successful sales meetings.

How To Lead A Sales Meeting

S ales meetings are one of the most consistent and visible ways to provide strong, supportive leadership. Sadly, sales meetings are often dreaded as the low point of the week by managers as well as salespeople. What causes this wonderful opportunity for group interaction to turn into a nightmare? Let's look at one type of meeting that salespeople dread. Then we will discuss ways to turn the situation around to make the meeting an event the entire team will look forward to. We will also look for opportunities to apply leadership principles discussed in the first three chapters.

* * *

Our fictional sales meeting starts out with the sales director calling it to order.

"Okay, boys and girls. We're already fifteen minutes late. I needed to make a call, but that's no reason for everyone else to be wandering around. Oh well. They'll get here when they get here. Let's get started.

"I have bad news and bad news. I'll start with the bad news first. We're three sales behind quota for the month. Come on, tigers, we can do better than that. Now for the bad news. It doesn't seem to matter whether we sell any homes or not, because production doesn't get them built anyway. Why should they? They're on salary.

"So, does anybody here have any good news?"

One salesperson speaks up. "I had two sales."

"Whoa, Nellie! After three weeks of goose eggs, Steve finally breaks through. Does this mean he could actually make his monthly quota? Anybody else?"

* * *

We don't need to take this example any farther to get a pretty good idea of the "tone" of this sales meeting.

The other kind of meeting which salespeople dread is this:

"Let's get started. We have a lot of numbers to crunch today. There are seventeen of us, and we only have two hours, so please hold your questions, and we'll see if we can squeeze them in at the end. When I call your name, I want you to read off your numbers. Take it slow, because you talk faster than I can write. I need your traffic for the week broken down by source, your contracts, kickouts, settlements, lot holds, contracts pending settlement, any settlements that have been delayed and the reason for the delay, number of specs started not sold, number of specs drywalled not sold, and number of specs completed not sold. Does anyone need that repeated?"

* * *

What should a sales meeting be like? And what about leadership? What does Alexander's Battle of Issus have to do with running a sales meeting?

As a leader, you need to start out by deciding what you want your meetings to accomplish. The most important principle to use as a guideline for your sales meetings is this: *Sales meetings must <u>benefit</u> the sales team.* Make this your leadership vision for sales meetings; then you can begin filling in the colors. What kind of support can you, as a leader, offer your team in sales meetings?

There are four primary benefits that sales meetings can provide: motivation, knowledge, training and problem solving.

Motivation

For salespeople, motivation means more than just "getting pumped up." It includes:

• *Belief in what they are doing.*

Salespeople must be assured that their work has real value.

• *Confidence that they can do it.*

They must believe that they have the ability and knowledge to success-fully achieve their objectives.

• *Belief that their work will be appreciated.*

While a paycheck has practical economic value in addition to its val-ue as a reward, a salesperson's identity is far more important. Instilling your salespeople with a sense of *dignity* and *respect* is one of the most valuable services you can provide as a leader. Showing consistent appre-ciation for their work will give a tremendous boost to their motivation, their feeling of self-worth, their sense of purpose and their productivity.

• *Assurance that they are being supported by those whom they depend on.*

It is hard for salespeople to stay motivated when they believe they are being undermined. They need to be assured that management, production and purchasing are being held accountable for their end of the bargain.

Each of these four elements of motivation has more value than the tem-porary shot of adrenalin that might come from a "pep rally." There is nothing wrong with pep rallies. They can provide one type of motivation. But they are no substitute for the four elements of motivation listed above.

In our first scenario at the beginning of the chapter, the sales team's motivation was consistently undermined. Here are some of the ways it happened.

• Salespeople are adult human beings, just as managers are. They are not "boys and girls," and they are not "tigers."
• The manager believed in a double standard. He required everyone but himself to show up for the meeting on time. He dishonored the team before the meeting started.
• He kept focusing on bad news. He conveyed the message that his team produces nothing of value. They are failures. Even the one success sto-ry was treated as a fluke. Humor has a place in leadership, but not when it turns to sarcasm.
• He promoted the idea that success was impossible anyway, because

there was no support system. Nor did he intend to do anything about it. Setting an example of company disloyalty is a deadly path to follow.

Whatever positive motivation the salespeople may have had when the meeting began was sucked away by the manager. Can you imagine their mental attitude as they leave the meeting to face their first customer of the day?

In our second example the manager did not undermine the team. He simply offered them nothing of value. The meeting existed solely for the benefit of the manager. Sales meetings are for salespeople. The team should leave the meeting *energized*.

KNOWLEDGE

The second benefit that sales meetings can provide is valuable information. Updates concerning the market, the company, product information, financing, individual achievements, etc., can help sales-people increase their understanding, awareness and, hopefully, their sales.

TRAINING

Knowledge and training can overlap, but we have separated them here in order to emphasize the different types of benefits that can be provided. When we discuss knowledge, we mean factual information which allows your sales team to be better informed. With training we are focusing on skill development. It is not important to classify your meeting as one or the other. The goal is to cover both bases. For example, if a vendor comes in to explain the benefits of a product to the consumer, that could be classified as both knowledge and training. The vendor is teaching you "what it is," and also "how to sell it." Examples of pure training topics are how to prospect, close or follow up.

PROBLEM SOLVING

With the company's entire resources of sales experience and brain power in one room, your sales meetings are the best opportunity for brainstorming and problem solving. This is one of the most significant benefits your sales meetings can provide, and it is the kind of meeting that salespeople most often request. Their comrades on the firing line are usually their most credible resource.

You do not need to provide all four of these benefits in every meeting. The meetings would be too long, and the benefits spread too thin. Your goal is to provide a consistent balance of these four benefits over the long term. They work together to enhance each other. A team that is motivated will benefit more from meetings on knowledge, training and problem solving. Teams that are better trained will be more productive in meetings on problem solving, just as they will be able to get more out of the knowledge meetings. They will also be more motivated. When all four benefits work together, the result is a successful team.

What are the benefits for you, the manager? In addition to the gratification of managing a successful team, you will gain a stronger, more credible leadership position. As we discussed in Chapter Two, *the key to successful leadership is the ability to provide an effective support system for your team.*

* * *

What are the steps you can take to make sure that your sales meetings are successful? There are four principles to focus on in order to lead the kind of sales meetings your team will look forward to, will help your team to be more successful, and will help you to be a successful leader.

1) MAINTAIN A DECISIVE DEMEANOR.

We have discussed the importance of decisiveness in effective leadership. Sales meetings are an ideal forum for displaying this strength. Your ability to do this is important for your team as well as for you because your decisiveness will be significant to their morale in the long run. There are several ways to demonstrate decisiveness in sales meetings, the first of which occurs before the meeting even begins.

• **PREPARE A WRITTEN AGENDA FOR THE MEETING.**

Set the stage. Let your salespeople know in the beginning where the meeting is going. Then guide it each step of the way to make sure you stay focused on the direction. The agenda should be written, and each salesperson should receive a copy at the beginning of the meeting. In situations where assignments are involved, the agenda can even be distributed in advance.

For most meetings it is helpful if you schedule a specific amount of time for each topic. This helps everyone to keep track of how the meeting is progressing, and helps cut down on frivolous, time-wasting tangents. Most people don't want to cause a meeting to fall behind. When you have to cut someone off you can say, "We have to keep moving to stay on schedule. If we have time at the end, we can come back to this." (For people who need one-on-one counseling, you can say, "I'll meet with you after the meeting to spend some more time on this.")

Stick to the schedule as closely as possible. Plan ahead for those topics that could take longer than you anticipate. Plan extra time for them, but don't use the time if you don't have to. It is better to be ahead of schedule than behind, and better to finish a meeting early than late.

Some topics may need to extend beyond your allotted time in order to be resolved. For that reason it is better to put the less important topics toward the end of the agenda.

If a new topic comes up that is more important than some of your agenda items, change your agenda in order to address the new topic *promptly* and *decisively*. Don't use the agenda as an excuse for side-stepping a crucial issue.

Try to build a little time into your agenda for people to raise issues for which they would like the input of the team. Fifteen minutes would usually be an acceptable amount of time, but this can vary depending on the overall length of the meeting and the other issues which need to be addressed.

• **PROVIDE IMMEDIATE ANSWERS FOR AS MANY ISSUES AS YOU CAN. FOR THE REST, MAKE A COMMITMENT THAT YOU WILL PROVIDE THE ANSWERS, AND WHEN.**

Meetings serve the purpose of *addressing and resolving issues.* When issues are discussed and then seem to suddenly evaporate, salespeople leave feeling frustrated. If an issue is important, pursue it *to a resolution* as often as possible. When an issue is resolved, restate the solution concisely to make sure that everyone agrees with it (or at least understands it).

When a decision is not possible during a meeting, explain the issues that are preventing the resolution, and tell what your own course of action will be in order to reach a decision. Commit to a deadline in front of the group. When you can promise an answer and then deliver on your promise, you have still acted decisively.

Decisiveness does not require dramatic bravado. It is not loud or bullying. It is simply the *ability and willingness to make decisions.* Decisiveness in a leader breeds confidence in those who follow.

• RESOLVE ITEMS WHICH ARE PENDING FROM THE LAST MEETING BEFORE YOU GET TOO FAR INTO THE CURRENT ONE.

This is important for the reasons discussed in the last item.

• KEEP THE MEETING UNDER YOUR CONTROL.

In addition to moving the meeting along from one agenda topic to the next, you will be looked to as the authority figure in the meeting. Unfortunately, most sales meetings do not stay orderly by themselves. The natural course for most meetings is to begin to drift. Comments become less relevent, private conversations spring up in various places around the table, and cynical remarks may begin to surface. While the tone of a sales meeting should normally be light and casual, a general feeling of order should still be present. You are the one who will be expected to maintain this sense of order. As the meeting begins to drift off track, don't be shy about bringing it back. While you don't want to be abrasive, gentle firmness is usually your best strategy. Examples of this tone would be:

"Okay, everybody, one at a time. Ellen, go ahead with the point you were making."

"We need to keep moving if we're going to finish on time."

"We have to wrap this up now. Does anyone else have anything on this topic before we move on?"

You are the one who brings closure to each event in the meeting. Make each topic relevant, but not overly serious. Casual levity is an important ingredient in a sales meeting, and occasional diversions can be rejuvenating. Just be sure the overall tone of the meeting is constructive, productive and uplifting. These were the elements that were missing in the examples at the beginning of this chapter. This leads to our second major principle for successful sales meetings.

2) Keep the tone of the meeting positive.

Positive meetings are more productive than negative ones. Sometimes negative information must be conveyed. There may be times when you have no alternative but a "chew-out session." These types of meetings must be handled very carefully, because even negative meetings must have a positive element in order to be productive. There are several ways to create a positive tone.

• OPEN THE MEETING ON AN UPBEAT NOTE WHENEVER POSSIBLE.

If your company filed for bankruptcy on Friday, it might be frivolous to open the Monday meeting with a pep talk. However, in most cases an upbeat opening can set the tone for the rest of the meeting. In both examples at the beginning of this chapter, the upbeat opening was avoided and the results were predictable. The opening message in the first example was, "Life around here stinks." In the second example the message was, "The No-Doz is in the cabinet. Take a handful."

Open your meetings with a piece of good news:

- Tell a success story on behalf of someone else, or the company as a whole.
- Ask for success stories from anyone in the group.
- If the team's overall sales for the week were good, start with that.
- Share news that is encouraging in the marketplace.
- Unveil the company's newest strategy for improvement in a particular area.

• USE SALES MEETINGS TO OFFER RECOGNITION TO YOUR PEOPLE.

Recognition is one of the most important elements in your overall support system. It extends far beyond simply the sales meeting, and will be discussed in detail in Part Three of this book, "Motivation." While there are many ways to provide recognition, it is always a key ingredient to successful sales meetings.

Recognition is much more than plaques. Recognition that is spontaneous is often the most appreciated. Many companies starve their salespeople in this critical area.

Go back to your vision of a successful department. What values do you want to instill? What standards are you trying to raise? What goals are you hoping to achieve?

As we said earlier, *if you want to create a pattern of behavior, reward the behavior when it occurs at random.* Let your salespeople know, by means of recognition in the presence of their peers, that you consider their accomplishment extraordinary. Let them know that their achievements exemplify your ideal. Allow them to enjoy their richly-earned recognition, and let everyone else see that this reward is available to them as well. Here are a few examples of the types of achievements that deserve special recognition in your meetings:

- Exceeding sales goals.
- Creating new ideas for prospecting.
- Making a sale using a new technique.
- Making a sale through extraordinary perseverance.
- Developing a new marketing strategy.
- Going beyond the call of duty to solve a problem, help a co-worker or serve a customer.
- Achieving extra sales from a diligent commitment to follow up.
- Adding a creative touch to the merchandising presentation.
- Extraordinary efforts during preconstruction sales.
- Overcoming challenges in a difficult community.

The list of possibilities for recognition is endless, and each incident of recognition provides four benefits. It provides reward and gratification to the salesperson who has earned it. It makes the idea or accomplishment available to the rest of the team. It reinforces the standard from your vision. And it establishes you as a leader who appreciates your people.

As you present recognition in your meetings, let people know, where appropriate, that you will also pass word of the accomplishment on to the builder or other managers. Salespeople need to realize that their extra efforts are appreciated by others in the company as well. It also helps others realize that your efforts to set high standards for your department are paying off.

• **DO NOT REWARD NEGATIVITY IN SALES MEETINGS.**

Another way to keep your meetings positive and productive is to maintain control over negative forces. As important as it is to reward positive behavior, you must be equally alert in your handling of negative behavior. For many managers this is one of the most difficult challenges they face in sales meetings. A sales team with no negative element is very fortunate, and fairly unusual. More often than not there is at least one person on any team of five or more who injects negativity into sales meetings. They may otherwise be productive employees, so that except for their negativity you are glad to have them as part of your team. How do you prevent them from undermining your efforts to create a positive environment in your meetings? How do you deal with negativity in general, regardless of the source? We have three suggestions.

• If there are particular individuals who are the primary cause of the negativity, speak to them privately and honestly.

"You know that I value your opinion. Everybody does. But I need your help in the sales meetings. My job is to keep the meetings positive so everybody can walk out and do their best work. It makes such a difference when getting together gives people a boost. It's the best kind of support the meetings should provide. Can you help me out with this?"

Using this approach as a starting point, you can then address the specific issue in whatever terms are appropriate.

This type of encounter drifts on to the outskirts of discipline. In our next chapter, when we go into more detail on discipline, we will discuss the principle that the best place to start is to make sure the salesperson can see the issue through your eyes. Get them to empathize with your responsibility as manager by asking, "What would you do if you were in my position?"

In this case the negative salesperson needs to understand that you are responsible for the welfare of the team, and that includes morale. Your job is to address any issue or behavior that threatens the team. The question is, do they share your concern? If they do, your challenge becomes much easier. If they don't, you may need to apply disciplinary action (see Chapter Five).

• Try to nip the negative statement in the bud.

Most salespeople genuinely dislike negativity in a sales meeting. They will not fight it, because they believe that's your job. They have no reason to wage war on their colleague in the meeting, so they go along with the negativity and try to lay low. Normally, however, they realize the destructive potential of *unwarranted* negativity, and welcome the opportunity to bring it to an end. For that reason, a constructive approach to a negative statement would be to ask the group, "Does anyone else feel the same way?"

This is a sincere question. If the concern is shared among other salespeople who have not spoken up, then it should be addressed in the interest of open communication. If, however, it was simply a negative remark by a negative salesperson, the failure of anyone else to offer support may send a message that the comment was universally unwelcome. If salespeople know that you will respond to their complaints in the future with this same question, they will become more selective with their complaints. Silence can be a very powerful weapon against a troublemaker.

- Establish a rule for your meetings that before a salesperson can bring up a problem, they must think of at least one possible solution. It does not have to be the perfect solution, but it must be a serious proposal that can serve as the starting point for a constructive effort to find the best answer.

- CONCLUDE THE MEETING ON AN UPBEAT NOTE.

We have discussed ways to set a positive tone for productive meetings at the beginning, and then to preserve the positive atmosphere throughout. It is important to finish up on a positive note as well.

- Create a sense of accomplishment about the meeting by reviewing the highlights and reinforcing positive messages.
- Review significant decisions that were made during the meeting.
- Commit to any unresolved items for which you owe answers or solutions, including a self-imposed deadline.
- Gain a similar commitment from salespeople on action items for which they are responsible.
- Create a sense of positive anticipation for the next meeting. Create a reason for salespeople to look forward to it.

3) ENCOURAGE INTERACTION FROM EVERYONE.

Our first two principles for leading successful sales meetings have concerned contributions that *you* make. The best sales meetings also rely on positive contributions by the salespeople. While you provide the structure and direction of the meeting, they provide its *richness*. Therefore, you want involvement from all salespeople.

Any salesperson good enough to be on your team has valuable insights to share. The stereotype that "all salespeople love to talk" is not true. Many love to sell but are not necessarily extroverts. They find talking in front of their peers much more intimidating than talking to customers. Perhaps they are simply not motivated to talk in meetings. Whatever your salespeople's reasons for participating or withdrawing in meetings, it is your job to create a balance. This is another expectation that your salespeople have of you as their leader. You should not let extroverts grab center stage week after week, nor should introverts escape without sharing their secrets of success.

On a sales team, everyone follows a unique path to success, and it is this success which qualifies them as experts. You are surrounded by a wealth of experience, expertise and insight. Your meetings are the team's best opportunity to pool these resources for brainstorming breakthroughs.

How do you create a balanced meeting in which everyone can make valuable contributions?

For those salespeople who are so comfortable in the spotlight that they tend to dominate, it is perfectly appropriate to say, "Let's give some other folks a chance."

For the salesperson who is more intimidated by the "risks" of speaking out in a group, the goal is to give them the confidence that the risk will pay off. Ask them questions in areas where you know they are strong, or where they have had recent successes.

"Eric, you've always been good at demonstrating models. What do you say to make your customers welcome the idea of you going with them to see the homes?" Then follow up on their answers in a way that makes them glad they shared.

Be very careful not to embarrass a salesperson in a meeting. Even in the case of someone who is disruptive, conduct your admonition in private after the meeting. Embarrassment in meetings can suddenly turn antagonistic. Even when it doesn't, it can be awkward for the group as a whole. Embarrassment is demoralizing, and therefore runs counter to your goal of conducting sales meetings which energize your team. Embarrassment also discourages interaction.

To gain the maximum brainstorming benefit from your sales meetings, provide problem-solving opportunities in the form of questions, real situations or hypothetical scenarios. Focus primarily on topics which apply to a majority of your team, and then solicit insights from as many salespeople as time permits. Let salespeople pose their own questions and challenges for the group as well.

Salespeople frequently consider these brainstorming sessions to be the most stimulating and beneficial of all their meetings.

"So much to do, and so little time." Earlier in the chapter we discussed four basic kinds of benefits which sales meetings provide: motivation, knowledge, training and problem solving. How do you accomplish them all? The answer lies in our fourth principle for conducting successful sales meetings.

4) Vary the format of your meetings.

Rotate the focus of your meetings so that one is primarily motivational, the next conveys information useful for selling, another focuses on selling skills, and the fourth is for brainstorming.

Vary your speakers as well. For example, you could lead the motivational session, or you could bring in an outsider. Experts from other departments in your company can lead the information meetings. Training meetings could be led by you, an outsider, or the salespeople themselves. In the brainstorming meetings you would serve as moderator for the group.

These four approaches can overlap as well, with one meeting occasionally serving several functions.

"Status updates" can always be a part of your meetings. However, when they become the central focus of meeting after meeting, you are letting the four primary benefits of sales meetings slip through your fingers, and you are also diminishing your own position of leadership.

Another way to add variety and value to your meetings is to assign a discussion topic to the group as a whole (or to several members of the group) for the following meeting. Presenting the topic in the form of an assignment allows the entire group to think about the issue prior to the meeting, even if they were not specifically assigned to present. You could supply the topics, or you could let the salespeople suggest them. The potential list is infinite. Just remember that the more people who can directly relate to the topic, the more valuable and energizing the meeting will be.

Here are ten examples of the kinds of topics which can be presented by several salespeople in a single meeting. These types of topics are designed to stimulate a *variety* of answers, so that everyone can walk away with new ideas to consider and new techniques to try. Your goal with these discussions is to enable everyone to learn from the successes (and failures) of others.

1) Tell about your all-time favorite sale.
2) What do you believe is the strongest part of your selling ability?
This question can be presented in several other variations:
- Why do you think people feel comfortable buying from you?
- What part of the selling process do you believe you perform best, and why?
- What is it about you that wins sales away from your competitors?
3) What is it about your community that makes you the best in the marketplace?
4) Give the details of your last sale, from beginning to end.
5) How did you close your last customer?
6) How do you sell your builder?
7) Tell about a strategy or technique that you tried once but would never try again.
8) Tell about a strategy or technique that you experimented with which surprised you by working.
9) Tell about a current customer that you can't quite seem to close and don't know why.
10) Have each salesperson come up with a challenge which they find difficult. Then pick out several challenges for everyone to think about prior to the next meeting, and then propose solutions at that time.

Summary

Your sales meetings are frequently the most visible and consistent element your support system. The purpose of sales meetings is to benefit salespeople. In addition to giving status updates, sales meetings should help salespeople sell more homes. Salespeople should look forward to meetings as opportunities to obtain four benefits:

1) Motivation.
2) Knowledge.
3) Training.
4) Problem solving.

There are four steps you can take to make your sales meetings successful:

1) Maintain a decisive demeanor.
2) Keep the tone of the meeting positive.
3) Encourage interaction from everyone.
4) Vary the format of your meetings.

Salespeople should emerge from sales meetings enriched, confident and invigorated. If they do, then you have provided powerful leadership.

DISCIPLINE IN SALES MANAGEMENT

THE TWO FACES OF DISCIPLINE

The word "discipline" provokes mixed feelings. It conjures up negative images as well as positive ones. This is sad, because the benefits of discipline can help an individual or a team to be more successful. Following are some of these benefits.

BENEFITS OF DISCIPLINE

• **HIGH STANDARDS.**

High standards create a more motivating and fulfilling work environment. They produce confidence. Confidence produces sales. We have been saying throughout this book that your top priority as a sales manager is to provide a support system to your team. The team's standards result from the quality of your support system. Discipline protects those standards. A commitment to discipline is a commitment to the success of your team.

• **MUTUAL TRUST AND RESPECT.**

High standards produce an environment of trust and respect, as long as everyone is playing by the same rules.

- **CONSISTENCY.**

Discipline assures that everyone does play by the same rules. A good system of discipline produces a level playing field. When everyone knows the game is fair, victory is more meaningful, and the motivation to succeed is stronger. Each of the members of the team will honor the standards with greater consistency when they know their co-workers are doing the same.

- **SELF-RESPECT.**

Just as discipline creates an environment for respect of one another, it also encourages self-respect. When people know that they are doing their best and maintaining a high standard in the process, they feel entitled to a sense of dignity. The company must help to provide this dignity: *recognition* of your employees' excellent performance and high standards gives them the satisfaction of knowing that their work has value to others.

- **FOCUS.**

An environment of discipline helps individuals, as well as the group as a whole, to stay focused on improving skills and achieving goals. An environment of chaos and inconsistency makes focus hard to sustain.

- **ACCOUNTABILITY.**

Your success as a manager and the success of your team will depend largely on the degree to which each of your salespeople feels personally accountable and responsible for their own performance. While it is important that salespeople know what you stand for, it is equally important that they know what you won't stand for. Companies or teams with little discipline often have little accountability. In these companies an individual's level of performance often seems less important than how good their excuse is when they fail (or who else they can blame for their failure). Teams with a strong sense of discipline foster an environment of individual accountability. Once the individuals on a team take personal responsibility for their performance, the team's system of discipline begins to take care of itself.

- **HIGH MORALE.**

The six benefits discussed so far lead to an environment of higher morale. Higher morale makes each of the six benefits even more valuable. A strong, fair system of discipline which is administered wisely and consistently helps this cycle to fuel itself. These seven benefits of discipline all work together to produce a bottom line benefit:

- **IMPROVED PERFORMANCE.**

The rewards of discipline are, in fact, very tangible. You have created not only a more fulfilling environment, but a more successful one.

These eight benefits make discipline sound like the key to a perfect world. Why, then, is the concept of discipline so controversial? Why does it produce so much anxiety for managers, causing stomach problems and sleepless nights? Why do so many managers avoid discipline altogether, even as morale and productivity continue to deteriorate around them? Why do so many salespeople rebel against it?

The answer is that many leaders abuse discipline. One of the greatest pitfalls of leadership is the abuse of power. Unfortunately, this happens in our line of work just as in any other. The abuse of power is the ugly side of discipline. It undermines every one of the benefits listed above, creating cynicism about one of the most valuable tools you have for providing a strong support system.

Here are several ways that discipline can be abused in sales management.

ABUSES OF DISCIPLINE

- **FEAR OF ENFORCING IT.**

There is no doubt that it takes courage to administer discipline. Not everyone responds well to it. Most people respect discipline, and respond well to it when it is enforced fairly and wisely. However, some employees cannot handle discipline, no matter how well it is administered. Managing these employees can be extremely difficult. It can even be frightening. This is why many managers avoid discipline. They take the path of least resistance, and survive another day in peace. But the price their teams will pay for this approach is very steep. Ultimately, the benefits listed above will be lost, and with them a lot of good people and a lot of money. The decision to go into management is a serious one, and discipline is one of the most serious issues of all.

• INCONSISTENCY.

Fear of enforcing discipline is, of course, one kind of inconsistency. There are many others, including:

- Enforcing a rule sometimes, but not always.
- Constantly changing the rules.
- Showing favoritism for reasons other than performance.
- Taking discipline more seriously sometimes than others.

Discipline only has value when it is consistently enforced. Otherwise your position of leadership deteriorates.

• UNFAIRNESS.

Not only must discipline be consistent, it must also be fair. Your rules must make sense, and must be tolerable. They must not undermine the dignity of your salespeople. If your salespeople tell you that a rule is unfair or insulting, hear them out and weigh their comments with sensitivity.

• GIVING RULES WITHOUT REASONS.

Employees always deserve an explanation for a rule or decision. Failure to give reasons risks your perception of credibility, sensitivity and wisdom in their eyes. It may also cause them to believe that you are not really interested in being fair.

• USING DISCIPLINE AS A DISPLAY OF POWER.

Managing means setting aside one's ego in order to encourage and develop the work of others. It requires a "big picture" perspective.

Once again, your goal is to provide a support system. The purpose of discipline is to empower your employees, not yourself. Your system of discipline empowers your people by providing the benefits listed above. If you use discipline to lift your people up rather than put them down, your own position of power will take care of itself. It will no longer be something which needs to be "displayed."

These are five ways that discipline is misused. The unfortunate result is ambivalence about the idea of discipline. If these mixed feelings exist within your team, the good news is that the problem can be fixed. Think of discipline as your commitment to their well-being, and not as a necessary evil of management.

So far this all may be sounding very idealistic, so let's look at some specific ways to bring these ideals to life in the real world.

HOW TO CREATE A SYSTEM OF DISCIPLINE

The purpose of discipline in a new home sales department is not to achieve perfection, but to create an environment for success. We are in an industry where a perfectionist can become a very unhappy person. You do not have to be a perfectionist to pursue high standards. The problem with perfectionism is that it winds up making everyone feel like a failure. You do not have to administer discipline every time a mistake is made. Your goal is to create an environment where everyone keeps improving.

The word "discipline" comes from "disciple," and therefore implies *teaching*. To discipline is to teach, not to command. The spirit of your system of discipline should be to *improve* your salespeople, not punish them. That is the spirit of this chapter. Punishment is sometimes necessary, and we will discuss that topic briefly. However, we will not include a section on "how to dismiss an employee" in this book. That is not our purpose here. Procedures for dismissal should be taught by your company's own personnel department or legal resources. Termination must be handled in a way that is fair, consistent and legal. We do not believe that a book such as this is the best place to learn dismissal procedures.

In order for a system of discipline to be successful it must be clearly understood by everyone. It is hard for employees to view discipline as fair when they do not understand what it includes and why.

You start by explaining your entire system to yourself — in writing. Refer back to your "Vision and Action Plan," where you set your standards for yourself and for your ideal department. Using this plan as your starting point, write down exactly what your standards are. If you can't put them into words, they don't exist. At least not in the form that can be upheld consistently and fairly. It is helpful if your salespeople can also have access to written standards. Many companies provide this information in the form of a policy manual. Some include it in a contract or written job description.

Your standards include your *expectations.* They must be clearly stated. There can be no doubts among your team about these expectations. The better your communication about standards, responsibilities and expectations, the less will be the need for disciplinary action later on.

As you explain your standards to your team — verbally or in writing — it is not always necessary to state the consequences for failure to comply. This is a judgment call, depending upon the group and the topic. Information concerning consequences can be conveyed on an as-needed basis, as long as it is consistent. However, it is certainly something you should carefully think through in order to be able to take a proactive approach to discipline. Talk it over with your personnel department. You don't want to be suspected of making discipline up as you go.

As you think through the ways you will administer your discipline program, hold on firmly to the idea that your purpose is to help, train and improve your salespeople. It is never to exert power or get revenge. Discipline is for their well-being, not yours. Your goal is to motivate, not stifle.

Your system of discipline motivates your people by demonstrating a commitment to excellence: they can take *pride* in their company, their work, their colleagues, and their own personal achievements. It trains and supports them by helping them up when they fall, not by knocking them again. As you help them up, you teach them how to keep from falling again.

To have a successful system for discipline, it is important to receive input from your sales team. Discuss your ideas and policies openly with your salespeople — one on one and in your team meetings. Welcome their ideas. Everyone should feel comfortable discussing their thoughts openly and honestly. The final word belongs to you. Once an issue has been discussed, bring it to closure before moving on. Don't leave issues dangling in uncertainty.

Be thorough in giving your explanations. Your salespeople deserve them. There is the rare occasion when the final explanation must be, "Because I said so, and I'm the boss." Sometimes this is the only way to break a deadlock where opinions will never be reconciled. Take this approach as rarely and gently as possible. Sensitivity to the dignity of each salesperson is especially important in these situations.

Finally, be willing to lead by example. As you design your system for discipline, make sure that there can never be any double standards. Your team will look to you not only to explain the standards, but to demonstrate them.

HOW TO ADMINISTER YOUR SYSTEM OF DISCIPLINE

You developed a "Vision and Action Plan" in order to define your vision of a successful leader and a winning team, and then established your plan for fulfilling that vision.

Now all of the members of your team understand the standards, expectations and responsibilities that go with their job. When a team member falls below the standard, you must help them make their comeback. Normally your efforts will begin with a one-on-one conversation. A group meeting may be appropriate when the team as a whole has fallen below the standard, but discipline is usually individual. Let's look at a few examples of situations where you need to confront an individual on a matter of sub-standard performance.

Suppose you have a salesperson who is frequently late getting to the sales office. Opening time is 11:00, but the construction supervisor has told you that the salesperson frequently arrives ten or fifteen minutes late, and sometimes as late as 11:30. How would you handle this situation?

Here is one scenario:

As the salesperson stops into the manager's office to drop off some papers after the Monday morning sales meeting, the manager says, "Joe, for three months now I've been hearing that you're coming in late. You know as well as I do that it's unacceptable. Plus it makes you look like an idiot to the whole world, and I'm sick of covering for you. If I hear about it again, you're history. Do you catch my drift?"

Does a manager have the *right* to take this approach? Sure. The salesperson's continual lateness is grounds for strong discipline. However, while the manager is within his "rights" to take this approach, it is not the best way to administer discipline. There are several problems with the way the manager handled this situation.

1) Why did the manager wait three months to address the problem, and then suddenly threaten the salesperson with dismissal? What if the salesperson had not needed to drop off some papers at the manager's office, could he have kept on coming to work late? Why has the manager been covering for the salesperson for three months if the problem were grounds for dismissal? Where is the consistency?

2) The manager attacked the salesperson by calling him an idiot. The salesperson's lateness is the issue, not his intelligence. The salesperson was humiliated. This situation calls for corrective action, not verbal assault.

3) There was no dialogue, only reprimand. People treat their dogs with more dignity when they housebreak them. Let the "defendant" have his say. That's the way our system works.

Here is a better approach. In this scenario, the manager did not follow up on the superintendent's first report of lateness, because the manager believed it was a fluke, and not worthy of a reprimand. However, a week later, he gets a second report. In this example we are not trying to depict a manager who combines the wisdom of Solomon with the charisma of George Washington. This type of situation can be handled very naturally by any manager with average ability, without the need for a commanding personality.

A soon as possible, he calls the sales office (to avoid the further delay of waiting until the next time he sees the salesperson) and says, "Joe, I understand that you're not always opening up on time. The next time we get together I'd like to chat with you about it and see if there's a problem."

If you took this approach you would be letting the salesperson know that you are aware of the problem, and that you consider it serious enough for a face-to-face talk. You would also be showing the courtesy that you don't want to catch him off guard.

The next time you see him, whether it's in your office or his, wait for him to bring it up. If he doesn't, then you can.

Manager: "Joe, about this lateness problem, what's going on?"

Salesperson: "Yeah, I've been late a couple of times. I never get any traffic before noon."

M: "Joe, whether you get traffic is not the issue. All of our sales offices open at 11:00. And opening on time is important. We've talked about it in meetings, and it's in the policy manual. Do you think it's not a serious matter?"

S: "I don't think it's all that serious. I'm one of you're top three producers. Somehow I manage to have the sales office open when customers want to buy houses."

M: "So have you decided to give yourself a pay raise by working a shorter day than everyone else for the same pay scale? Everybody else seems to think opening up on time is important. I think it's important, and so does the company. Making sales is just one part of your job. There are a lot of other responsibilities, too, including having the sales office open when we tell the public it will be. There's no doubt about it, you *are* an outstanding salesperson, and everybody knows it. It's very much appreciated, and you have a lot of respect around here. Why do you put all that at risk? Let me ask you something. One day you might be in my position. If you are, what would you do now? You need to run a department fairly, and you must maintain high standards. Without that the morale dies and nobody wants to work for the company any more. So what would you do?"

S: "Okay, I get your point."

M: "What's the next step?"

S: "I'll be on time."

M: "Great, I really appreciate that. Is there anything I can do for you?"

   Some people might say this manager's response was too long-winded or wimpy. There are certainly plenty of right ways to handle the situation, if this approach does not suit your style. However, let us make several points about what was accomplished in this scenario.

- The manager sought to help the employee, while also protecting the support system by upholding the team's high standards.
- He addressed the problem promptly. The longer a problem is left unconfronted, the more the integrity of the team and the manager are compromised.

- His position was clearly stated. He did not waffle, apologize or back down.
- His message was conveyed gently, but firmly. When the salesperson's response was mildly rebellious, the manager displayed an appropriate amount of impatience without blowing his cool.
- He used the discipline situation as an opportunity to expand the salesperson's thought process, rather than simply to issue a reprimand. He got the salesperson to think through the situation, and the implications of his lateness which the salesperson had apparently not considered. The manager helped the salesperson to see the situation from the manager's perspective, and to increase his understanding of the issue. He wanted the salesperson to think, learn, and correct his behavior.
- He dealt with the problem fairly. He put the offense into the correct perpective, not making it larger or smaller than it really was.
- He showed consistency. He referred to the fact that the issue had been discussed before, and was also in the policy manual. The same standard applies to everyone.
- He made it clear that his commitment was to the entire team.
- He conveyed respect to the salesperson, balancing an appreciation of success with a disappointment of failure.
- He allowed the salesperson to express an opinion, in case there was an excuse that the salesperson considered legitimate. In this case the salesperson's explanation was fairly brief. If it had been longer, the manager would have listened and weighed the salesperson's side of the story.
- By asking, "What would you do?" the manager gently introduced the issue of consequences into the discussion. Since the salesperson was a successful employee who had gained respect aside from the tardiness problem, the manager did not feel it was appropriate to beat him over the head with a threat. The salesperson agreed to cooperate, so it was not necessary for the manager to kick him again by saying, "And if you don't..." A salesperson's long-term track record should be considered in these types of encounters.
- The discussion ended with a specific resolution, a commitment by the salesperson to improve, and a final gesture of gratitude and support by the manager.

Presumably the problem will not arise again. If it does, then a specific warning should be issued which spells out clearly that the next violation will result in dismissal (if that is consistent with company policy). The specific offense, the prior history of the offense and reprimands, the plan for improvement, and the consequences for failure to improve should all be put in writing, with a copy to the salesperson and a copy in the salesperson's personnel file. Consult with your personnel department for the official procedure for dismissal.

What about dismissal? There is a theory floating around that says "a failure by an employee is a failure by management." The implication is that if you as a manager have to dismiss someone, then it is your failure, not the employee's. That philosophy can destroy a company. Your job as manager is to set standards, and then to personally set the example of those standards. The employees' responsibility is to support those standards.

A sales director is hired to be a leader, a boss and a manager, not a savior. If you do your job, and provide the support necessary for them to do theirs, the truth is that sometimes employees will still fail. An employee who continually undermines the team's standards and damages its morale, when you have done your best to provide support, is not your failure. Your failure would be to continue to allow their damage to spread.

You, your sales team and your company deserve good people who will show you the same loyalty you give them. Many companies suffer unnecessary injury by holding on to the employees who are hurting them the most. Beyond the damage they cause, the manager causes even more by sending the message to the rest of the team that poor performance is acceptable. Few things are more demoralizing than watching a bad employee be rewarded. The good employees view this as a sign of incompetence, blindness or cowardice on the part of management. That becomes a far greater problem than the bad employee alone.

If you have an employee who cannot or will not honor your standards, the problem must be addressed courageously and honestly. Do not let the employee twist in the wind, hoping that over a period of time they will get discouraged and quit. That is an injustice to everyone. Everyone deserves to be treated fairly and honestly, regardless of their attitude or performance.

No one should ever be surprised by a termination. With the exception of gross or illegal acts that *demand* immediate dismissal, employees should be warned and provided with a plan for improvement, with each step documented as necessary.

Let's look at one more example. Suppose you have a top producer whose poor paperwork continues to cost other employees time and the company money. It also creates misunderstandings with buyers. Except for paperwork, the salesperson's performance is outstanding. Still the paperwork problems continue to wreak habit with production, accounting, the lender and the settlement attorney. Sometimes the types of problems that arise make you wonder if the negotiations with the customer were entirely above board. You have decided that no matter how good the salesperson is, the paperwork problem must end. It is so notorious that it has become a morale problem for other departments, and for other salespeople who work long hours to get their paperwork right. To make matters worse, the salesperson has been taking an uncooperative attitude toward improvement.

M: "John, I have another problem on your latest contract. You sold one option for the wrong price. On another one you didn't fill out the form correctly for production. We have to go through this on three out of every four of your contracts. It's getting to the point where production and accounting dread it every time you sell a home, which is not the way it should be. We keep having this conversation, but it doesn't seem to make any difference to you. You're a very intelligent guy, and I know you can do the paperwork right if you want to. If this problem is never going to get any better, I need to know it now."

S: "What are you going to do, fire me because the paperwork's wrong? I'm your top salesperson and you know it. Why can't the secretary fix the paperwork so I can do what you're paying me to do — sell houses."

M: "John, we're paying you to do a lot more than just sell houses. That's why we have job descriptions. You're paid to do the whole job, not just your favorite parts. I've shown you how to correct your mistakes quite a few times. Whether the problem is ability or attitude, we need to resolve it once and for all, right now."

S: "I think you're blowing it out of proportion. Everybody has weaknesses, except you, I guess. But my weakness is paperwork."

M: "Unfortunately, John, it's more than just a weakness. It's a real problem for the other departments. I've been asked more than once why I put up with it. If everyone turned in paperwork with this many problems our whole operation would be in turmoil. Your job includes submitting correct paperwork. Are you telling me that you can't do that?"

S: "I don't understand what you're getting at. Is my job in trouble or not?"

M: "That depends on your answer to my last question. Everyone in this department works very hard to get their paperwork right except you, and your paperwork is causing big problems. If you're saying it's not going to change, then, yes, you're job is in trouble."

S: "Well I don't think that's reasonable."

M: "Then let me explain it to you. I have an entire team to worry about, and if everybody gets to have their own favorite set of rules, then I have no team. I've got low morale and chaos, and eventually a bankrupt company. I know you are a top salesperson, but the company depends on the rest of your job, too. I depend on it. So do the other salespeople. If your paperwork is bad, and I accept that, then I have to accept everyone else's failures, too, whether it's no sales or drinking on the job or lying to customers. Where do I draw the line? You tell me."

S: "I know you're under a lot of pressure."

M: "That's not the issue. The issue is that for the good of the team and the company, I need for you to commit that you're going to get your paperwork straightened out. I need for you to tell me that from today on, your paperwork is going to measure up to the standards of the rest of the team. Can you do that?"

S: "I'll try. I admit, I really do have a problem staying focused on the paperwork. I hate it and I'm terrible at it. And I didn't see what the big deal was about losing a few dollars or asking someone else to work with me. But I see your point, and I'll try harder."

M: "It's very important. I'm going to have to put a letter in your file this time, and I want you to consider the situation serious. There will be no more discussion of your job being on the line if it gets better. I know it won't be perfect every time. But it should be most of the time. We can talk about it again in a month, and see how it's going. Thanks for understanding."

This scenario was obviously very exasperating for both people involved, and required tremendous persistence on the part of the manager. It's okay to get exasperated, and to show it, as long as your demeanor remains calm and rational, and your approach fair and consistent.

Here are several things that this manager did right.

- She remained very firm about her dissatisfaction with John's work without attacking him as a person.
- She kept the conversation focused on getting a commitment for improvement.
- Her approach was fair. The problem had grown beyond the point of reasonable tolerance, so that a warning of dismissal had become appropriate. Dismissal without warning would not have been.
- While she referred to the fact that other people had asked why she tolerated the problem, she did not use it as the excuse for this reprimand. It is vital that you take personal responsibility for the reprimands that you give. When managers try to pass that buck to someone else, it lowers the position of the manager and the tone of the discussion.
- She continued to reinforce her loyalty to the company and the sales team. She used a "big-picture" perspective in order to teach the salesperson to view the problem in the same way. She explained the entire situation and its consequences to others. She was trying to help the salesperson to understand, and not just obey. She showed empathy for others as she attempted to encourage John to do the same.
- Her approach was consistent. There had been other similar conversations leading up to this one. She referred to the job description, and kept the playing field level with the other salespeople.
- She not only spoke, but also listened. She did not try to force him to be quiet. She responded firmly to his remarks, but with an appropriate amount of sensitivity.
- She was as specific as she needed to be about her expectations for his future performance.
- She got him to commit to doing his best to meet those expectations.
- She set a timetable for improvement, as well as a specific time for a followup conversation to review the progress.

The principles discussed in these two examples apply to most types of situations which require a confrontation. When improved performance is necessary, it should be done one-on-one, face-to-face. It should not be done by memo alone, or in the presence of others. Don't try to make an example out of one person. It is more likely to humiliate and demoralize them than help them improve.

As with other aspects of management, the discipline part of your job can be more successful if you can handle some of it proactively. Naturally, there is a part of discipline which must be reactive. But there are other parts where the initiatives you take when there are no problems can make a difference. We have already discussed the importance of planning, communication and leadership by example in helping your team to achieve high standards. There are two other commitments you can make to your team which will help promote excellence and prevent problems: continuous counseling and performance appraisals.

CONTINUOUS COUNSELING

Like almost everyone else, salespeople need attention. For a social profession, new home sales has a very lonely aspect to it. There is also a high level of frustration. Salespeople need a sounding board for their problems as well as their ideas. They also need consistent feedback as to how their performance is viewed by the company and by you, their manager.

One of the frustrations most frequently expressed by salespeople is that managers are never around when you need them. Availability to salespeople must be a top priority for sales managers. There must be a way for them to reach you by phone when they need a specific answer, or at least a way for you to return their calls promptly (such as a beeper). You also need to be able to schedule time with each of them just to talk. This part of your support system is usually accomplished most effectively in the field — "on their turf." We will discuss site visits in detail in Chapter Nine as part of our section on training. In addition to the training benefits which site visits offer, they also provide the opportunity to:

• Discuss challenges the salesperson faces in selling.
• Discuss problems in getting customers to settlement.

- Let the salesperson sound off about anything that is bothering them.
- Review the salesperson's performance (including appreciation for the salesperson's achievements and discussion of areas where the salesperson needs to improve).

During these encounters it is important to listen as much as you talk. People joke about how psychological counselors just sit there and ask, "What do you think?" But the reason they keep doing it is because it keeps working. They teach their client to work through a thought process while they team up with the client to solve problems. As a managing counselor, your role is very similar. You help salespeople to improve their ability by working with them to expand their thought processes.

Supportiveness and honesty are two other elements of effective counseling. Find out what they need from you in order to improve. If there is an area in which they are not meeting your expectations, bring it up now, while the atmosphere is casual and supportive. Talk it through and try to develop a plan for improvement before the issue reaches the "reprimand" stage.

If the salesperson has a complaint about someone other than you, don't fuel their fire. Commiseration is dangerous business for a manager. Stay focused on solutions. Encourage the salesperson to take intitiative in solving problems. If there is no solution, try to help the salesperson endure the challenge. Encouraging their complaints about production or the designated lender without providing a solution can lower the salesperson's morale, and highlight your own helplessness to remedy the situation. Instead of being their buddy, you will have them wondering, "What good are you?"

Managers need to be cautious in what they say about other people. In the managerial world of shifting alliances, today's friend can become tomorrow's enemy. "True confessions" can backfire on you, too. As a manager you should make it your policy not to say anything that you don't want repeated.

Although a consistent commitment to counseling requires a significant investment of time, it is one of the most valuable functions you will perform as a sales manager. Managers who neglect this duty on the grounds that they don't have time pay dearly for their misplaced priorities. Unfortunately, so do their salespeople. A consistent commitment to counseling will enable you to:

• Maintain a high level of communication with your salespeople.
• Work with your salespeople to maintain high standards.
• Work with your salespeople to solve problems.
• Resolve small performance issues before they become large ones.
• Take the time to give complete explanations to your salespeople so that they can see issues from all points of view and understand the reasoning behind management decisions.
• Follow up on issues which have been discussed before.

PERFORMANCE APPRAISALS

If you are continuing to support and evaluate each of your salespeople's performance and needs through one-on-one counseling, why do you also need performance appraisals? The more formal atmosphere of performance appraisals complements the day-to-day counseling by providing a specific time to review the salesperson's performance *as a whole*. Performance appraisals offer an additional way to help salespeople sustain high performance (or improve mediocre performance) because these appraisals are formalized, anticipated and continuous.

• *FORMALIZED*

They are based on real *results*. They are also documented, with copies going to the salesperson and the salesperson's individual personnel file.

• *ANTICIPATED*

Because they are serious, and because everyone knows when they are coming, they provide a target date for achieving performance goals.

• *CONTINUOUS*

Each performance appraisal provides measurable changes from the last one and measurable goals for the next one. Performance appraisals should be specific. You can use any method of measurement you want, as long as you and the salespeople understand your system of measurement in the same way. Even subjective items such as attitude can be measured, as long as the standard of measurement is clearly expressed.

Company goals, such as sales, settlements and profit margins can be included. So can specific issues, such as punctuality, paperwork, model maintenance, Realtor visits, prospecting, follow up, and competitive shopping. Although the overall format for your appraisals should be consistent for your entire team, it can be tailored to meet the specific needs of each individual.

While performance reviews focus on specific *results* and *progress,* it is still important to encourage each salesperson to express his or her point of view during these meetings.

Many managers avoid giving performance reviews, finding them awkwardly judgmental. It is important that these reviews be perceived as a service to your employees. If their performance is excellent, they deserve formal as well as informal recognition. If their performance needs improvement, it needs to be addressed head-on in a serious but supportive way. Most salespeople would rather succeed than fail, and will welcome help as long as their dignity is protected. For those who don't care, a conscientious appraisal enables you to warn them, and to give them a fair opportunity to redeem themselves and keep their jobs.

People must see themselves through the eyes of a leader whom they trust to keep them on the path to greater success. They need to know what they are doing right so that they can build on it, and what they are doing wrong so they can improve.

Performance appraisals provide an opportunity for you to work with your salespeople to provide a plan for their long-term success, and for yours.

SUMMARY

Discipline adds a valuable dimension to your management support system, as long as the motivation behind it is to *teach* and not to punish. It creates an environment in which your salespeople can enjoy the satisfaction of continuous improvement on a team which shares high values, and in a company which rewards excellence.

A consistent system of discipline will help your sales team achieve a higher level of success by providing eight benefits:

1) High standards.

2) Mutual trust and respect.
3) Consistency.
4) Self-respect.
5) Focus.
6) Accountability.
7) High morale.
8) Improved performance.

When discipline is abused, its creates cynicism which lowers morale. Five examples of the abuse of discipline are:

1) Fear of enforcing it.
2) Inconsistency.
3) Unfairness.
4) Giving rules without reasons.
5) Using discipline as a display of power.

To create an effective system of discipline:

• Put your standards and expectations in writing, at least for yourself.
• Consider providing your expectations to your sales team in writing. This can be done with a written employment contract, job description or policy manual. Some companies prefer not to put this kind of information in writing. In this event, be sure that your standards, expectations and the salesperson's job description are clearly understood by everyone on your team through verbal communication.
• Provide explanations to your salespeople so that they will understand the thought process behind your standards.
• Invite input from salespeople as to how the discipline system can be improved. Open-mindedness is an important part of discipline.
• Lead by example.

To administer an effective system of discipline:

• Address problems quickly, decisively, consistently and fairly.
• Address problems with individuals face to face, one on one.
• Do not attack or humiliate the salesperson. Stay focused on the issue, and on the goal of helping the salesperson.
• Recognize the salesperson's positive achievements. Show that you still

respect them and appreciate what they have accomplished in the past.

- Use the discipline situation as an opportunity to expand the salesperson's thought process about the issue, its implications and its consequences.
- Show that your commitment is to the entire team, and to the company. Explain ways in which the salesperson's actions have jeopardized that commitment.
- Allow the salesperson to express his or her opinion. Listen and respond fairly to that opinion.
- When necessary, ask the salesperson, "What would you do in my position?"
- Do not blame someone else for the fact that you are forced to administer disciplinary action. You must personally stand firm behind the action you are taking.
- Conclude discussions with a specific resolution, a plan for improvement, and a timetable for that plan to be accomplished. Provide written documentation when necessary (see your personnel department or legal resources).
- Understand the consequences of keeping employees who continue to be unproductive or who undermine your team and its standards, even after you have done everything you could to help them improve.

Make a commitment to one-on-one sales counseling for all of your salespeople, whether they ask for it or not. Your counseling is an important part of the overall communication process. It helps your salespeople to keep their perspective. You have more time during these meetings to provide meaningful explanations to your salespeople. It enables you to work with them as a team to resolve challenges. It helps you to address small problems before they become large ones.

In addition to the informal coaching and counseling which you provide, you can also help salespeople to achieve a higher level of success by providing periodic performance appraisals. These appraisals add a dimension to your support system because they are formalized, anticipated and continuous.

Providing this level of individual support to your sales team requires a commitment of time which is often quite difficult to make, given the other responsibilities which will inundate you. Therefore, let's move on to the final chapter in our management section — "Time Management."

MANAGING YOUR TIME

SETTLING IN

M any new sales directors are surprised by the work load. As a salesperson you were responsible for yourself and your production. Now you wear many hats — "people, paper and profits." If you are finding it overwhelming, do not regret your decision to become a sales director. It really will get better. It is not unusual for a sales director's first six months to be very difficult. It seems impossible to reconcile the infinite amount of work with the finite amount of time. You are working sixty hours a week and getting farther behind. You can't keep this pace up forever. You're not sure that you want to.

Well, the good news is you won't have to. The tough parts of the job will get easier. The awkward parts will become more natural. The new parts will become familiar. Although your sixty-hour week may never become forty hours, it will get shorter.

It is important to realize that this initial struggle with time management is normal. It does not mean you are incompetent. It simply means you are mastering a new challenge.

You must fight off self-doubt during this time. Self-doubt is one of the biggest hurdles for a new sales director to overcome. Where does this self-doubt come from? There are several sources.

- You may think everyone else seems to have their job under control better than you do.

For a while this may be true. They may have "caught the rhythm" of their job by now. They are farther along their learning curve, and they have figured out which parts of their job demand worry and which do not. But remember, at some point they were starting out, too. In addition, as we discussed earlier, the transitions you have made in becoming a sales director (peer to boss and field to office) include some uniquely difficult challenges.

- You may have someone advise you to "work smarter, not harder."

Somehow that comment often seems to make things worse, especially when it comes without an explanation. Don't allow the remark to make you question your own intelligence. The fact is, you *do* have to work harder, at least for awhile. As your skills and confidence improve, the job will get easier. Learn to "work smarter" at your own pace.

- An expert might tell you to manage your time better by establishing your priorities as A's, B's, and C's. Do the A's, delegate the B's and leave the C's for another day.

Once again you feel foolish because you can't make this work. Completing the A's while you try to handle all of the interruptions seems to consume your entire day. No one else knows how to do the B's, and the C's really do need to be accomplished soon.

There is no doubt that *prioritizing* and *delegating* are two of the most important ingredients for effective time management. Let's see how you can develop a foothold for managing your time as a new homes sales director.

PRIORITIZING

The reason companies hire sales directors is to increase income. You are perhaps the company's most important income producer. Prioritize your use of time with this idea in mind. What allocation of your hours will produce the most income for the company? The answer is: *Manage your time so that activities which increase sales get most of your weekly hours.*

Make a list of those responsibilities that contribute directly to increased sales. Your list will include:

- Training, coaching and counseling salespeople.
- Helping salespeople to solve problems in the field.
- Solving sales-related problems with other departments that are beyond the authority of the salesperson.
    — Product design, features and options.
    — Communication problems that adversely affect sales.
    — Construction-related issues within your realm.
    — Sales strategy and policy issues.
    — Marketing issues.
- Managing settlements.
- Working with mortgage lenders to assure that your salespeople have the best possible financing products and service for their customers.
- Visiting the competition.
- Supervising the salespeople's strategies for generating their own traffic.
- Monitoring and evaluating each salesperson's activity, including follow up.
- Maintaining high standards of model and community presentation.

Add to this list any other functions specific to your company that will help your salespeople sell more homes, or sell their homes more profitably.

Next make a separate list of all your other responsibilities. Your goal in time management will be to develop a schedule that allows you to accomplish this second list as efficiently as possible. You must accomplish these items correctly, without jeopardizing your primary commitment to the first list — the income-producing activities. The second list could include:

- Reporting.
- Contract ratification and related paperwork.
- Other paperwork.
- Budget management.
- Miscellaneous office meetings.
- Responding to non-sales-related phone calls, memos and special requests.
- Miscellaneous interruptions.
- Office socializing.

Each of the items in our second list plays an important role in the smooth running of a company. Even the last two are necessary for a sales director to allocate some time for. The challenge is to establish the correct proportions. That is time management.

How can you set the best priorities for your company and your sales team? Once you have set them, how can you stick with them in the real world of continuous surprises?

The first step is to sit down with your supervisor and create a plan for your time management that you both agree on. You will need your supervisor's support in order for your plan to work.

Discuss your "Vision and Action Plan" with your boss, and tell him or her how you see your role as sales director being fulfilled most effectively. Also find out what he thinks, in as much detail as possible. How does he think you should be spending your time? What does he think your priorities should be? You will need to reach an agreement on these issues in order to have your boss's full support; and there will be times when you need it.

You may have to compromise on some of your priorities in order to reach this agreement. Be willing to trust your boss's experience enough to re-evaluate some of your own ideas. At the same time, if there is an issue that you feel very strongly about and are confident that you are right, ask your boss to give you the benefit of the doubt. Reassure him that you are willing to take full responsibility.

One important question that you will need to agree upon is, "What percent of your time should you spend in the office, and what percent should you spend in the field?" This decision provides the cornerstone of your time management plan, and you must force yourself to abide by it in order for your plan to succeed.

Your supervisor can help you stick to your plan by respecting the commitments you make away from the office. In fact, the entire company must support your time management plan, just as they must support the needs of any other employee. Your ability to provide consistent field support will prove to be a significant factor in your company's overall success.

The percentage of time spent in the field vs. the office varies from one company to the next, and is affected by the way administrative and marketing responsibilities are divided. In companies where a sales director also carries most of the department's administrative and marketing responsibilites, the sales director may only get to spend 20% of his or her time in the field. Beware that this approach will probably not allow your team to receive the coaching and problem-solving support they need.

At the other extreme is the sales director who has very few responsibilities other than directly helping salespeople. These sales managers may spend 80% or more of their time in the field. Some do not even have a desk at the corporate office. Your company may not agree to the level of staffing necessary to allow you to spend this much time in the field. They may also believe it is better for the company that you have more involvement in administrative details and marketing strategy. Whatever your company's position, be sure you weigh the cost of every hour that is taken away from the direct support you can offer your salespeople.

Generally you should be prepared to commit at least 50% of your time to field support, with the other half committed to office responsibilities. Your goal is to be a "field general" at least as much as "office general," and hopefully more. If you cannot give 50% of your time to the field, you are running the risk of providing inadequate support to the income-producing arm of your company.

Here is how to allocate your time so that at least 50% is devoted to the field.

Decide the total number of hours per week that your job requires. (We will use 50 hours per week as an example.) Then decide how that time will be allocated. In our example, we will commit 25 hours to the office and 25 to the field.

Now make a list of every activity that you believe will require your time in the office, and every activity in the field. Allocate a specific number of hours that you plan to commit to each activity, *beginning with your field responsibilities.* It is absolutely essential to assign times to your field activities first, and then make your office responsibilities fit into the hours that are left over. If you start with your office responsibilities, you will probably hit 40 hours very quickly, and then be tempted to lower the number of field hours. Fulfilling your office responsibilities in no more than 50% of you total hours may be your most difficult time management challenge. On the other hand, 25 hours for field support may not seem like enough, either, depending on the number of people you are coaching and distance you must travel.

Review your time management plan with your supervisor. If he endorses the plan, ask him to commit to helping you protect it. Ask him to explain the importance of your program to other upper level managers who might also be in a position to disrupt your commitment.

Explain your time management commitment to your salespeople so they understand your system as well as your other responsibilities that could occasionally interfere with your time for them.

Of course, every sales director's schedule will be slightly different. Here is an example of how such a schedule might look. This is not intended to serve as a model for your schedule, but rather to show how the concept can work.

Field Responsibilites	Average Hours per Week
1) Driving to sites	5
2) Working with salespeople	12
3) Walking the models and sites	2
4) Visiting construction offices	1
5) Meeting with homeowners	1
6) Visiting Realtors	1
7) Visiting competitors	3
Total Hours	25

Only items #1 and #2 would occur with every site visit. The other items would be rotated in order to produce the average number of hours listed above.

Office Responsibilities	Average Hours per Week
1) Weekly sales meeting	2
2) Other meetings	2
3) Paperwork related to contracts	2
4) Paperwork related to reporting	2
5) Other paperwork	3
6) Phone calls	4
7) Fulfilling needs of other office people	3
8) Problem solving	3
9) Miscellaneous interruptions	3
10) Socializing	1
Total Hours	25

While some of the time allocations listed here may seem unrealistically low, remember that your being in the field will help some of these numbers. For example, some of your time commitment for items #3, #6, and #8 will now be shifted to your field schedule. Hours needed to fulfill #7, #9, and #10 will be reduced simply because you are not there. Some of these needs can be delegated to others.

One obstacle to effective time management is interruptions that occur in the office while you are doing paperwork. In our example we committed 9 hours to office paperwork. Any paperwork assignments which can be completed before 8:30 or after 5:00 will go much faster than when they are tackled during regular business hours. This will free you up for more time in the field. The options of coming in early, staying late or taking paperwork home may actually shorten your work week instead of lengthening it.

Try not to get bogged down in paperwork, unless you are on a strict deadline. Be willing to put it aside in order to fulfill your other responsibilities, and then return to the paperwork later. You may even be more energized and attentive for paperwork with your other commitments in order.

DELEGATING

Delegating can be difficult for a sales manager because so many of your tasks demand that you be personally responsible for decisions and their results. Much of your work seems too risky to delegate. Frequently, it seems to take more time to delegate an item than to complete it yourself.

Remember that one of your greatest achievements as a manager will be helping your people to grow in their careers. The two best ways to help people grow are to *teach* them and *empower* them. Combine this fact with your own need to make your enormous range of responsibilities more manageable and you have a perfect situation. Help your people to grow by training them and empowering them to share in your reponsibilities. It sounds simple enough, but how can you really make delegation work without leading your whole company out on to a very thin limb?

You must first decide which responsibilities you could delegate if your employees (salespeople and office employees) can learn to think like you.

Then perform the task one time yourself in the presence of your employee. Explain each step so that the employee understands your entire thought process as well as how the task is executed.

Have the employee accomplish the task as you look on. Ask him to explain his thought process each step of the way.

Now the employee can perform the task without you present. Review his work carefully when he is finished, remembering that correct completion of the task is still your responsibility. Don't forget to express appreciation for the fact that the employee has successfully relieved you of the task.

In time you may reach the point where you feel comfortable allowing employees to implement their own decisions without your approval, although the ultimate responsibility for any work you delegate is still yours.

If employees become scapegoats for failures of delegated work (especially when the work is beyond their basic job description), they will be reluctant to accept additional responsibility in the future.

An example of a task you might delegate could be the selection of exterior home elevations and colors at a community where these items must be preselected. When the time comes to choose these selections, meet with the salesperson and explain exactly how and why you make your choices for each home. Next time have her do it under your supervision. These two steps should be accomplished during a site visit. The third time allow her to make the selections alone and have you review them. Eventually you will become confident that your involvement in the selections will no longer be necessary. Make sure to express appreciation when tasks are completed successfully.

Delegating these types of responsibilities does not happen overnight. However, it can be accomplished in a way that will eventually relieve you of significant decision-making responsibilities, one at a time, so that your own time and energies can be channeled more productively.

Empowerment

Empowerment is a very important management tool, serving several valuable functions:

• *It is motivational.*

It shows your employees that you respect and trust them.

- *It is efficient.*

Empowering your employees allows you to distribute your work load.

- *It makes good business sense.*

When the decision-making person is also responsible for its success, the decision is carried through with greater conviction, and is therefore more likely to succeed.

- *It is a reward.*

Good salespeople frequently want more authority. Granting this authority is one way to reward their successes and initiatives. You do not need to empower everyone equally. Reward each employee according to their own success and ability to fulfill previous empowerment opportunities.

- *It provides an opportunity to evaluate employees.*

Some employees will take more initiative than others, or will accomplish tasks more successfully than their peers. Give everyone the same opportunities from the start and train them equally. Some will grow faster than others. Some will feel they should be *given* promotions or opportunities, while others want to *earn* them. By watching your salespeople respond to the challenges of empowerment, you can help each of them to set the most appropriate course for their future.

- *It will make it easier for you to replace yourself when the need arises.*

It is always sad to see an employee's achievements and potential limited because the manager feels personally threatened. What a waste! Managers should take pride in the growth and success of their employees, rather than be frightened by it. A great leader enables followers to exceed even their own expectations. Companies should encourage this ideal: when an employee succeeds with a manager's support, both should receive credit.

New opportunities may arise for you within the company. Sometimes you will be able to take advantage of these opportunities more quickly if your system of empowerment has helped to develop one or more employees to take your place.

There are risks with empowerment. Unfortunately, these risks discourage many managers. There is the risk that an employee will make a costly error. Another risk is that an employee whom you spent time and energy developing will attempt to go after your job at your expense. You should be cautious, but not afraid. As a manager, your job is to develop employees. The risks of letting your people grow are smaller than the risks of refusing to let them grow.

An effective time management plan will not make life run perfectly. There will be times when you simply cannot do it all. You will have days of crisis management, when everything you do is reactionary. All you can do is get through those days, and then get back in control as quickly as possible.

Even with your best efforts to prioritize and delegate, something important may fall through the cracks. As you prioritize, you will have to neglect items on your "To Do" list, and sometimes you will neglect the wrong item. Make your judgments as carefully as you can, weighing consequences proactively.

Do not feel inadequate if you begin your management career working more and accomplishing less. It takes time. You learn to handle mail more efficiently (handle it once and then process it, trash it or file it). Phone calls become less burdensome as you learn to keep the caller focused. Co-workers learn to schedule meetings around your schedule, or relieve you of the need to attend. You get better at keeping your desk organized, and cleaning it off once a day. You become more organized, productive, decisive and in control.

Make sure your boss expresses his or her expectations of your performance as specifically as possible. Then establish your priorities and develop a system of scheduling and empowering that is consistent with those priorities.

SUMMARY

There is no way that new home sales can prepare you for the challenges of time management that you will face as a sales manager. The two jobs are so very different. If you are finding this part of your transition to be especially difficult, don't worry. You're in good company.

Two important elements of effective time management are *prioritizing* and *delegating*.

To effectively prioritize your use of time, plan a schedule in which you spend as many weekly hours as possible on activities that increase sales. Make a firm decision as to what percentage of your total hours you will commit to providing field support outside of the office. Ask your boss to help you deflect some of the unnecessary office distractions.

To provide the support system necessary to help your team achieve its full potential, you should plan to spend at least 50% of your time in the field.

As you plan your specific allocation of time for field and office responsibilities, plan your field time first, so that the office responsibilities will not consume more than their rightful share. One way to cut down on interruptions that keep you chained to your desk is to do as much of your paperwork as possible outside of normal business hours.

The key to successful delegation is *empowerment*. Empowering your employees enables them to grow, which in turn enables you to grow.

There are six reasons why empowerment will make you a better manager:

1) It is motivational.
2) It is efficient.
3) It makes good business sense, because the person making the decision will be responsible for its success.
4) It is a reward.
5) It provides an opportunity to evaluate employees with respect to their future potential.
6) It will become easier to replace yourself when the need arises.

Provide the support and take the risk to let your people grow. Take this risk cautiously. Their failure may not be your fault, but it will be your responsibility. Still, enabling employees to grow is the greatest service a manager can provide.

We have reached the end of the management section of this book, but the theme of helping your salespeople will be continued in the section on "Sales Training."

PART TWO

SALES TRAINING

GIVE YOUR TEAM A HEAD START

TRAINING HELPS EVERYONE

Willie Meyers' big day was finally here. After a year and a half in the minors, he was about to fulfill a dream that began when he was seven years old. Willie Meyers has been called up to pitch in the major leagues. As Willie sat in front of his locker, Gus Ames, the team's manager, walked up from behind and put his hand on Willie's shoulder.

"Welcome to the big leagues, Willie," Gus said. "I've been keeping up with your stats, and right now you're the brightest hope we have for getting out of the cellar. We're all counting on you, son."

"Wow!" Willie thought. "You're putting the whole world on my shoulders pretty fast. I know I'm good, but am I that good?" Suddenly Willie's confidence turned to doubt. But he couldn't let it show, at least not today.

"I'm here to give it all I've got, sir," Willie answered.

"Good man," Gus said. "We really need a change in our luck here, so I'm putting you on the mound tonight."

"Tonight?" Willie said. "That's kind of sudden. I haven't even met the guys yet."

"You will. They'll be along in a few hours."

"What about the coaches?" Willie asked.

Gus looked puzzled. "What do you mean, coaches?"

"You know, sir, coaches."

"We don't have coaches here, Willie. What makes you think we use coaches?"

"Excuse me, sir, but all major league baseball teams have coaches."

"That doesn't make sense, Willie. Why would major league teams need coaches? That kind of stuff is for minor leaguers. When you get to the majors, you leave your coaches with your diapers. In the big leagues you sink or swim on your own."

"I'm sure I can do the job, sir, but I was hoping I could keep getting better."

"We're hoping you will, too, son. But not with coaches. They're not in our budget."

"How will I be able to stay in a groove?"

"Just stay focused, son."

Willie was getting scared. How could he succeed without a coach? Everybody has coaches — football players, boxers, tennis players, everybody. No matter how good you get, you never stop needing a coach.

He was afraid to ask, but he had to: "What if I get in a slump?"

"You've gotta think positive, Willie. Just don't think about slumps. If you get in a slump you're history. There's plenty more people out there who would love to have your job. We're a baseball team, not a babysitting service."

"Yeah," thought Willie. "A baseball team that's learned the secret to finishing last."

* * *

What a ridiculous story! No manager would ever say, "Major leaguers don't need coaches." Big league ballplayers continue to get top flight training and coaching on a regular basis, no matter how long or how well they play. They would never consider playing for a team that could not provide this coaching.

New home salespeople need consistent training and coaching in exactly the same way. Any company that sells new homes owes its sales team a serious commitment to high quality training. Even companies that only hire veterans need sales directors to provide training and coaching as part of their total support system.

No matter what a salesperson's level of experience may be, a consistent training and coaching program will increase their success in the following ways:

1) EXPOSING SALESPEOPLE TO NEW IDEAS.

Variety is an essential part of a total training program. The more diverse your sources of information are, the better you will be able to expand your salespeople's horizons, no matter what their level of experience. There are always new concepts and techniques to be tried, or old ones to be revisited. Experimenting is vital to growth in new home sales.

2) HELPING SALESPEOPLE TO STAY SHARP.

Selling is repetitious. It is tempting to conserve energy by taking shortcuts. In new home sales, shortcuts can become very costly. In baseball, if a runner takes off from first base to third without touching second, he will be called out. It works the same way in new home sales.

Training helps salespeople stay focused on the entire task — touching each base, and then moving on to the next one. It helps salespeople to stay sharp, in their thinking as well as their actions, through each stage of the selling process.

A good training program provides different ways for salespeople to *practice* their skills. Practice helps salespeople stay in a successful groove. It helps them to prevent slumps and maintain their competitive edge.

3) HELPING SALESPEOPLE TO GET OUT OF SLUMPS.

Although a strong training program will help prevent slumps, the perfect vaccine against slumps has not yet been developed. Therefore, training can also help salespeople to get out of slumps by:

a) Helping them to refocus.
b) Helping them to re-evaluate their approach and revise it as necessary.
c) Energizing and motivating them.
d) Showing them that they are not alone: management is still committed to their success.

4) INCREASING THEIR UNDERSTANDING.

Successful new home sales does not result from rote memorization. It comes from *understanding* the product you are selling, the benefits you offer, the market in which you are competing, and the overall businesses of real estate, homebuilding and financing. Training provides the understanding necessary to give your salespeople a competitive edge. This in turn gives your customers a higher level of confidence in their buying decision.

5) Providing solutions to the ever-changing challenges that a salesperson faces.

A good training program does not end with generic selling information. It teaches salespeople how to solve specific problems they will face today and tomorrow.

6) Directing them to seek self-improvement avenues on their own.

Effective training creates a thirst for knowledge. It challenges salespeople to develop their own methods of self-training.

Starting Off Right

Training begins with the first day.

In Chapter Three we discussed the importance of a proactive recruiting program. Since salespeople sometimes leave suddenly, you may need to hire suddenly. You do not want to find yourself backed into a corner where you have to lower your standards to fill a position. Always be prepared in advance for the fact that someone on your team may leave without warning.

Just as you would take a proactive approach to recruiting, you should do the same for training. No matter how experienced a salesperson is, he should never be thrown into a sink-or-swim situation. All salespeople should start out with a comprehensive program that will teach them about the company, community, product and procedures. They need to be able to sell with confidence their first day in the sales office.

It is ideal for an orientation program to be completed before selling begins. If this is not practical, then the orientation process should be completed as soon as possible, with as few interruptions as possible. An orientation program can run concurrently with the beginning of sales responsibilities, but it must be the salesperson's top priority until it is completed. It rarely works well when it is postponed.

The purpose of your orientation program is to provide salespeople with their most powerful weapon — knowledge. Knowledge is what builds confidence to be effective on the front lines. In order to establish a competitive advantage through superior expertise, salespeople need training in more than just how to sell. They need training from your construction department, from engineering, customer service, purchasing, marketing, accounting, and from your lender. Therefore you will need cooperation from others in your company to provide your salespeople with more expertise than the competition. To get this cooperation you may need to emphasize to others the importance of your sales team's expertise for the well-being of the rest of the company.

ESTABLISHING YOUR ORIENTATION SCHEDULE

Set up a complete and specific orientation program with agreement from others who will participate, and then stick to the schedule as closely as possible until it is completed. Once you establish a program that works, follow it as consistently as possible with each new person you hire.

There are many ways to design an effective orientation program. The following is one example of a two-week orientation which you can customize to meet your company's needs. In order to make our example as specific as possible, we will make several assumptions:

• The salesperson starts on Monday, June 1.
• He or she is taking over a community which is already selling.
• The sales office hours are 11:00 AM to 6:00 PM, and the days off are Wednesday and Thursday.
• The salesperson would work from 8:30 to 6:00 on Monday, Tuesday and Friday for their first two weeks.
• Saturday and Sunday would be normal hours in the sales office.

The following is an outline of the salesperson's first two weeks:

**Monday, June 1** (Sales assistant or substitute staffs the community)

8:30 - 10:00 — Attend regular group sales meeting to meet other sales-people and get the flavor of the company.

10:00 - 11:00 — Fill out the paperwork that is required for new people.

11:00 - 12:00 — Meet various people in your office in order to become acquainted with them and to learn their responsibilities with the company.

12:00 - 1:00 — Lunch

1:00 - 1:30 — Meet and talk with the top executive in the company to get a first-hand version of the company's corporate philosophy, standards, values and position in the marketplace.

1:30 - 6:00 — Accompany you to the community and meet with the sales assistant. Spend the rest of the first day learning the basics about the community, location, product, position, strategy and paperwork. (It is also important to itemize the assistant's responsibilities during this meeting.)
    This is a good time to introduce the salesperson to the construction superintendent, and to get the superintendent's permission for the sales-person to spend time with him on Tuesday.

**Tuesday, June 2** (Sales assistant staffs the community)

8:30 - 11:00 — Spend the morning in the field with the construction superintendent(s).
    This initial chance for the salesperson and superintendent to get to know each other is important for several reasons:
• The salesperson can communicate a desire to learn, to serve and to be a team player. This vital relationship needs to start off right.
• The salesperson can learn about the product.
• The salesperson can learn what procedures are important to the smooth operation of the construction function. He can also learn what flexibili-ty the superintendent believes does or does not exist.

Since only a limited amount can be accomplished in this brief period, a followup period is provided in the second week. After that the salesperson would spend time as needed with the superintendent in the morning prior to opening the sales office.

Priority items to be accomplished in these two initial meetings with the superintendent include:

1) The construction schedule.
   a) Sequence of construction.
   b) How to quote estimated dates to the customer.
   c) Deadlines for selecting options.
2) Policies concerning non-standard extras.
3) Rules for letting customers on to the construction site, or into homes in which they have a purchase agreement.
4) Construction-related paperwork.
   a) Establishing an effective system of communication and paper flow between sales and construction.
   b) How sales paperwork is used by the construction department, and by subcontractors.
5) How the home is built.

The salesperson should learn the building process from the ground up by accompanying the superintendent through inspections of homes in every stage of construction. You may even want the salesperson to tape-record discussions during these inspections in order to create an outline for presenting features, advantages and benefits to customers. Information would include:

   a) Materials, and why they were selected.
   b) Techniques, and why they were selected.
   c) Special construction features which can be translated into sales benefits.
   d) Specifications.
   e) Construction standards — what is your company's definition of "acceptable"?
   f) Conveying the correct level of expectations to the customer: what to say vs. what not to say about guarantees, quality and service (also see customer service section on Friday, June 12).
6) How the permit and inspection processes work.
7) How to read a complete set of blueprints using an architect's ruler.

You may consider this last item to be too big a burden to place entirely on a busy superintendent. In that case, you should train the salesperson on as many blueprint issues as you can during one of your first site visits, and leave only the questions you cannot answer to the superintendent.

8) Learning the superintendent's interpretation of the division of responsibilities between construction and the salesperson. The salesperson and superintendent should have a clear understanding of their mutual expectations as early in the relationship as possible, although you may wind up intervening if there is a difference of opinion on this issue. Harmony and mutual trust in this relationship are worth many dollars to your company's bottom line, so the relationship is worth nurturing.

11:00 - 2:00 — Spend more time with the assistant getting the "rhythm" of the community.

1) Why have customers bought there?
2) What has worked and not worked in the sales approach?
3) Are there particular problems or objections to be prepared for?
4) What are the main selling points and pitfalls of each of the models?
5) What does the assistant know about the location?
6) What does the assistant know about the competition?
7) What does the assistant believe are his/her own strengths and weaknesses in selling?

2:00 - 6:00 — Learn the location.

The salesperson should visit those local features that will offer benefits to his buyers so that he will be able to describe them and tell how far they are from his community.

If it is impossible to provide a substitute or assistant for six days during this first week, then you could change the agenda for this afternoon. If the salesperson needs to cover the job himself, you may want to work with the salesperson on site during this time, and reschedule the above agenda for the next convenient day. Or you may want to give the salesperson an agenda of your own for the afternoon, such as going through certain sales materials, or developing a sales presentation for you to discuss with him sometime before the weekend.

Friday, June 5 (Sales assistant not required)

8:30 - 9:00 — Meet with an employee in your company's accounting

department for an overview of those financial procedures that relate to sales.
1) Financial processing of items relating to sales contracts, options and settlements.
2) Explanations of any matters relating to the spending or purchasing authority of salespeople.
3) Issues the salesperson may need to know relating to payroll, submission of commission vouchers, or processing of sales assistant's compensation.
4) Any of the company's financial procedures (such as prompt payment to vendors) that may help to sell the company's credibility or financial strength.

9:00 - 11:00 — Meet with main office sales administrator/coordinator/secretary.

Friday may be the best day for this stage of the orientation if Monday or Tuesday are typically the sales administrator's busiest days.
1) Learn how the salesperson's responsibilities relate to those of the sales administrator.
2) Learn proper preparation of purchase agreements, option sheets, sales reports and other sales-related paperwork, and how these papers are processed.
3) Learn how to schedule and prepare for settlements.
4) Learn needs of the sales administrator as they relate to salespeople.

11:00 - 6:00 — Salesperson works a regular day at the sales office, learning the files, becoming better acquainted with sales office displays and equipment, model homes and homesites, and developing strategies for the weekend.

Sometime during this afternoon there should be a one-to-two-hour meeting scheduled at the sales office with the primary loan officer to review:
1) How to qualify buyers using your lender's current ratios.
2) How to sell available financing programs.
3) How to quote closing costs.
4) How to prepare the customer for the loan application process so that it is comfortable and familiar to the buyer when it occurs.
5) How long the approval process typically takes, and how to anticipate the more common pitfalls.
6) Agree upon what, if any, involvement the customer should have with the loan officer before signing a sales contract.

Saturday and Sunday are treated as regular selling days. Naturally it is an advantage if you can spend one of these two days on site with the salesperson during his first weekend. The more contact you can have with the salesperson throughout the orientation period, the more successful your program will be.

Monday, June 8 (Sales assistant not required)

8:30 - 11:00 — Regular sales meeting.

11:00 - 6:00 — Salesperson works a normal day on site. Priorities for study in the sales office should be:
1) The warranty (as this will be reviewed with the customer service representative in the Tuesday morning segment of the training program).
2) Available information on the surrounding area (schools, shopping, recreational facilities, churches, etc.) to the extent that this was not completed June 2.
3) Homes association documents.

Tuesday, June 9 (Sales assistant required)

8:30 - 10:00 — Meet with a representative of the customer service department. You may also wish to attend this meeting to make sure that everyone is on the same wavelength.
1) Understanding what the warranty says, how it is enforced and how it is to be sold.
2) Understanding the customer service procedure.
    a) How walkthrough items are handled.
    b) How new items after settlement are handled.
3) The salesperson's role in customer service.
    a) How the salesperson should represent customer service.
    b) How to use customer service as a selling tool (and how not to).
    c) Conveying the correct level of expectations to the customer.
4) How the customer service department and the sales department can work together to promote referral sales.

10:00 - 12:00 — The salesperson has a second session in the field with the construction department.
1) Pursue new questions with the superintendent.
2) Meet other construction employees and key subcontractors.

12:00 - 6:00 — The salesperson should visit his primary competitors.
1) If your company uses competitive analysis forms, these should be taken on the visits.
2) Find out from each competitive salesperson why customers like their community (they will usually feel more comfortable divulging this kind of information than why people do not like them).
3) Find out from each competitor who they believe is *their* main competitor, and why they believe they are better than their competition. Through this avenue your salesperson can eventually determine the weaknesses of all competitors.
4) Your salespeople should develop good rapport with their competitors by demonstrating a willingness to share information equally, so that they can call competitors on a weekly basis if necessary.

Friday, June 12 (No assistant required)

8:30 - 11:00 — Meet with the employee in the engineering department who is most directly responsible for the salesperson's particular community.
1) Overview of the land development process.
2) How approvals and permits are obtained.
3) How to read and sell from a site plan using an engineer's ruler.
4) Specific features of the site which are relevant to the selling function, especially those which may be overlooked by a salesperson.

* * *

At this point the primary portion of your salesperson's orientation is completed, and he can spend Friday afternoon preparing for his second weekend.

In the next several weeks there are three other activities which will help your salesperson to increase his confidence and expertise.

• Attend a pre-settlement customer walkthrough.

- Attend a settlement.
- Spend an afternoon with several other salespeople whose techniques and insights would benefit the new salesperson.

Prepare a checklist that includes each portion of the orientation for your salespeople to initial upon completion. As they proceed through those parts of the orientation at which you are not present, it is important for you to follow up with them at the conclusion of each stage in order to get feedback concerning items which need further explanation, or which may have caused concerns to them.

Another useful tool at this stage is a comprehensive handbook in outline form for the salesperson to complete and personalize as they move through the orientation. This manual will become their community "bible" to expand and modify throughout the life of the community.

A high-quality orientation program will not only improve your salespeople's level of skill and knowledge, but also the level of confidence they have in your company, its products and its service. This level of confidence will in turn increase your salespeople's long-range motivation level, and will help establish a position of strength for them in the selling arena.

The salesperson's level of expertise is just as important in conveying value to your customers as your price per square foot or the number of standard features included in your base price. A salesperson who can explain subtleties of purchasing, marketing, engineering, construction and finance has an enormous competitive advantage over the salesperson who can only sell product, price and location.

SUMMARY

All new home salespeople need and deserve a consistent support program that includes training and coaching. It will help to increase the success of your sales team by:

1) Exposing salespeople to new ideas.
2) Helping them to stay sharp.
3) Helping them to get out of slumps.
4) Increasing their understanding.
5) Providing solutions to their ever-changing challenges.

Whenever you hire a new salesperson, no matter what their previous experience, provide them with a comprehensive orientation program which allows them to understand the following before they are held accountable for their sales performance:

1) The company's philosophy, standards, policies and position in the marketplace.
2) The company's internal systems which are relevant to selling.
3) The product.
   a) Features and benefits.
   b) Value.
   c) Construction and engineering.
4) The location.
5) The community.
6) The paperwork.
7) Financing.

In this chapter we have provided an example of a two-week orientation program. Since some hiring situations may require a salesperson to begin selling immediately, our example shows how the orientation can be combined with selling time during these two weeks.

A comprehensive orientation program will provide each of your salespeople with a full tank of high-test gas to start out on the road to success. It is a long journey, however, requiring constant refueling.

If you have salespeople already working for you who have not benefitted from such a program, allow them to participate in any portions of your orientation program that would be helpful.

Once everyone has received the basic information to help them compete successfully, your continuous training and coaching program takes over. This support program will help to assure the consistent, long-term excellence of your entire team. Let's move forward to see how you can create a complete training program which will enable you to fulfill your vision of a successful team.

How to Provide Complete Sales Training

Is It Really Worth It?

B elieve it or not, sales training is a very controversial subject in the homebuilding industry. Many companies do not offer sales training. Others provide a little. Some companies believe that sales training probably has some sort of value, but does not merit a line item in the annual budget. Very few homebuilding companies (or their representative selling companies) offer a consistent commitment to training that is supported by a significant budget. Why is this? There are several reasons.

1) The value of sales training is often seen as intangible, and therefore difficult to measure. The accounting department would love to hear that $10,000 in training would yield an additional $50,000 in profit, but without evaluating the results they are unable to prove it.
2) Many salespeople have had bad experiences with sales training. They attended a seminar which was not geared to their needs. They were subjected to a role-playing exercise that seemed designed to embarrass them. They have felt ridiculed, criticized or insulted by the trainer or the program. They felt treated like children, when in fact the trainer had less sales experience than the salespeople themselves. Or they felt treated like money-grubbing mercenaries at the bottom of the moral

totem pole.

3) A company does decide to spend a significant amount of time and money on training, only to wind up feeling that the money is wasted when salespeople leave to go work for another company who makes more enticing promises.

Feelings run high on all three of these issues, and they each deserve to be addressed frankly.

1) How do you justify the expense?

Money spent on sales training must be considered an investment, not an expense. This is the same theory we use on most marketing expenses (research, merchandising, advertising, etc). Why not consider sales training the same way?

Many companies budget $100,000 for merchandising the model area more easily than they would budget $10,000 for training the salesperson. Suppose that instead of budgeting $100,000 for model presentation, you budget $90,000 for the models and $10,000 for training support. The second way would bring you a greater return on your total investment.

The best advertising campaign and the most elaborate merchandising will be worthless if your salespeople are not prepared to maximize their opportunities. With an insignificant reduction in yearly advertising you can provide top flight training for your sales team.

While a token training effort will rarely justify the small expense, a consistent effort will easily justify the larger expense. This is because consistency is such a critical part of the training process in sales, just as it is in athletics.

As a sales director, you should go through your entire budget, line by line, and ask yourself which items on your list will provide a higher or more certain rate of return, dollar for dollar. You should find it very easy to reallocate enough money to fund a very high quality, year-round training program for your entire team. This program could easily increase your sales by 20%. Ask your accountant how much money 20% more sales would bring to the bottom line in the next 12 months.

The problem is that you cannot prove at the outset that your training program *will* increase sales by 20%, so you have a chicken-and-egg problem with allocating the time and money. The only way you can resolve this issue is to bite the bullet and commit to a program and budget for a year. Then see how it works, and decide whether to renew it for a second year. While this may sound risky, it is actually one of the least risky ventures, with one of the highest rates of return, of any investment you will ever make. After all, advertising does not promise traffic, nor does merchandising guarantee increased sales.

2) How do you make sure the training will be beneficial?

To have value for your salespeople, your training program must include the following characteristics:
  a) It must be credible. It must be taught by bona fide experts whose credentials are respected by your salespeople.
  b) The material must be relevant to their real selling needs.
  c) The format must offer dignity and sensitivity to salespeople.
  d) It must offer new ideas which have value, as well as reviewing old ones which are time-tested but may have fallen into disuse.
  e) It must provide a challenge for change and improvement.
  f) It must insist on practice to perfect new techniques which are learned.

3) How do you live with the "waste" of training people who leave?

This is a copout. In fact, retention is likely to increase with training. Many people switch companies due to lack of support and training. The fact that some people may leave is no reason not to train them. It is better to train them and risk losing them than not to train them and keep them. Our business is transient, but a commitment to training will still prevail. A thorough support system provides one reason for people to stay. People want to work for a company who stands behind them. If there are other reasons why people are leaving, address those issues rather than depriving your entire team of the training that will help them prosper. Keep the issues of training and turnover separate. Just as you expect your salespeople to give their best effort to some customers who will not buy, you must give your best effort to some salespeople who may not stay.

MAKING IT HAPPEN

Throughout this book we have mentioned the importance of a complete, consistent training program as a vital part of your overall support system. The time has come to look at exactly what a top flight training program should include.

The first thing you need is a *commitment.* Your commitment begins with a *budget* and a *plan.*

Your budget will depend partly upon what training resources you already have available. Some companies have a full-time sales trainer on staff who is part of corporate overhead. This can, of course, lower your line item budget. The same would be true if you, the sales director, happen to be blessed with sales training skills. If not, then allocate some expense to outside resources. These resources can include trainers, books, cassette tapes, videos, seminars and mystery shopping.

Your plan should be laid out for the entire year at the time you establish your budget. It is important to commit to a long-range plan, and to make your sales team aware of your commitment. It is okay to change your plan as specific needs arise, as long as you never diminish the plan. Salespeople derive pride and true motivation from working for a company that offers a serious, long-term commitment to their training.

We will discuss a wide variety of elements your plan can include. Do not try to include them all; you will spread yourself too thin and make it difficult to maintain continuity. Evaluate the real needs of your sales team today. Then focus on several avenues of training that you feel will meet those needs.

Before making any training decisions, ask your salespeople what kind of training they believe would be most helpful, relevant, effective and enjoyable? Add to this whatever training you feel will provide the greatest value to them. Provide a variety of experiences. Occasionally you may want to offer a type of training they specifically say they don't want. You have the right to ask them to try it once and give it a chance. Realize, however, that if the training provokes antagonistic feelings, any benefits it might offer are likely to be lost.

It is important that one person takes responsibility for the success or failure of your company's sales training program. Unless you have a specific Director of Training in your company, then the person responsible should be you. Do not share the responsibility for your training program with a second person. Responsibilities that are shared are usually fulfilled less successfully than those for which one person is accountable. By placing your reputation on the line, you will convince others of the seriousness of your commitment. Sometimes you will need support from others in order for your program to succeed. Showing your commitment in your leadership can make it easier to get support when you need it.

Your training program should revolve around three priorities:

1) PROVIDING KNOWLEDGE.

There is often a great variation in the level of knowledge among salespeople. Your training program should strive to share the knowledge that already exists within your sales team, and also to increase everyone's knowledge through exposure to new information. Among the types of knowledge your program should teach are:

a) Product knowledge — specifications, features and benefits.
b) Construction and engineering knowledge.
c) Architectural knowledge.
d) Financial expertise.
e) Awareness of the market.
f) Awareness of the industry as a whole.
g) Understanding of company policies, procedures and standards.
h) Business management as it relates to the sales level.

2) TEACHING THOUGHT PROCESSES.

You seek not only to provide information, but also to teach your salespeople to be successful *thinkers*. When you can expand a salesperson's thought processes, you can expand the horizons of their potential. Better thinking produces faster growth.

Examples of training topics which can enhance thought processes would include:

a) How to maintain a *focus on closing* throughout the entire selling process.
b) Making *transitions* from one stage of the sale to the next.
c) Helping customers to develop a *decision-making rhythm*.
d) How to convey your product's *unique value*.
e) How to sell against your immediate *competition*.
f) How to build *momentum* into your selling process.
g) Getting your customers to understand your *concept* as well as your features and benefits.
h) How to *overcome objections*.

i) How to *compete against discounters* or lower-priced competitors.

j) How to gain *control of the selling environment.*

k) How to establish *rapport* with customers so they will be attentive to your message.

Success in each of these tasks relies on more than merely learning successful sales techniques. While techniques are helpful, the overall attitude or thought process of the salesperson is what will allow these techniques to be used effectively at the right time. These types of tasks require an understanding of the selling process on a deeper level.

Of course, selling skills are also critical to success, and are the third major priority of your training program.

3) Teaching Sales Skills And Techniques.

Here we are talking about the specific techniques which make salespeople effective in each stage of the sale. Techniques should be taught for each of the major selling initiatives:

a) Handling incoming phone calls.

b) Greeting and establishing rapport.

c) Using the sales office.

d) Demonstrating models.

e) Showing homesites.

f) Explaining financing.

g) Closing.

h) Follow up.

i) Prospecting.

You will also want to devote some of your training to continuous refining of "people skills" (including communication) and time management skills.

At the end of this book is an Appendix consisting of six sales training seminars that can be led by you or by members of your sales team. They are interactive, and provide an example of how you could use group meetings to teach thought processes and selling skills simultaneously.

As you plan and budget for the training program you will provide over the next twelve months, try to include a wide variety of learning experiences. You do not have to offer all of the available possibilities: the focus, commitment and consistency of your program are the priorities. For the rest of this chapter we will discuss six different ways that you can provide training support for your sales team. While you could offer an outstanding program without using all six training methods, the more bases you can cover the richer the training experience will be.

SALES MEETINGS

In Chapter Four we said that sales meetings can provide four primary types of benefits to your sales team: motivation, knowledge, training and problem solving. We suggested that you rotate the primary focus of your meetings between these four benefits.

For example, if your sales meetings are scheduled for two hours every Monday morning, devote one meeting a month to training. During this meeting you may need to spend the first fifteen minutes on status updates. You might also have additional needs for the next fifteen minutes, such as conveying information, delivering a motivational message, brainstorming a particular challenge, or leading a general discussion. You would still be committing an hour and a half of your two hours to training. Try not to let other business cut any further into a meeting you have designated for training.

Training that is provided during your regular sales meetings offers several benefits which other kinds of training cannot offer:

1) It is always relevant to the immediate needs of your salespeople.
2) It allows on-the-spot discussion and application. Salespeople can question ideas they disagree with or do not understand. They can also give specific examples of how a principle has worked for them. Interaction and workshop formats help salespeople stay more involved.
3) It can be combined with all three of the other benefits of sales meetings as you apply your material to specific knowledge, problem solving or motivational needs which are important to your team at that moment.
4) It allows you to assume a position of leadership in the training.

Here are several different ways that training can be provided in sales meetings:

Training Led by You

You can lead the training meeting yourself, basing your presentation on:

1) Your own personal sales knowledge and experience.
2) Something you have read, heard or seen that would be helpful to your team.
3) Questions you ask which enable your salespeople to share their knowledge and experience.
4) Material prepared by others. The six-meeting training program provided in the Appendix at the back of this book would be an example of material from outside sources you could use as your own training tool.

If you do not consider yourself to be a polished speaker, don't worry. That is not necessary for this type of training. Your meetings will be successful as long as:

• Your information is helpful, relevant and credible.
• You allow plenty of interaction.

Techniques as well as information for leading these meetings successfully are found in the Appendix.

Training Provided By Experts From Other Departments Within Your Company

Once again, the goal with this type of meeting is not to bring in the most charismatic speaker, but to teach ways to sell your company's advantages. You can draw together the benefits of knowledge and training by bringing in experts from your architectural, construction, engineering, legal and lending resources. You are able to teach the information on these topics at the same time you discuss selling techniques which bring the information to life with value and impact on the selling floor.

Topics for sales meetings from these types of experts could include:

1) How to read and sell from architectural plans, using an architect's ruler.
2) How to read and sell from engineering plans, using an engineer's ruler.
3) Construction systems, techniques and specifications.
4) How the homes are designed. How architectural priorities are established and decisions made.
5) How a site plan is designed.
6) How to explain your sales contracts to customers.
7) How and when to explain financing and tax benefits to first-time buyers.

Naturally, the scope of this list can grow very large. While you do not want to be too repetitious of material which is taught during the salesperson's initial orientation program, you need to be sure your salespeople have enough understanding to achieve a competitive advantage in selling skills. Ask your salespeople where they feel that more knowledge would bring them more sales, and then add topics for areas where you would like to see improvement.

TRAINING LED BY INDIVIDUAL SALESPEOPLE

Salespeople can gain tremendous enrichment from training meetings that are led by their peers. Many companies encourage salespeople to take turns leading training sessions which they prepare in advance. Interaction tends to be comfortable and productive. There are several ways to give this approach credibility:

1) Have salespeople select the topics, and then choose from among themselves who is best qualified to teach each topic. This approach is especially beneficial because each salesperson has unique strengths which will help the others to become more successful. For your team, the whole really can become greater than the sum of its parts.
2) From your own analysis of the sales team, decide what topics are most needed, and who is best qualified to teach them. The advantage of this approach is that you can create a balance and assure that each member of the team makes a valuable contribution. If you have a lot of topics and participants, you can limit each presentation to thirty

minutes. Shortening the topics will allow you to cover three or four in a session, or to do a single one in each meeting along with other agenda items.

Make a selection, based upon your own observations as well as a consensus among the team, of who is the best person to present material on such topics as:

- Building rapport.
- Conveying value.
- Demonstrating models.
- Showing homesites.
- Overcoming objections.
- Closing.
- Follow up.
- Prospecting.

To set a tone of credibility and enrichment, it is important for salespeople to be diligent in preparing their assigned topics.

3) In a single meeting, ask each salesperson to take between five and fifteen minutes (depending upon the number of salespeople) to discuss either of these two closely related topics:
   a) "What is it that makes me a successful salesperson?"
   b) "How do I win sales from my competition?"

4) Use training materials generated by a respected outside resource, with salespeople leading a meeting based on those materials. For example, you could use a book on new home sales, with different salespeople each assigned one chapter. The Appendix of this book can also be used in that way.

TRAINING MEETINGS WHICH INCLUDE ROLE PLAYING

Role playing is a powerful training tool. It helps put new knowledge into action. When you include role playing in training meetings, your salespeople can immediately begin to apply and practice the principles they have learned. They can refine new techniques before trying them out on customers.

For role playing to be successful you need to create the right atmosphere. No matter who leads the rest of the meeting, it may work out better for you to take over when the time comes for the role-playing session. You are the one best able to make sure that the role playing portion of the meeting stays on track and the atmosphere remains positive.

Unfortunately, role playing is sometimes labeled "a salesperson's nightmare." It does not have to be. You can make role-playing sessions enjoyable and productive. First they must be non-threatening. No one wants to be embarrassed, so you must create an environment in which it is okay to stumble. Role playing is a time to try out new ideas without the fear of being judged. The best way to create this atmosphere is to explain your goals for the role-playing session before you start; then, if necessary, volunteer to be the first one on the spot. Allow yourself to be in the vulnerable position of playing the salesperson's role first, and let your salespeople take the role of the customer. Let them see you stumble a little as you get your feet wet. After they have seen you weather the storm, then you can let them take over the role of salesperson. The less vulnerable they feel, the more relaxed they will be, the better they will perform, and the more everyone will benefit from the experience.

Some managers use scripts for role-playing sessions, especially for a less experienced team. The script includes lines for both the salesperson and the customer. It is not intended to force everyone into a canned presentation, but only to start out the exercise more comfortably and help keep it on track. You should write the script if there is a particular way you want it to read. If not, then you can have your salespeople do the writing. Naturally, a script would not be appropriate if you are asking salespeople to develop their own techniques during the session.

Initially it helps to divide up into teams and practice with a partner before making a presentation in front of the group.

Make role playing fun. For variety, clip out newspaper ads for items such as furniture, tools or cars, and have the teams move through the selling sequence with a different product.

As you go through your role playing exercises, evaluate each exercise as soon as it is completed. Try to avoid interrupting with criticism during the role playing. Interruptions are distracting, and people may not know until it's over how the total strategy will unfold.

In your evaluation ask your salespeople the following questions:

1) What did you learn from the exercise?

2) Will you incorporate the techniques you have seen into your own presentation? If so, why? If not, why not?
3) Ask the person playing the salesperson how they felt, and why.
4) Ask the person playing the customer the same question.

These last two questions can gain you some surprising insights. Even though this is a staged exercise, the emotions of both the "buyer" and the "seller" can become very real.

Make sure you lead these follow up discussions in a way that does not offend the participants. The fastest way to kill a role-playing program is to cause embarrassment. Be especially sensitive to those salespeople who have "stage fright." Even though they "perform" their role every day with customers, it is one-on-one in their territiory, and there is no audience. For many salespeople, role playing is dramatically (and traumatically) different from selling. If a salesperson really is terrified, let them go later, or even not participate in the first session. Let them practice with one other salesperson in private, or with you, before the next meeting.

Don't be afraid to do "silly" things to make your role-playing sessions more comfortable. Some of these techniques may sound odd at first, but once people understand the spirit, they become more comfortable, and the meeting becomes more productive. Silliness makes the environment less formal, and therefore less threatening. Whether you choose this type of approach should depend upon the type of team you have.

One example of a silly technique for a role-playing session on overcoming objections is "throwing the pillow." During the session the pillow represents an objection and is thrown from one person to another. The person throwing the pillow raises an objection as the pillow is thrown. The symbolism of the pillow is that the person catching it must "cushion" the objection. Once the catcher answers the objection, he or she then throws it to another person with the *same* objection until everyone in the group has had a chance to answer the objection in their own way. Then you move on to another objection. To start this exercise off more comfortably for your salespeople, let them throw the pillow to you first. If someone believes they have a good answer to the objection, they can ask for the pillow to be thrown to them. As the exercise progresses along, you will get to the point where you can say, "Who wants the pillow next?" and salespeople will become more willing to accept the challenge. It is important that role-playing be enacted with sound techniques, and not as a joke.

As with other role-playing exercises, when you are finished be sure you take time for discussion. Feedback is a critical part of the learning experience. It is during this discussion time that many of your team's most significant breakthroughs will occur.

The various stages of the selling process can be topics of separate role-playing sessions. If you try to accomplish the whole process in a single session it will be too superficial to have many of the benefits which role-playing produces. Breaking the sessions into specific topics will allow more time to fine-tune your team's techniques and strategies. Each of the following topics deserves a complete session:

1) Greeting and qualifying.
2) Selling location.
3) Selling the builder.
4) Giving a community overview (including the site plan).
5) Demonstrating models.
6) Selling features and benefits (this session may be conducted separately or combined with demonstrating models).
7) Demonstrating homesites.
8) Overcoming objections.
9) Explaining financing.
10) Closing.
11) Follow up phone calls and letters.

Tape recording your role-playing sessions gives them even greater value. This is another aspect of role playing that many salespeople find intimidating, so it needs to be approached in a non-threatening way. It should be made clear that taping is solely to enhance the learning experience, and is not a tool for evaluating the performance of salespeople. The fact that a salesperson may "perform" worse because their presentation is being taped should be understood and dealt with sympathetically.

Videotaping can be even better. The video allows you to fine-tune more than just the words. The salesperson's smile, body language and overall demeanor can have as much impact as the words they use. When salespeople can *see* themselves, and compare the appearance of their presentation with that of others, the role-playing experience reaches a higher level.

Incorporating role playing into your in-house sales training can add a whole new dimension to it. Many companies are reluctant to take the risk for fear of adverse reaction. It takes a lot of work — as well as humility — on the part of managers to prepare the sessions and then make themselves vulnerable. But the effort will be handsomely rewarded if the program is enjoyable and enlightening.

Role playing is a form of "participatory education." This learning technique has unique value for several reasons:

1) If it is enjoyable and well-prepared, participatory education has been proven to create a superior learning environment to a textbook or lecture environment.
2) It produces a higher rate of retention than other learning formats.
3) It allows you not only to learn the principles, but to put them into action as quickly as you learn them.
4) It provides the benefits of interaction and group feedback.
5) It enables participants to increase their confidence, and put fear of inadequacy behind them.
6) It provides a greater sense of satisfaction when it is completed.
7) It complements the other elements of your training program, and allows you to apply those principles as well as the ones in your script.

If you don't currently use role playing as part of your training program, you might want to give it a try. Role playing is the best way to lead your team to practice their techniques. Often it is not the lack of knowledge that prevents salespeople from reaching their full potential, but rather the reluctance to put their knowledge to work.

Talk with your salepeople about it first. Don't try to shove it down their throats. Explain what you believe will be the benefits, and that it will not be used as a tool for evaluation or criticism. Prepare for it sufficiently that your salespeople will know you have made a personal sacrifice because you believe in the benefits.

USING VIDEOS, TAPES AND BOOKS IN YOUR TRAINING MEETINGS

When we discussed ways that individual salespeople can lead training meetings, we suggested one format could be for each salesperson to lead a discussion of a different chapter of a sales training book. In meetings where a book is used, whether you or a salesperson lead the discussion, be sure that everyone reads the assigned chapter prior to the meeting and is prepared to comment.

You can also buy a video or cassette series for use in your meetings. Be sure you allow time to discuss each segment once it is completed. The follow-up discussion is where the real value of the tape or video will be realized.

Training Meetings Led by an Outside Speaker

From time to time you may want to enlist an outside expert to discuss a particular topic that is especially important to the success of your team. Outside experts offer the benefit of being exposed to a wide variety of ideas and techniques from other successful salespeople, companies and training resources.

Outside resources add variety to your training which, as we said earlier, will enrich your overall program. You can also enhance the quality of your training meetings by varying the location, expecially if your normal meeting room is small or without windows. Model homes can provide a change of pace. Construction and engineering training should take place in the field. If your budget permits, you could even conduct a few of your meetings in conference facilities of local hotels.

Regularly scheduled sales meetings may prove to be the core of your group training program. They are the easiest format to plan and execute consistently. There is a another format for group training which is familiar to many salespeople. This is the second of the six types of training which we will discuss in this chapter.

Sales Training Seminars

Many sales training specialists offer full-day or part-day seminars which are motivational as well as educational. There are several unique advantages to this type of training:

1) When salespeople from different companies attend, these seminars provide opportunities for your salespeople to network with their peers as they are gaining knowledge.
2) The speakers provide a wide range of information in a relatively short time.
3) The learning experience is usually provided in an exciting, enjoyable and

beneficial way, because public speaking is the presenter's profession.

Sometimes a company will try to save money by sending only one salesperson to a seminar, and then have that salesperson give a condensed version at the next sales meeting. This is usually not a good idea for two reasons:

1) The rest of the salespeople miss the *presentation* of the material, which is an important part of the learning experience.
2) Each salesperson will benefit from the seminar in a slightly different way. Seeing a seminar through the eyes of one person may filter out those parts which would have been most valuable to others. It is better to research the seminar as thoroughly as possible in advance and then decide to send everyone or no one.

If your budget permits and the value is there, you may decide to bring the speaker in for a day with your salespeople alone.

Whether you send your salespeople to a seminar or bring the speaker in, ask your salespeople to take notes in a way that will allow a follow-up meeting within a week of the seminar. At this meeting, ask you salespeople to evaluate the seminar and discuss the following questions:

1) What were the most valuable things you learned? How will you apply them?
2) How valuable was the information as a whole? Would you want to attend another seminar by that speaker in the future?

As we said before, the follow-up discussion is often the most important part of training with outside resources.

We have discussed the two primary ways to conduct group training: meetings and seminars. The next four types of training are each administered on an individual basis.

ONE-ON-ONE COACHING FROM YOU

In previous chapters we have discussed the importance of visiting your salespeople at their sales offices as consistently as possible. This part of your support program is so critical that we will devote the entire next chapter to it. While training is not the only purpose of your site visits, it is a vital part of them. Brainstorming and role playing are two of the training functions you can provide during these visits. Reviewing their past performance and future strategies are equally important. This coaching function must be taken very seriously, because your ability to help them in this way will become a large factor in your credibility as a leader.

Since we will be discussing on-site coaching in detail in Chapter Nine, let's move on to a related form of training support.

On-Site Coaching By Outside Experts

If you have access to a professional sales trainer to work with salespeople on a one-on-one basis, this service can be enormously beneficial to salespeople. It offers several benefits which other types of training cannot offer:

1) With proper preparation, the trainer can relate specifically to the needs and challenges of each individual salesperson.
2) The training session can follow its own course with more flexibility as specific issues arise.
3) If on-site training is one of the trainer's specialties, then he or she can provide examples of how other salespeople they have worked with face similar challenges successfully. The insights and techniques of successful colleagues have special value and credibility for salespeople.
4) One-on-one, face-to-face, interactive training often has greater impact and more lasting value than other forms of training.
5) Salespeople appreciate that their company is willing to go to the expense to provide the individualized support of "their own personal trainer and consultant."

Mentoring

Some companies hire a combination of veterans and rookies, with veterans serving as mentors. While you would offer your regular training program to the team as a whole, veterans provide additional, individualized training to the rookies. This is usually accomplished by having one veteran and one rookie work together as a team to sell a community. Both salespeople are paid a commission on every sale made by either salesperson (the veteran's commission is higher, of course), so that there is no competition to jeopardize the training. In this kind of mentoring program, you must still monitor the progress of the rookie's training on a regular basis with both the rookie and the veteran. If this type of program is not practical for the way your team is structured, you should still provide opportunities for your salespeople to see each other in action. You may need to supply coverage for their community so they can visit someone else's.

Another kind of mentoring can be administered by you personally, at least to a limited extent. For many managers the hardest part of mentoring is finding the time and making the commitment. There are so many other demands on your time that seem more urgent. For that reason, let's take some time to discuss the concept of mentoring in general. It is an important idea to consider for the long-term success of every department in your company. In our discussion of mentoring we will review several principles from the management section of this book.

Mentoring is one of the most valuable services that any manager can provide. Mentors help employees to fulfill their potential. They also help entire companies to be more successful.

Mentoring can occur at any level of a company. A president can mentor a vice president, who can in turn mentor a sales director, who can pass this service along to on-site salespeople, who can then mentor their assistants. Anyone can benefit from having a mentor, and the bonus is that the benefits of mentoring go both ways: the mentor and the "mentee" both profit from the relationship, while the entire system operates more effectively.

WHY SHOULD WE MENTOR OUR EMPLOYEES?

The most important reason for mentoring employees is simply that it is the right thing to do. We all deserve the opportunity to learn the skills and the knowledge to help us do the best work we are capable of. Personal mentoring is the only way that much of this skill and knowledge can be meaningfully conveyed. Yet there are also many practical reasons why mentoring should be a top priority of any management strategy:

1) It is good for the company.

Personal mentoring raises competence and morale to a higher level. All other things being equal, employees will feel a higher degree of loyalty to a company that shows a sincere commitment of *individual managers* (not just abstract "mission statements") to providing real support to every employee who is supporting the management team.

2) It is a sign of competent management.

When managers seem too immersed in daily crises, month after month, to provide the mentoring fuction, it can appear as though they are "in over their heads." When managers can find the time to solve problems and also develop employees, the employees have more confidence that problems are under control and that the company is committed to improving itself each day. Seeing this commitment is an important part of an employee's belief that he or she is working for the right company.

3) It is good for the employees.

Personal mentoring not only improves employee's skills but also shows them they are important as individuals with unique value who can excel in unique ways.

4) It sharpens the other parts of the company's training program.

Mentoring should not take the place of formalized training. It adds a critical dimension to a company's training program, and helps employees to sharpen the skills which the formalized training introduces.

5) It is an excellent way to train employees for problem-solving.

Salespeople not only receive help in solving problems which may be beyond their initial capabilities, but they learn to address future challenges with greater confidence.

6) It allows the company to promote from within.

Many companies who desire to fill a management position from within the current ranks are afraid to do so because:

a) They have not developed the skill of their employees, or

b) They have not recognized skills which are there.

A strong mentoring program can solve both of these problems by taking the company's formal training to a deeper level.

7) *It can increase the manager's opportunity of being promoted.*

When managers commit to mentoring employees, they often find they can move more quickly into new areas of responsibility, because they have groomed someone to step into their shoes on short notice.

WHO MAKES A GOOD MENTOR?

Anyone can be a mentor if they are willing to make a serious commitment, because commitment is usually the hardest part. If you are honestly willing to make the commitment of time, energy and sacrifice to help other people grow, the chances are excellent that you will be a fine mentor. Characteristics of a good mentor include:

1) Confidence

One of the saddest situations in corporate life is when managers "hold their employees down" because the manager feels threatened. Such managers do their companies far more harm than good, and have no business in a management position. Good mentors have the kind of confidence that makes them delight in the success of others, even when their salespeople do a better job than they would have done themselves. Managers who lack this quality fail to realize that as sales directors they will gain a different kind of recognition: they will be viewed as managers who help others grow. That is the highest calling of a manager, and the rewards are exhilarating.

2) Patience

Mentoring can be frustrating as well as time-consuming. Not every moment of the mentoring process is gratifying, especially with those salespeople who "just can't cut it." An effective mentor must think long-term as well as short-term. Avoid squandering your time mentoring low producers who provide you with no positive results for your efforts.

3) Vision

Good mentors have a vision of a better company that will result from their mentoring commitment, as well as a vision of their salespeople and themselves at a higher level of performance. They see their salespeople as they are, but also envision what they can become. Many salespeople attribute their success to a mentor who believed in them and nurtured them until they blossomed into highly skilled professionals.

10 Ways To Be a Good Mentor

Effective mentors are creative in devising fresh ways to help their salespeople reach for new horizons. Here are a few ideas to help you mentor those you lead:

1) Make a consistent commitment of time.

Block out a certain number of hours *every week* to devote to mentoring. Do not let your mentoring commitment become a casualty of crisis management.

2) Tell your salespeople that you have made a commitment to mentoring, and that you want your commitment to include each of them.

Encourage your salespeople to take initiative so they can benefit from the mentoring opportunity which you are offering.

3) Ask your salespeople their goals.

If your mentoring allows them to achieve their goals more rapidly, and if their goals are also in the best interest of the company, then you may want to focus more of your mentoring in that direction.

4) Provide opportunities, without necessarily making a commitment.

It is important that your mentoring not be construed as a guarantee of future growth. You are offering a service, not a promise. Once that is understood, there will be times when you may want to give certain salespeople special opportunities: trying out a new idea, serving on a committee, handling a new responsibility. Encourage your people to move into new areas. Lead them out of their comfort zone to test new horizons.

5) Be willing to delegate.

When a salesperson has earned your confidence, be willing to let go of one or two responsibilities in order to help them grow, and also free up more of your time.

6) Be willing to take risks.

Special salespeople must sometimes be "given the opportunity to fail." The problem is that this could be dangerous for the company, or for you. The salesperson's failure may also be your failure. Therefore, when you take a risk by giving them responsibility in which they might not succeed, stay close to the situation. Be their safety net by watching every move the first time.

7) Let the salesperson tag along.

Let them learn new responsibilities by being a part of the task as you perform it.

8) Do a significant part of your mentoring "on their turf."

Most salespeople are more comfortable "where they work" than "where you work." Visiting them at their sales office can make your mentoring time more productive, and you can address specific problems relating to their sales challenges while you are there.

9) Give honest feedback.

If they are doing well, be sure to let them know. In some companies, the closest that employees ever come to receiving positive reinforcement is a situation in which "no news is good news." Salespeople need more than this. Likewise, if they are not meeting your expectations, it is important to convey that information honestly. They need to know where they stand in order to evaluate themselves realistically. They need to know if they are capable of more, and whether they are willing to pay the price to take that next step.

10) Let others offer the mentoring service, too.

Allow your salespeople to be exposed to the special skills and knowledge of others in your organization. In some companies there are formalized cross-training programs. If your company does not offer this, it can still be accomplished informally on a one-to-one basis.

Mentoring overlaps with coaching. There will be many times when you will be performing both functions simultaneously. However, mentoring and coaching are not quite the same. Coaching helps salespeople develop their skills, while mentoring helps them develop their careers.

MYSTERY SHOPPING

Mystery shopping is the final element of a total sales training program we will discuss in this chapter. It is unique among the six types of training because it is the only one that allows salespeople to hear and see themselves in action in a real selling environment. Hiring shoppers to evaluate your team with a written report, as well as an audio tape of the visit, enables your salespeople to have an objective view of their sales presentation. We recommend that all shopping visits include a tape in order for salespeople to hear what they are doing right as well as to recognize areas for improvement.

"Mystery shopping" can be a valuable part of a company's support system for its sales department. Here are eleven guidelines which will help make the experience productive and meaningful for your salespeople.

1) Shopping should be part of a total commitment to sales training, not something that is done in place of sales training.
2) Shopping should also not be a substitute for your own observation and evaluation of salespeople. It should only be one small piece of a very large picture. There is no substitute for your own time spent on site with salespeople.

3) The purpose of shopping is to *help* your salespeople, not to judge them. You need to convey to your salespeople that shopping is a positive experience — one more tool to enable them to continually improve their skills.

4) Your salespeople should know in advance that shopping is part of your support system, and that all salespeople will be evaluated periodically. You don't have to say when they will be shopped, only that it is part of your program. During the hiring process a consent form for tape recording should be signed.

5) Assure your salespeople that the marketing presentation of the community will be evaluated as well as the sales presentation.

6) Make sure that shoppers represent themselves as bona fide customers. If the shoppers are not in a position to make a buying decision (that is to say, if they are not ready, willing and able prospects for your community), your salespeople will feel tricked, especially if they get a bad report for "not closing." It will be very difficult to derive any positive benefit from an experience in which your salespeople were expected to close an impossible situation.

7) Review the results of the shopping report and the tape as soon as possible after the visit has occurred. Allow your salespeople to evaluate themselves first, and make sure the channels of communication stay completely open. Keep the experience upbeat.

8) Focus on strengths as well as weaknesses in the presentation.

9) Set up a training plan with the salesperson in order to improve areas of weakness. Both you and the salesperson must follow through with your commitment to implement that plan.

10) Offer some sort of recognition or other reward for a good evaluation report.

11) Continue the shopping evaluations periodically in order to track the salesperson's progress.

12) Use the first shopping report of each salesperson to create a "base line evaluation." This will assist you in determining training needs. Future shopping reports can then measure the salesperson's individual improvement.

You may also need to train your salespeople how to make the best use of their shopping reports. Here are four attitudes you can teach them:

1) They should treat the evaluation as an opportunity, not a criticism.

Its greatest value comes when it is considered with an open mind.

2) They should think of it as a unique opportunity to see themselves in action, as though they were watching a video of their golf swing, or their facial expressions, or the way they walk.

3) They should not get down on themselves over one bad shopping report. If it wasn't their best effort, they should try to understand why.

4) They should consider their strengths at least as much as their weaknesses. Often we don't spend as much time as we should reflecting on our strengths. It is our strengths, after all, that make us win. We should have a full understanding of what our strengths are, and how to use them to our best advantage. The shopping report is an opportunity for them to enjoy their strengths as well as improve their weaknesses.

The best approach to mystery shopping views it as an opportunity to help your salespeople reach a higher level of success. When shopping reports improve from one to the next, they can provide an additional source of satisfaction and motivation to your sales staff. They can testify to the success of the manager's support system as well as the salesperson's performance.

* * *

We have discussed six different types of sales training you can provide for your team. Given the limits of time and resources, very few companies offer them all. Try to provide at least several so that the training portion of your support system will be comprehensive and balanced.

We would like to make two other points about training in general before we move on to the specifics of on-site coaching.

First is the issue of scripts. While a few companies require their salespeople to work from a script, most do not. While we do not endorse the idea of selling new homes verbatim from an inflexible script, we do recommend that salespeople commit themselves to the exercise of *writing* a script. The process of writing a complete script for a hypothetical sales transaction will help salespeople organize their thoughts and objectives. Reviewing the script from time to time will help salespeople avoid the shortcuts that eventually produce slumps. Reviewing scripts can also be rejuvenating. Once salespeople put the effort into writing scripts, rereading them can provide a renewed sense of purpose. Scripts help salespeople to stay focused on what they are trying to accomplish in their presentations. They enable salespeople to *envision* the entire sale, which helps them to go as far as possible with each interaction.

There should be a script for each part of the selling process. Begin with the customer's first incoming phone call. Then plan a script for each part of the face-to-face interaction: in the sales office, the models and out on the homesites, concluding with the attempt to close. Finally prepare a script for the follow up call for customers who have not yet bought. Salespeople should try to anticipate the range of customer responses to their statements and questions. Revising their scripts as necessary will help salespeople to keep their presentations fresh.

Writing and practicing scripts really does enable salespeople to stay sharper and more focused. While the script may never be used word for word, it will still provide a competitive edge. There is perhaps no bigger turn-off than a "canned" presentation, but a *prepared* one will help salespeople to maximize their selling opportunities.

* * *

We have one final point to make in this chapter on sales training. Do not fall into the trap of making your greatest commitment to your lowest producers. Sometimes your weakest salespeople are also the most demanding, even though your efforts never seem to help them. Your best salespeople may not demand your best support, but they deserve it. Your weakest salespeople also deserve your best support — for a while. But don't let your support for weak salespeople turn into a crusade. You have an entire team to care for.

If you have a "high maintenance" top producer, then you need to make a judgment call. If giving that person more attention makes them more productive, and they are upholding the standards you have set, you may decide it's worth the effort. However, if your best efforts with a weak salesperson are not producing results, you must not bear the guilt for low performance. They are simply on the wrong team. You owe it to the rest of your team, and to your company, not to sacrifice support for your best people in order to prop up one or two who are not carrying their share of the load. Neglecting your responsibility to your top people in order to provide extra support to hopeless ones will only cause the overall morale of your team to deteriorate. While your top people may be self-sufficient, the support you provide them through your site visits, your availability, and your entire commitment to their success will contribute significantly to their long-term success.

SUMMARY

Salespeople and athletes share important similarities:

1) They are in highly competitive fields, where some people win and some don't.
2) They both benefit from intense focus and a driven desire for excellence.
3) They need constant improvement of their skills in order to keep winning as the competition gets tougher.
4) They deserve a consistent support system of training, coaching and motivating which helps keep them at peak performance.

Providing a support system that will allow your salespeople to compete successfully is an important part of being a sales director. There are a variety of ways that you can provide training support. In this chapter we have discussed six:

1) Sales meetings.
2) Sales training seminars.
3) One-on-one coaching from you.
4) One-on-one coaching by outside experts.
5) Mentoring.
6) Mystery shopping.

Your three most important training objectives will be to:

1) Provide knowledge.
2) Teach thought processes.
3) Teach skills and techniques.

Plan your training program, and budget it, for a full year in advance. Revise it as necessary, but do not let it slip down on your list of priorities. In the face of your day-to-day firefighting responsibilities, your training program must remain intact.

One of the ways that salespeople can make the best use of their training is to commit to the exercise of preparing a script for each part of the selling process. The purpose of this exercise is not to be able to recite the script. It is to organize their thoughts and objectives, and then to be able to review the script in order to sustain their focus and purpose.

Commit a sincere effort to your weaker salespeople, as you would to your stronger ones. However, if your support efforts are not helping your weaker salespeople to improve, you should replace them. Do not take time away from supporting your stronger people in order to continue supporting those who do not have the desire or ability to succeed. They do not have the right to drain your company's resources away from those who have earned them.

After seeing an overview of a total training program, let's move in for a closer look at the third type of training we discussed in this chapter: one-on-one coaching in the field.

On-Site Coaching

For many top sales directors, on-site coaching is the highlight of their job. The opportunity to return to your roots in the field and use your expertise to help others build a successful career provides enormous gratification. It also makes a big difference in your company's bottom line. Many of the principles of leadership, management and training we have been discussing throughout this book come to life during site visits.

Sales directors who "can't find the time to get out into the field" are depriving themselves of the greatest joy of new homes sales management. They are also depriving salespeople of their greatest service and support. Candidates for sales management who lack the confidence or desire to give consistent, one-on-one field support should not be considered for a position as a sales director.

Many of the best sales managers believe that on-site coaching is the most important function they perform. We agree. It is therefore appropriate that this chapter on coaching would be our most comprehensive. Site visits cover a broad range of management issues. There are so many ways in which site visits can enrich salespeople and help them to stay consistent at a level of peak performance. We will explore many types of challenges that can arise during site visits, and suggest specific ways you can use your management skills to meet these challenges.

SETTING UP YOUR VISITS

In our chapter on time management we suggested that you plan your commitment to your field time *before* you schedule the time to fulfill your office commitments. This approach can help you resist the temptation to compromise your field commitment when the office threatens to consume you. We suggested a commitment of 25 hours in the field and 25 in the office, and then gave an example of how these hours could be allocated. However you structure your own time commitments, it is important that you have the support of your builder or supervisor in order to protect your commitments. Often it is an impromptu meeting requiring your attendance that creates havoc with your schedule. Your supervisor's understanding of your commitment to the field can help keep these disruptions to a minimum.

Consistency is critical. If you do not have consistency, then you do not have a commitment. It won't take long for your salespeople to figure out where they stand on your list of priorities. If your salespeople realize that they are your top priority, they will trust you more, and your position as a leader will be stronger.

In our time management example in Chapter Six, we committed 20 hours to site visits, including driving time and visits to the construction office. This did not include the 5 hours for visiting Realtors and competitors and meeting with homeowners. Your numbers will probably be different, depending upon the number and location of your communities, and your own job description.

Crisis management can cause a lot of disruption to a sales director's schedule. There are times when you have no choice but to create your schedule as you go — one day at a time. Use the principles for prioritizing explained in Chapter Six as much as possible to balance your field commitment with your firefighting responsibilities. You may need to plan for more office time in the fourth week of the month than in the first three, if that's when firefighting demands are greatest. Commitments by salespeople (such as contract appointments) may also force you to change your site visit plans at the last minute.

In the face of all these challenges, your ability to honor the 20-hour commitment (or whatever your plan calls for) will still play a major long-term role in the success and morale of your team.

In our example in Chapter Six, 12 of the 20 hours would be spent working directly with your salespeople (14 if they go with you through the models and to the homesites). For 6 or 7 salespeople, this would allow you about 2 hours with each person every week.

Sometimes you will want to visit a salesperson unexpectedly, just to check in with them. Other times you will have to pay an unannounced visit because of a last-minute schedule adjustment. However, your site visit program as a whole will be more productive if salespeople know you are coming. They should prepare issues they want to discuss with you, and you should prepare a list of your own. As with your sales meetings, the better prepared everyone is, the more you can accomplish. There is so much ground to cover during site visits that it is impossible to do it all in a single visit. Rotate your objectives from one visit to the next. Most of the time *their* issues should be your top priority, with your agenda filling the remaining time. If you have an urgent piece of business that cannot wait, go ahead and bring it up first in case you get interrupted later. At very busy job sites you may need to schedule visits before opening hours if you have a lot of business to cover.

For the rest of this chapter we will discuss some of the objectives of site visits. While the list is quite long (and will be longer with your own additional priorities), it will give you an idea of how important a consistent commitment to site visits can be. This list will also show the value of planning your visits in advance so that your objectives can vary from one visit to the next.

GOALS TO ACCOMPLISH AT YOUR VISITS

1) COMMUNICATE INFORMATION FROM THE OFFICE

As a leader you are a communicator. As a sales director, you seek to improve communication between the office and the field, and between sales and construction. Toward the end of this chapter we will discuss your role with construction. For now let's take a closer look at communication between the office and the field.

As we said earlier, effective communication is a challenge for many homebuilding companies. For some, it is their largest single corporate problem. Decisions that affect sales and marketing stategy are often made at the office without input from salespeople which could have helped make the best decision. Then the problem is compounded because the decision is not effectively communicated back to the salespeople. Sometimes the decision is never conveyed at all. Other times it is conveyed incompletely. Often when a decision is communicated, it is still delivered with no explanation because "salespeople don't need an explanation." Explanations help salespeople to understand all the factors that produced the decision. They provide the knowledge which enables sales associates to execute the decision more confidently and effectively. They also show salespeople that their acceptance of the decision is valued by management.

For issues awaiting a decision, let your salespeople know that their imput is important. Pass their opinions on to the appropriate authorities so that these opinions can be part of the decision-making process. If you disagree with the salesperson's opinion, or if you are certain their wishes will not be satisfied, be honest about it up front. Don't allow salespeople to be shocked by the decision if you can prepare them in advance.

If a decision has already been made, take the time to explain the factors and the reasoning that went into the decision. Not only do salespeople deserve this, but it can help them sell the decision to others more successfully.

2) Ask Your Salespeople What They Need

Determining what they need should be part of each salesperson's preparation for your visit. As with communicating information from the office, the salesperson's needs should be discussed during every site visit. What are their greatest challenges, and what can you do to help? Sometimes the solution will be their own responsibility. Tell this to them frankly; then brainstorm with them how they plan to meet the challenge. In other situations the solution may be your responsibility. Make a specific commitment as to what you will do and when you will do it.

3) Evaluate Your Salespeople's Knowledge

Site visits are the ideal time to find out what each salesperson knows and doesn't know. You should not try to accomplish this in group meetings, because some of your salespeople will feel more threatened than others. They should not feel threatened by this discussion at your site visits. Your purpose is to learn the areas in which they need more training, and how you can provide this training. Ask them questions in any areas where you are uncertain of their level of knowledge: product features and benefits, construction, the site plan, location, financing, competition, paperwork, etc. Make sure they realize you are performing a service, not conducting an inquisition. You would perform this function whenever you think it is needed, but not on every visit.

4) EVALUATE THE MODELS AND HOMESITES

This task would also be performed periodically, but not every time. You have several objectives in this part of your site visit.

You want to check the quality of your presentation in the sales office, the model area, homes which are nearly completed, and the job site as a whole. While the salesperson is responsible for items within his authority (and for reporting those which are not), a second pair of eyes never hurts. Try to view each of these items as though you were a prospective purchaser visiting for the first time. We are in a very competitive business where superior presentation really does convey superior perceived value.

Many companies supply a form for rating the various aspects of a model and site presentation. This form can help salespeople maintain high quality in those parts of the presentation that may be hard to notice on a daily basis.

For areas in need of improvement, gain a commitment as to when and how the improvement will occur. If there is a dispute between sales and production as to who is responsible, and the on-site team cannot resolve the dispute, then you will need to get involved.

On some of your visits your salespeople should accompany you through the model so that you can review their selling strategy for each home (including features and benefits), and any new objections that have arisen. Discuss ways in which each model may be the best one for a particular customer as you brainstorm ways to overcome objections.

Go through the same exercise at each of your available homesites. What is good about each homesite? What are the objections? Do any of the homesites require a specific remedy, such as fencing or additional landscaping?

Your role as coach becomes important here, as it does with our next goal for site visits.

5) HELP YOUR SALESPEOPLE SOLVE PROBLEMS

The second goal for site visits we listed was, "Ask salespeople what they need." One of the issues we raised was, "What are their greatest challenges, and what can you do to help?" Whatever problems your salespeople may be facing, they expect you to help solve them.

As you talk through these problems, stay focused on solutions. If solutions are not possible, then discuss ways to accept the problem by creating a positive picture of the situation as a whole. Don't let the discussion become a gripe session that winds up going nowhere. If you allow salespeople to bury themselves deeper into their problems instead of digging out of them, then your site visit is doing more harm than good.

Let's take a closer look at nine different types of problems that salespeople may have to deal with, and then explore ways you can help your people resolve them. While there are many other challenges we could add to our list, we chose these nine because they allow us to discuss a variety of concepts you can adapt to other types of challenges.

A) PRODUCT OBJECTIONS

Ask the salesperson to describe the objection as carefully as he or she can, and to give examples of times when the problem may have prevented a sale to someone who *otherwise would have bought.* The salesperson must do his best to distinguish between objections from people who would buy except for the objection and those who would not. Keep your salespeople focused on the idea that your homes were never intended to sell to everyone. You know that your homes cannot be all things to all people. The question is, if the product objection were eliminated, would you really sell more homes, or would "the cure be worse than the disease?"

For example, suppose you are selling single family homes with two living levels and a basement. The laundry room is located on the upper level. The salesperson says customers are complaining that they would rather have it someplace else. The company gave the decision a lot of thought before finally locating the laundry room upstairs. You want to be open-minded in dealing with the salesperson's challenge. At the same time, you want to evaluate the salesperson's thought process in dealing with the challenge. You could address the issue this way:

Manager: "What do you think is the best location for the laundry room?"

Salesperson: "All I know is that a lot of people are objecting to it being upstairs."

M: "Why are they objecting?"

S: "They say it's inconvenient and that it takes up too much space."

M: "Where would they rather have it?"

S: "Some want it near the kitchen, where it's more convenient. Others want it in the basement, so they can have more space on the other two levels."

M: "That's the problem with a laundry room. There's no perfect place for it, because people have different ideas about where it should go. It seems like no matter where you put it, you're going to make two-thirds of the market unhappy."

S: "Why don't we make the location optional then?"

M: "I wish it were that simple. The problem is that we would have to make a lot of changes on each level in order to offer it as an option. People forget what a laundry room can do to a kitchen, or how far the basement is from the upper level. The home isn't large enough to put a full-size laundry room on the main level and still keep the other rooms spacious. We feel that we're making the best decision for this market by putting it upstairs. If a customer objects, it will help to explain why we designed it the way we did, and why other people like it. We chose the upper level because it's more convenient to the bedrooms and allows us to give the best use of living space on the main level. Consumer research backs up our decision. Do you think you can sell this idea to customers as the best *overall* use of space for the money?"

If your home had the laundry room already located on one of the other two levels, you would handle the discussion in the same way using different reasoning. If you become convinced that your company really is losing sales because the laundry room is poorly located, you could pursue a revision on the management level while you attempt to help the salesperson continue to sell its current location. However, most customers will accept an unsatisfactory laundry room location if they feel they have found a home that is best for them otherwise.

Here is what this approach to solving a product objection attempted to accomplish:

- The salesperson was encouraged to express his experiences and thoughts.
- He was also encouraged to extend his thought process farther. So far, all he had considered was the problem. He had not thought through the problem to a solution or its consequences. He had also not organized his thoughts as to why the existing plan might be the best alternative.
- The manager showed the salesperson how to make the transition from *reactive* to *proactive* thinking.
- The manager gave a patient, thorough explanation of how the company's decision was reached.
- The manager suggested a specific way for the salesperson to overcome the objection.
- The manager concluded by asking if the salesperson believed in the proposed solution (in this case a verbal explanation to customers) enough to sell it. He left the door open for the salesperson to argue that the manager's solution was not satisfactory. If the salesperson does not buy into the solution, then the discussion may need to continue.

As we have said earlier, your goal is to train and stimulate your sales-people's thought processes so that they can provide more of their own solutions.

There will be times when a product revision may be required. In that case you should work with salesperson to propose a mutually agreeable solution to upper management. You must then commit yourself to getting a decision on your proposal as quickly as possible. Product decisions that remain in limbo are very frustrating for salespeople.

B) HOMESITE OBJECTIONS

Some of your visits should focus on walking each of your available homesites with the salesperson to determine how he or she plans to present them. For the tougher homesites, try to think of reasons why a customer might find that specific site desirable. If all lots are priced the same, do not expect the salesperson to sell the less desirable ones first. Set out a reasonable expectation of how long it might take to sell each homesite, assuming that the best ones will go first. Selling the best home-sites first is a very valid way to create urgency.

Do not put too many homesites on the market at once.

Superior homesites often justify a higher sale price. When selling these sites, refer to them as "premium homesites" (implying added value), not "homesite premiums" (implying added cost).

Sometimes you will have several homesites which are so inferior that you know a favorable sales presentation will not be enough. In this situation there are three basic approaches you can take:

- Offer them at less cost on the grounds that they really do have less value.
- Add features to enhance the value of the homesite, such as landscaping or fencing.
- Be willing to wait longer to sell them. There will be times when patience will pay off. Not everyone demands the kind of homesite that we might consider ideal. Some people really don't care that much about having a great homesite. Some will accept a certain site for the same reason that others will reject it. A steep hill might offer them privacy, or a view, or a walkout basement, which means more to them than a usable yard. Some will prefer a smaller yard for the same price if they know there is no pricing flexibility. They may like the features of the home that was sited there, and rationalize the smaller homesite on the basis of less maintenance for space they would rarely use anyway. The truth is that a 9000 square foot site offers very little function or privacy that a 7000 square foot site does not offer.

Help your salesperson to stay focused on the fact that thousands of less desirable homesites are successfully sold every year. We may have to show it twenty times instead of five, but we can plan for that. It is very important to establish your expectations and selling strategies for the entire section of homesites in advance with the salesperson. Determine what buyer profile would benefit from each homesite and why.

Be prepared to share with your sales associate how *you* would present the homesite. This is a great opportunity for role playing, with you in the role of the salesperson. That's the kind of coaching they want most. It will only make their problem seem more insurmountable if you tell them, "You're the salesperson, you figure it out. That's why we pay you the big bucks."

If you believe that *you* could not sell the site as it is for the going price, that is something to consider very thoughtfully. You may want to go ahead and design a backup plan to put into action if the homesite is not sold within a certain period of time.

Assuming your homesites are accessible, it is better to go through these exercises on each homesite than in the sales office over a site plan. The more you can work side by side with your salespeople to develop specific solutions to real problems, the more value you will have to them as a manager.

c) Location objections

Your company chose to invest its money in this location as opposed to others. What was the thought process behind that decision? If the customer can understand the value which caused your company to invest its money, it may help them to justify investing theirs.

Third-party endorsements are important here, too, as they are in overcoming other kinds of objections. Why have other people chosen this location? In some way they must have felt it was the best location for the money — all factors considered. Share those reasons with prospective buyers.

Salespeople need to be proactive in selling location. Early in their presentation, they should ask what the customer already knows about the location. If customers are unfamiliar with it, give them an overview of its benefits. If they have a favorable impression, reinforce it. If they have and unfavorable impression, ask them to be specific in their concerns. When addressing those concerns, explain why other customers have found the location desirable.

Bring the location to life with historical and current anecdotes, local features and amenities, and information which conveys the "feeling" of the area.

The community and location overview should usually be accomplished before you begin selling the product.

d) Price resistence

From time to time you will need to visit the competition for each of your communities. You must be convinced in your own mind that your values are competitive. How would *you* sell your community's value against the competition? Make a list of all of the features of your product, community, location, and builder reputation that you offer which the competition does not. Then perform the same exercise yourself from your competitor's point of view. Attach a value to each feature which is different and bring all of the values for both communities to the bottom line. If you believe the competitor is offering a better value, you need to present your analysis to upper management. Your salespeople depend on you to correct uncompetitive pricing. At the same time, your mission is to help your salesperson overcome the price resistance to your homes and compete successfully by realizing the value they *are* offering.

If salespeople are having a hard time establishing a competitive pricing position, accompany them on their competitive visits. Discuss sales strategy as you walk through the competitor's models together. If your salesperson expresses concerns, take the lead in seeking positives, but be honest about any value deficiencies which your homes may have. Not everyone can offer the best value on a purely objective basis.

If your competitor is offering a better overall value and there is nothing you can do about it, then work with your salesperson on articulating the advantages that you do have. Fortunately, there is also a part of value that exists in the eye of the beholder — the subjective part. Your advantages will be worth more to some customers than to others. (This is one of the reasons that learning their needs is so important.) Certain customers will attach more value to your benefits than to those of your competitors. While you may not outsell that competitor in numbers, you could still get your share of the market. Help your salesperson to stay focused on why your homes and neighborhood *have* sold rather than why they have not, even if a competitor is outselling you two to one.

Customers rarely do a competitive analysis in the same way we do. We must teach them how to keep score in order to overcome their price resistance. If you have put extra money into your site and construction, let the customer know why you spent more. Show them how the extra expense will improve their quality of life and protect their investment. Even if the homes and lots are identical and the only difference is that you have higher overhead or profit margins, show the customer how this translates into better service and more attentiveness to the well-being of the community.

If customers are expressing price resistance, abstract claims of better "quality" or "value" are unlikely to change their minds. You will need to show specific examples of features that translate into better quality of life for a very small additional cost per day.

E) COMPETING AGAINST COMPETITORS WHO ARE DISCOUNTING

This is an extremely difficult and frustrating challenge for many salespeople. As in dealing with price resistance, salespeople must stay focused — and keep the customer focused —on the *total package* which they are providing. In addition, the selling focus must also remain on the *bottom line value* of your home vs. the competitor's, and not the size of the discount alone. This is where buyers can get confused. They sometimes believe that the bigger discount is the better deal, as though everyone's original price was equal to begin with. The salesperson must help the customer to understand that a discount is not the same as a deal. It is only one type of pricing strategy. Every builder still wants to sell their home for as much as it is worth. The discount is only the builder's admission that his asking price is unrealistic. The salesperson takes on the role of a *counselor* in these situations, explaining to the customer how the principles and strategies of real estate pricing work, and how each builder adopts a different strategy in order to compete. The salesperson then explains to the customer why your company believes your pricing strategy is the best for them.

Shopping the competition with your salesperson will help you both to gain a better understanding of why the competitor is forced to give such large discounts, and to explain it to customers in a professionally discreet way on those occasions when it is absolutely necessary in order to defend your pricing position.

If a competitor is discounting in order to liquidate inventory, it may be necessary for you to simply wait it out until their inventory is gone rather than try to match their discounts. Their discounting strategy either will work (in which case it will end when the inventory is gone) or it won't work (which means the market is not accepting their homes). For you, there is light at the end of either tunnel.

As with price resistance, help your salespeople maintain their position of strength against discounters by showing how your homes provide a better quality of life for a very small amount more per day. Reinforce those features and benefits in your homes, homesites, community and location that may have cost you more to provide, but also offer the customer real living benefits.

On some of your site visits you will want to discuss the competition with your salespeople. They must know their competition very thoroughly in order to be able to articulate their own competitive advantages. At the same time, your salespeople must not let their knowledge of the competition consume them. It is not realistic to expect to be able to defeat every competitor on every feature and still offer a lower price. Nor should salespeople become depressed over sales which are lost to competitors to the point where they believe their own package is inadequate. The competition is entitled to their share, too. Presumably, they are trying to compete just as hard as you are. The salesperson's goal must remain focused on fulfilling their own customers' needs, and showing customers how the concept, features and benefits you offer will provide value and improve their quality of life, regardless of what the competition is doing. While awareness of the competition is a very important part of the salesperson's expertise, their primary focus must still remain on selling their home to their customer that day.

F) UNQUALIFIED OR UNMOTIVATED TRAFFIC

A salesperson's complaint that traffic is unqualified or unmotivated should be studied very carefully. There could be any number of explanations. It could be a problem of advertising, merchandising, product, pricing, or overall market conditions. Unfortunately, it may sometimes turn out to be the salesperson. It is very important to determine correctly which of these factors is the real problem.

Some sales directors are reluctant to go through individual customer cards during site visits for fear that the salesperson will consider it degrading. You do not need to have this concern. Naturally, if you have reason to doubt that a salesperson is maximizing his opportunities, you have the right to discuss customer cards in terms of how the salesperson has handled specific interactions, and what they are doing to follow up. However, even if the salesperson's performance is outstanding, discussing cards helps you to do a better job of managing. Discussing individual customers enables you to understand your market better, and also to understand *trends* that are occurring at each neighborhood. This information will help you and your team to develop the most effective sales and marketing strategies for each community. It is especially important when you are trying to address a problem of unqualified or unmotivated traffic.

Are the people walking in your door the ones you have been trying to attract? For example:

• If they are not serious buyers, you may not be advertising in the best medium.
• If they are disappointed by what they see, your advertising may be con-

veying the wrong message or creating unrealistic expectations. Or your merchandising effort could be inadequate.

• If they cannot afford your homes, your ads could be conveying an inaccurate picture of what your typical home really costs.

What is the purpose of advertising? Some managers (and many ad agencies) believe that the sole purpose of advertising is to generate traffic. We disagree. We believe that the purpose of advertising is to help salespeople sell homes. Ads that set visitors up for disappointment work against the goal of selling homes. They force the sales interaction to start off with the salesperson back-peddling instead of moving forward. They place the salesperson into a position of weakness instead of strength.

The goal of an ad should not be to draw hordes of unqualified traffic, but to bring in a manageable number of qualified buyers who want what you are selling. Handling unqualified traffic is time-consuming and takes your sales associates away from opportunities to prospect, present and follow through with ready, willing and able buyers. It does nothing more than reduce a salesperson's closing ratio.

Ads should help customers understand the concept of your homes, the selling advantages which your salespeople can reinforce, and the approximate cost of a typical home you are trying to sell. When a salesperson can reinforce and then build upon an ad message instead of skirting or denying it, the selling interaction will be more productive. If your traffic is better qualified and more prepared to appreciate what you are offering (even if total traffic numbers are lower), then your advertising has supported the selling effort instead of undermining it.

Merchandising should convey the warmth, function and personality of a home which the target market can relate to as they aspire to it. This means merchandising a slight notch above the market's current level of affluence, while exhibiting a taste that the target market will be comfortable with. Merchandising should enhance the space, not overpower it.

As you review customer cards with your salespeople, evaluate the effectiveness of your advertising and merchandising as a support system for the sales effort. Discuss specific customer responses to your homes, community, builder and price. Weigh the opinions of "A" and "B" prospects more heavily than "C's." What objections are arising? Are they isolated occurrences or consistent trends? How is the salesperson handling them?

Help your salespeople create prospect profiles from their guest cards to help you target your advertising audience.

Reviewing customer cards also provides a comfortable transition into role playing for specific situations.

What is the salesperson's closing strategy for interested customers on their first visit? What about subsequent visits?

What is the salesperson's follow up strategy?

Which customers are the result of the salesperson's prospecting? What is the prospecting strategy?

The answers to all of these questions really *are* your business. They allow you to understand the skills and strategies of your salespeople, and to learn ideas from one salesperson which you can use to help another. It also gives you the opportunity to pool your experience with that of your salespeople to brainstorm ideas for selling and for solving problems. No matter how successful a salesperson may be, two heads are still better than one.

To focus specifically on your salespeople's progress with their best prospects, ask them each to keep a "Top Ten Prospects" chart which details the customers' history and current status as well as the salesperson's plan of action. It is important to know where the customer is in their buying cycle. Are they just getting started, or are they ready for action? Again this is intended primarily as a brainstorming tool, not an accountability tool.

All of these strategies become especially important for constructively addressing the problem of unmotivated traffic.

G) CREATING URGENCY

A variation on the problem of unmotivated traffic is the challenge of creating urgency for customers to go ahead and make their buying decision today. What can your salespeople do to speed up the buying cycle?

When the market is hot, there is the built-in one-two punch of "They're going fast" and "It will cost more tomorrow." However, when the market is average or below average, and the pressure is on your salespeople to increase volume, they will often come to you as their coach and say, "Tell me how I can create urgency."

Sometimes they will be fortunate enough to have circumstances which enable them to create urgency with certain customers. These kinds of circumstances would include:

• A limited selection of a home the buyer really wants.

- Availability of homes that match the customer's time frame better than those of the competition.

There will also be times when your company will be able to offer assistance in creating buyer urgency, such as:

- Added value incentives such as landscaping, decks and upgrades.
- Price incentives "for a limited time only."
- Below market financing or locked-in interest rates.

What about creating urgency when none of these factors exist? This is the real challenge for your salespeople, and for you as a coach.

As we said earlier, one of your goals as a coach is to train your salespeople in their *thought processes* as well as their knowledge and skills. You need to train them in an entire *attitude* about creating urgency that does not rely solely upon your ability to provide a "gimmick" or "crutch" to get them through one week at a time.

Here is a suggestion for training your salespeople to develop a thought process which understands urgency on a higher level than just giving discounts. Begin by asking your salespeople to consider other types of sales that do not typically rely on rapidly rising rates or limited selection. Two examples of this are:

- Selling cars, where even if the selection at a particular dealer is limited, there may be a competitor nearby offering identical models with similar pricing incentives.
- Clothing, where there may be ten of the same item in the same size on the same rack for the same price.

Successful selling in these kinds of circumstances often requires simply getting the customer to the point where they would rather buy than not buy. If we take this approach to creating urgency in new home sales, how can we get our customers to reach the point where they would rather buy than not buy?

There are six conditions where a customer can develop a sense of urgency. These conditions could also be called the six "elements" of urgency:

1. The customer must be *excited* about the home. This is the *emotional* element. In cars and clothing, the goal is to get the customer *involved* in the product. In car sales this is accomplished largely dur-

ing the test drive. In clothing it develops as the customer tries on the item. In new home sales it occurs during the model demonstration and the trip to the homesites.

2. The customer must believe that you are offering *the best available alternative for them in the market* (and also an alternative better than where they live now). This is the *rational* element, which combines with the emotional element to create urgency. As important as loving the home (the emotional element) is in the buying process, emotions alone will not necessarily be enough to force a buying decision. For "desire" to become a "decision" the customer must also believe that what you are offering is the best for them. It is the combination of 1) *loving the home* and 2) *believing the home is best* that ultimately provides the basis for *fear of loss*.

3. If the customer loves your home and believes it is the best for them, they must then believe that *there is one home in your selection which is better for them than the others.*

4. Once these first three conditions have been met and the customer believes that there is one best home, you can build a logical case that this home could be the next one to sell. After all, why would the next customer feel any different? Again, this is an approach with both rational and emotional overtones. It is rooted in common sense, rather than in an overt threat that "Someone else is interested in that same site, so you'd better move fast." Yet this rational thought can produce the emotional reaction of *fear of loss* without antagonizing the customer. If your community is selling one home a week, it is logical to assume that in the next two weeks their favorite choice could likely be claimed by someone else.

5. Customers can also feel a sense of urgency if they believe they are *in the right place at the right time.* If there is anything at all which is special about the particular moment or situation in which the customer is making their decision, it could contribute to their feeling that perhaps this decision was "meant to be."

6. Finally, customers must reach the point where they believe that *there is no reason to postpone improving their lives.* Using the

examples of cars and clothing, people often buy these expensive items, even when they don't actually "need" them, simply because they don't want to be without them any longer. They love the item, they are convinced that the item is best for them, and they are now at the point when they must decide whether or not they believe their lives are worth improving. They are ready to get the decision behind them and continue on with the business of their lives. Our job is therefore to help customers envision a better life in the new home than the life they are living now. We must persuade them to relish the fact that the sooner they take the step that will improve their lives, the sooner their mediocre current existence will become a part of their past.

In the end, true urgency is more a result of these six elements than of contrived gimmicks. While gimmicks and circumstances can often be helpful in creating urgency, and should be maximized whenever they are available, it is also important to look beyond these "props" to the larger concept of urgency, and to where its motivations really come from. Developing these motivations is the true art of selling. While new home sales is different from other forms of selling in many ways, it is helpful to understand the universal principles behind creating urgency in selling, and then to develop strategies to apply these principles in our profession.

Help your salespeople to think of creating urgency in terms of the progression of these six stages, whether there are any other urgency factors available to them are not. The principles discussed here are also part of the training program found in the Appendix.

H) PROBLEMS WITH A SALES PARTNER

Some companies put more than one salesperson in a community in order to handle traffic more productively and increase sales. It can also be an effective way to train new salespeople. Naturally, in order for "sales partnerships" to succeed, there must be enough commission potential for all salespeople to achieve their financial goals. Regardless of whether salespeople are compensated individually or commissions are shared, if there is not enough to go around morale will be threatened. Other problems can also threaten morale in a sales partnership:

• One partner may be a stronger salesperson than the other.

- One partner may take more initiative than the other, be willing to sacrifice more, or be more diligent.
- The salespeople simply might not like each other.
- The salespeople could be too competitive to work as an effective team.

When factors in the partnership threaten morale, there is a high risk they will threaten sales and service as well. What should your role be in these types of situations?

In order to protect morale in a partnership situation, make sure the lines of communication are open at all times. Salespeople must be willing to communicate their feelings to each other in a constructive way. If a salesperson brings a grievance concerning the other partner to you, insist that they talk it through with the partner first. Help them to prepare what they will say to the partner if they feel they need this kind of help. At the same time, you must be willing to talk to them about the partnership — together or one-on-one — whenever your assistance might be helpful. Most partnership problems can be handled more easily than it might seem as long as they are discussed openly and honestly. Individual strengths and weaknesses of each partner must be kept in balance, and the division of responsibilities must be kept fair. Getting involved in some of these situations, especially with newer partnerships, is an important part of your management role. What the partners need from you is the authority, as well as the wisdom and support, to make sure that issues which threaten morale are resolved quickly, and not allowed to drag on.

If you sense that one salesperson is producing more or shouldering an unfair share of the "busy work," you must take the initiative to rebalance the situation rather than waiting for one of the partners to "rat" on the other. At the same time, if both partners believe that the situation is fair, then it may be best to leave it alone, even if their definition of fairness seems unusual to you. They may have reached a mutually agreeable arrangement that allows them both to achieve maximum productivity because they are each handling the responsibilities they enjoy most, and the other enjoys least.

There are many different ways that partnerships can be successful, and some of them may seem unorthodox to you as a manager. In partnership situations, you are performing your management role effectively when:

- The channels of communication are open.
- Both partners are producing.
- Both partners believe the arrangement is fair.

• Both partners feel their teamwork method is helping each of them to sell more homes.

1) PROBLEMS WITH THE CONSTRUCTION DEPARTMENT

Just as problems can develop between sales partners, they can also develop between a salesperson and his "partners" in the construction department. As with sales partnerships, the sales and production "field team" should make every effort to resolve their problems before taking them to the manager. If they cannot be resolved, and you need to intervene, follow the same principles that we discussed for resolving problems between sales partners. You may also need for your own counterpart in the construction department to be involved. Make sure everyone sees that your objective is not to blame the construction department, but to work together with them to achieve a fair solution which is best for the company.

When salespeople see your commitment to helping them solve problems during your site visits, they will view your visits in a more positive way and prepare for them. They will also be more receptive to those parts of your visits that may be difficult for them, such as going through guest cards, or the next objective of your visits which we will discuss.

6) WATCH YOUR SALESPEOPLE IN ACTION ON THE WEEKENDS

Some salespeople will be quite comfortable with this part of your coaching program, but others will not. You must explain to your salespeople that your purpose in visiting sites on weekends is not to spy or intrude, but to support. Your weekend visits are necessary in order for you to understand what kinds of support will help them sell more homes.

You need to get the "rhythm" of each community first-hand: how it is sold; what the traffic is like; what the customer's responses are; what the challenges are. You also need to understand in detail the individual selling style of each of your salespeople. You will learn techniques and strategies from one person that you can teach to another. Of course, you may also find ways to use your own experience to help the person you are observing.

You are the manager and the coach. There is no reason for you to feel self-conscious about watching your salespeople sell, any more than a sports coach watching an athlete perform. There is also no reason why salespeople should feel uncomfortable. You are there to help, not criticize.

Before you visit salespeople on a weekend, talk it over with them. Where would they like you to sit? What will you be doing while they talk with customers? What would make them and their customers most comfortable? If they get tied up, how would they like you to handle additional customers who walk in? If you have an idea while they are talking, do they want you to interrupt with it or keep it to yourself? Do they want to introduce you to customers and then work with you as a team, or would they prefer that you remain anonymous? Discuss these issues with salespeople in advance to reassure them that your sole purpose is to assist them and to learn what other sales or marketing tools you can offer them that might help them become more effective.

If you have suggestions for ways to improve their selling skills, don't be shy about sharing them. That is one of the reasons you are there. Be open-minded to their responses, yet firm and straightforward when you need to advise them. If you want them to adopt a new technique, ask them to give it a try, just as a sports coach would. You're not demanding that they make a lifetime commitment to it, only that they make an honest effort to see if it works.

On weekends, you want to be especially sensitive not to hurt their morale or dampen their enthusiasm. If you have a negative message that can wait, hold off so that it does not weaken their confidence or their selling intensity.

Another very important benefit of weekend site visits is the opportunity to have hands-on experience with customers.

7) MEET WITH YOUR PURCHASERS AND PROSPECTIVE PURCHASERS

Many companies neglect this vital management function. Your own first-hand experience with the various markets you are serving will play an enormous role in the success of your company's sales and marketing strategies. As with watching your salespeople in action, you should discuss you plan for meeting with customers in advance with your salespeople to be sure that you are not jeopardizing their selling efforts as you go about your marketing business. Once the ground rules have been agreed upon, you can seek out opportunities to improve your products and strategies with input from your real market.

Over time you will have opportunities to speak with customers who:

- Have already bought from you.
- Are considering buying from you.
- Have decided not to buy from you.

Information from all three of these groups is valuable.

When you meet customers who have already moved into your community, you have the opportunity to learn what is being done correctly, and what could be improved upon. Several types of questions you could ask are:

- Why did they choose to buy from you, and not a competitor?
- What other communities did they consider, and what were their impressions of those communities?
- How did they first hear about your community?
- What motivated them to search for a new home?
- How did they feel about the various experiences in their homebuying process?
    - a) The salesperson.
    - b) The lender.
    - c) The walkthrough.
    - d) The customer service department.
- How did they respond to the various elements of your marketing presentation?
- What suggestions do they have for how you can improve your product or procedures?
- Would they recommend your company to a friend?

Buyers appreciate this kind of interaction with managers of the company who sold them their home. Prospective buyers often appreciate interaction with managers as well.

If a customer is interested in your homes but has not yet purchased, your position of authority can sometimes help you gain a competitive edge. But again, you must be careful not to do anything which could inadvertently undermine your salesperson. Some of the questions listed above can be appropriate in your conversation with visitors as well as homeowners. Just remember that if the customer is a potential buyer then your first priority is to help your salesperson, while your second priority is to gain marketing insight.

When you learn that a visitor is not a viable customer, you may still find that they will enjoy talking with you about a variety of sales and marketing topics. Some people like to be helpful, and are flattered that you value their opinion. If you find that you have such a visitor, and they seem to represent a part of your target market, then ask them some of the difficult questions that you frequently find yourself wrestling with. Their input can be valuable, even though they have chosen not to buy one of your homes.

Before you begin asking a visitor questions, make sure they know who you are — your name and your position in the company. When you talk to a customer for the pupuses of gaining marketing information, explain to them that you are there because you are a marketing person, and your company has a policy of asking the market what it wants in order to continually improve their products and services.

Your interaction with customers should be relaxed and casual so as not to feel like an "exit interview." Customers will usually offer deeper insights when they feel more comfortable. In addition to questions about your product, your presentation, and the customers' motivations, you can ask discreet questions about your competitors.

- Who else did they like, and why?
- How does the competition compare to you?
- What are their primary criteria for deciding who is best?

As you receive answers to these types of questions, listen open-mindedly, but weigh their answers cautiously. Do they represent your target market? Are their responses typical or unusual? If you made a change, would you gain more sales than you would lose?

This last question is especially important in sales and marketing strategy, and one that you may sometimes need to focus on with your salesperson. Theoretically, every major marketing decision we make will gain sales and lose sales. We must not fall into the trap of thinking that we need to change our product or strategy every time we lose a sale. The perspective from which we should make our sales and marketing decisions is this: we must evaluate, as knowledgeably and honestly as we can, whether our decisions are gaining us more sales than they lose, or losing us more sales than they gain. As we said earlier, we never intended to sell to every person who walks in the door. We only intended to sell a certain number per year. Do we have the best overall strategy for achieving that number?

8) VISIT THE CONSTRUCTION DEPARTMENT

Another valuable purpose of site visits is the indirect support system you provide to the construction department. We have discussed the role of the sales director in the company's overall communication process. Communication between sales and construction, in both the office and in the field, is one of the issues that affect your success as a manager very directly. It is important that you be willing to take the initiative in this communication.

While it may not be practical to stop at the construction office on all of your visits, try to stop in periodically.

The healthiest on-site environment is usually one in which sales and production treat each other as equals. One message that your visit to the construction office conveys is that you are at their service. Is there anything you can do to make their world function more smoothly?

On the other hand, if you have a request for them, you should have an agreement with your counterpart in the production department as to what the appropriate channels of communication should be.

It is important to realize that in many cases the construction people need this contact with you very badly — not necessarily to blow off steam about their problems, but simply to know that the channels are open. You are part of their support system and want them to be a part of yours. As with your salespeople, you should follow up on any production needs which apply to you as quickly as possible.

You may choose to do your site visits with your production counterpart if the scheduling is compatible. You could split up so each of you could meet separately with your own people, and then regroup as a team. These types of joint visits will send a healthy message of cooperation and support to your on-site team.

9) PROVIDE INTERIM REVIEWS

In our discussion of performance reviews in Chapter Five we said that information in your formal reviews should not surprise your salespeople.

Once again, consistent, effective communication again the key. Your coaching visits should be characterized by an atmosphere of openness and honesty. For your coaching to be effective you must let your salespeople know how you think they are doing on a continuing basis. They want this. Lack of feedback from management (especially positive feedback) is perhaps the number one frustration of salespeople nationwide. Those who receive feedback from their managers that is correctly balanced between positive and corrective are very fortunate indeed. Not all of your site visits need to include a performance review. However, your visits are an excellent opportunity to show appreciation for good work and to point out deficiencies which need to be addressed.

If you have standardized forms for certain areas of performance (such as model maintenance), refer to these forms during your site visits. From time to time discuss topics that will be a part of the next formal performance evaluation (or were a part of the last one) to make sure that you and the salesperson are on the same wavelength with respect to their progress.

If you have a salesperson who is doing especially well, show your appreciation, and convey the appreciation of the company as a whole. When salespeople feel appreciated they will gain more satisfaction from their careers, and they will be more productive. You will also be more successful in retaining good people.

Give salespeople the opportunity to talk about their successes and reflect on what it is that is making them successful. Take notes while they are talking so you can remind them of these successes in the future if they get into a slump. Encourage them to keep a diary during a hot streak that they can review later to remind themselves of what they were doing right. See what you can learn from them that you may be able to use in helping others.

If you have a salesperson whose performance is poor, or who is not living up to your team's standard in other ways, use the site visit and opportunity to agree upon a solution. If there is anything you can do to help them, commit to it on the spot and follow up diligently. Demand the same from the salesperson.

Chapter Twelve will discuss ways you can help your salespeople prevent slumps and burnout. Here we will propose several steps to help a salesperson whose sales volume is below your expectations.

a) Ask them what they think the problem is.

b) Ask them what they think the solution is.

c) Tell them what you think the problem is.

d) Tell them what you think the solution is.

e) Ask them what they would do if they were in your shoes.

f) Propose a new plan of action, and a timetable for implementing the plan. Make sure that you and the salesperson both agree on the plan.

g) Be specific about your expectations for their future performance.

Be totally honest about their situation. If their job is in jeopardy they have a right to know it.

As with your top salespeople, have your less successful salespeople reflect on successes they have had, and how they achieved them. Help them to focus on why their homes *do* sell rather than why they don't. Keep them thinking about the advantages they have, rather than those of the competition.

When your salespeople are failing and yet you believe they have the ability to succeed, balance your concerns with your appreciation of their accomplishments to help them retain their sense of dignity as you address ideas for improving their performance.

If they tell you they need something in order to succeed, be sure that they are reacting to *patterns* and not to isolated incidents.

As you go through the salesperson's customer cards with them, try to pinpoint a specific stage in the sale where the transactions are ending most often, and role play that part of the selling process with your salesperson. What techiques can you employ to get the sale to go one stage farther?

If you are addressing a problem of discipline (such as those discussed in Chapter Five) instead of performance, you can still follow the same seven steps discussed earlier. Discuss the problem and a proposed solution from their point of view and yours. Ask them what they would do in your shoes. Agree upon a plan for improvement and a timetable. Be sure your expectations are specific, and that the salesperson understands them and believes they are reasonable. If the salesperson does not buy into your expectations, make another attempt to "sell" them on your position, and then hold them accountable to the standard of performance outlined. Balance your positive and negative feedback to them according to their performance. Help them to keep the problem in its correct perspective: no more important or less important than it really is.

Unless you are giving a warning to an employee who is on the verge of dismissal, end your visit on an upbeat note. This applies to all your visits, whether you have been evaluating the salesperson's performance or pursuing any of the other objectives discussed in this chapter.

Your on-site coaching is your most personal commitment to your salespeople, and is therefore your most important. Commit to the preparation and consistency which will make your visits effective. Then create the environment to allow your salespeople to be enriched by your commitment.

SUMMARY

Your site visits can make an important contribution to the success of your salespeople and your company. As a sales director you will find many responsibilities competing for your time. In the face of a barrage of administrative assignments and firefighting challenges, it can become difficult to maintain a consistent commitment to visiting all of your job sites on a regular basis. However, many top sales directors have successfully organized their time management system so that they can spend at least 50% of their time out of the office. They schedule their paperwork responsibilities during hours when there will be fewest interruptions. Much of their firefighting is handled on the road. More importantly, the training they provide during their site visits enables their salespeople to handle or prevent many of the problems which would otherwise have found their way to the sales director's desk. In fact, site visits become a time management tool when scheduled with planned consistency.

In order for you to be able to use your own time most productively, you must train your salespeople so they understand your own thought processes for preventing and solving problems. You must then empower them so they can take the action necessary to solve their own problems. Then you will be free to spend more of your time coaching and counseling your salespeople to greater success.

The hands-on experience you gain at each of your communities increases your own management expertise, and helps you to provide the best marketing strategies and training programs for your salespeople.

Site visits provide an enormous range of possibilities to use the skills of leadership, management and training that we have discussed throughout this book. In this chapter we have discussed a number of objectives for your visits to salespeople at their communities. Here is an overview of these objectives:

1) Communicate information from the office.
2) Ask your salespeople what they need.
3) Evaluate your salespeople's knowledge.
4) Evaluate the models and homesites.
5) Help your salespeople solve problems, such as:
   a) Product objections.
   b) Lot objections.
   c) Location objections.
   d) Price resistence.
   e) Competitors who are discounting.
   f) Unqualified or unmotivated traffic.
   g) Creating urgency.
   h) Problems with a sales partner.
   i) Problems with the construction department.
6) Watch your salespeople in action on the weekends.
7) Meet with buyers and prospective buyers.
8) Visit the construction department.
9) Provide interim reviews.

This completes our section on supporting your sales team with training and coaching. We are now ready to look at ways you can use your leadership and management skills to motivate your sales team.

PART THREE

MOTIVATION

CREATING A MOTIVATIONAL ENVIRONMENT

WHAT IS MOTIVATION?

I f we are motivated, what does that mean? Does it mean we are excited? Pumped up? Energized? Clearheaded? Intensely focused? There is no doubt that each of these attributes can help us succeed. But do any of them (or all of them combined) represent the true meaning of motivation?

What if they do? How do we provide this kind of motivation to every salesperson every day? How can we be assured that we will always have pumped up, clearheaded, energized salespeople who are chomping at the bit, waiting to sink their teeth into that next challenge? What if we cannot provide them with this kind of motivational atmosphere on a daily basis? Does that mean they will be unmotivated?

Naturally, there will be days when salespeople will feel tired, perhaps even overwhelmed. They may have a lot on their minds — construction delays, settlement problems, difficult customers, difficult coworkers, a tough market, or personal concerns. Sometimes they will be a little depressed mentally, while other times they won't be 100% physically. Is it your job to keep jump-starting your salespeople under all of these conditions? Of course not. Life is complicated, and none of us has the power to make it simple. What does all of this mean about motivation? And what is your responsibility as a sales director in keeping your salespeople motivated?

The key to motivation is found in the word itself. To be motivated simply means to have a motive. To provide motivation means to provide a motive. We all need a *motive* for success. Our motive becomes our motivation. It's that simple.

This is good news, because it means you don't have to lead daily pep rallies or hire motivational speakers twice a week. If you do not have a "cheerleader" personality, it means there are other ways you can provide personal motivation to your team. Motivation is not merely a "stimulus-response" concept. It runs much deeper.

While some salespeople will be better "self-motivators" than others, sales directors have the responsibility to help all of their salespeople achieve a *consistently* high level of motivation on a *long-term* basis. This means providing the kind of motivation that will reach that deeper level. If deep-rooted, long-term motivation can be achieved, then the shorter-term, high-impact benefits of motivation (such as being pumped up, energized, clearheaded and focused) become easier to generate. They also last longer.

Jump-starting the battery of your car won't produce lasting success unless the rest of the electrical system (the battery's "support system") is in good working order. As long as the battery is not damaged, and the rest of the system is doing its part, then the battery will be "motivated" to provide the engine with all the energy it needs.

To be a good motivator, then, you need to keep your salespeople's support system in good working order. You can also help them maintain their peak level of performance by understanding how they each pursue success in their own unique way, and why. What are their *motives* for success? If you understand their motives, you can help them to stay motivated.

MOTIVES FOR SUCCESS

Not every salesperson's motives for succeeding in sales are the same, so salespeople cannot all be motivated in the same way. There are some types of motivation you can offer your team as a whole, while other types must be provided individually.

During your site visits, ask your salespeople one-on-one what motivates them, and remember what they tell you. Why did they choose this profession? What achievements have given them the most satisfaction?

What previous motivational tools have they found most effective? What kinds of rewards or recognition do they appreciate? What makes them enjoy their job? Why do they want to succeed? You may even ask each of your salespeople to think of five or ten influences which motivate them to be successful. You are not promising to provide all of those things. You simply want to learn what they are so you can do your best to help your team.

If you find motivations which are shared by all (or most) of your team, you may be able to use these motivations to design programs for the entire team. Where the motivations for success vary between salespeople, try to provide them with *personal* gratification in those areas. Remember, the key to successful motivation is to help your salespeople fulfill their motives.

Of course, the list of individual motives could be infinite, and you may find some motives that you do not believe should be fulfilled. However, there are ten motives for success which are expressed frequently in new home sales. We will discuss each of these motives, and suggest ways that you can help your salespeople achieve fulfillment from their successes.

1) MONEY

We listed this motive first because it is the most obvious, not because it is the most important. It may provide the top motivation for some salespeople, but not for others. As we will see in this chapter, there are many different motives for choosing a career in new home sales. It is important not to make value judgments about which motives are more valid than others.

The motive of money needs to be treated with respect. It is a real need as well as a symbol of achievement. The rules for compensation need to be clearly understood so that salespeople do not feel "ripped off" by earning less than they expect. Salespeople are at risk enough with construction delays and fluctuations in the market. When a misunderstanding or a change in policy causes them to feel deprived of income they believe they earned, the consequences on future morale and productivity can be devastating.

Naturally, money is a big topic in sales, and the issue of compensation in new home sales can become quite complex. For that reason we will devote part of the next chapter to compensation as a motivational tool.

2) QUALITY OF LIFE

One reason that money is a motive in selling is because it can help a salesperson achieve a higher quality of life. All other things being equal, more sales mean fewer financial worries. However, the motive of *quality of life* often extends beyond money. Many salespeople seek a balanced life, with time for commitments to family, friends, outside interests and spiritual pursuits. New home sales can threaten this balance because of constant weekend work and frequent evening appointments. While it is fair to say that this is "part of the deal" for new home salespeople, managers still need to be aware that seeking a well-rounded, balanced life can be an important motivation for many salespeople. Achieving this balance can make them more productive.

Management must respect the fact that salespeople have a life, too. Some companies will schedule commitments for salespeople on their days off, while they would never dream of scheduling a commitment for other employees on the weekend. The message this sends is that management believes the personal life of a salesperson has less value than that of other employees. While salespeople may be more liable for inconveniences on their days off than other employees, the matter should be handled with sensitivity. Comp days can be offered when it is appropriate.

Management's attitude is important. An inconvenience that cannot be avoided is different from the consistent assumption that salespeople have no right to privacy. A company that shows it values its salespeople's quality of life will have a more motivated team. Some companies offer occasional weekend days off for salespeople above and beyond the standard vacation allowance.

3) RESPECT AND APPRECIATION

With quality of life we discussed one way companies need to demonstrate respect for salespeople. Respect is a tremendous motivator. Appreciation is closely connected. Remember that salespeople sink or swim every day based on their ability to win approval for their efforts from others. As much as they need this gratification from their customers, they need it even more from their managers.

Companies frequently underestimate the importance of respect and appreciation to salespeople. Some companies believe that a salesperson's pay check is their reward. Beyond that the approach is "no news is good news." If the salesperson hasn't been fired, then they must be acceptable. What more do they want? As a result of this communication void, the number one disappointment that salespeople experience in our industry as a whole is "lack of respect and appreciation from management." What a sad irony!

The entire mystery of motivation can be solved with one basic principle:

People are motivated when they believe they have value.

If you use this principle as the guidepost for your motivational strategies, as we have for the ten motives we are discussing, you will achieve long-term motivation for your team. You will also achieve an environment in which your short-term, shot-in-the-arm motivational strategies (tapes, videos, pep rallies, etc.) will have greater value.

You convey respect and appreciation to your salespeople through your consistent commitment to a quality support system. Recognize positive achievements, give fair and balanced feedback, and resolve personnel problems which jeopardize the morale of the team. Involve salespeople in decisions that affect them. When they come up with good ideas, make sure you give them the credit. When they perceive that decisions are working against their best interests, take the time to convey the whole picture to them. Help to understand the benefits of working for a company that practices sound business management and keeps a watchful eye on the bottom line.

The twin motives of respect and appreciation are very powerful. Satisfying these motives will create an atmosphere for loyalty as well as motivation. The next two issues are related to respect and appreciation, but include additional dimensions.

4) CONFIDENCE OF OTHERS

If we know that our efforts will win us the confidence of others, we will pursue that confidence. Confidence feeds on itself in a cycle. The confidence of others is a testimony to our success, and allows us to increase our confidence in ourselves. With this increased confidence, we will become even more successful, further winning the confidence of others, and so on.

As a manager, your belief that a salesperson will succeed increases their chances of success. The so-called "Pygmalion effect" has been proven to be very significant. If we believe that one salesperson will be more successful than another, we tend to set into motion a series of events which creates a self-fulfilling prophecy. We express more confidence in one than the other, which affects each salesperson's level of confidence. We then provide a better support system to our favorite, which increases the favorite's success, but hurts the other. Beware of the consequences of favoritism.

You must express your confidence in each of your salespeople on an individual basis as well as to the group as a whole. You should also express confidence in employees in other departments, and encourage their managers to express confidence in yours. Be on your guard against employees who undermine the confidence of others, and address the occurrences of this undermining promptly. Winning your confidence, and that of other colleagues, is a powerful motive for success for salespeople.

5) CONFIDENCE IN THE COMPANY

Salespeople need to have confidence in the organization they are working for. Confidence in the organization contributes to a salesperson's pride in their work. Managers need to make sure their own personal frustrations with the company do not undermine their salespeople's sense of purpose. Your own belief in your company, its standards and direction will help salespeople sustain their sense of purpose. The stereotype of salespeople as "mavericks" or "mercenaries" does not apply to the majority. Loyalty is a very strong motive for many salespeople. As a sales manager you can nurture and fulfill that motive by upholding high standards and being a symbol of the company's excellence.

6) BELIEF IN THEIR WORK

We said earlier that "people are motivated when they believe they have value." In the same way, *people are motivated in their work when they believe their work has value.* Compensation is, of course, one way that companies express the value of work. But there is so much more. It is a shame to see companies express the feeling that "salespeople are over-paid" or "are only looking out for number one." When companies treat salespeople as outsiders just because their work schedules are different, there can be a severe loss of motivation for the sales team as a whole. Companies must not take away their salespeople's sense of purpose or direction by belittling or ignoring their occupation. The stress and the peaks and valleys of sales cause enough doubt as it is without manage-ment adding to this doubt.

From time to time you may need to reinforce a salesperson's sense of purpose in a private conversation. We all want to be proud of the work we do. Whenever it is appropriate, remind salespeople of the value of their work — to customers, to the company and to you personally. New home sales is truly a high calling. Salespeople play an important role in enabling people to improve their lives. They also pump the life blood to the company's heart which allows coworkers to be paid. From time to time salespeople need to be reminded of the enormous value of their occupations.

7) SERVICE TO CUSTOMERS

It may surprise cynics to learn what an important motive this is for so many salespeople. For some, this is actually the highest gratification they receive, especially in companies where managers do not express appreci-ation or provide encouragement. The ability to have a significant positive influence on the lives of so many customers provides the motivation for many salespeople to achieve consistent success in an inconsistent busi-ness. Some salespeople cite this satisfaction as the primary factor pre-venting burnout.

This motive for success also benefits the company, as long as salespeo-ple maintain the perspective that their primary loyalty is to their builder.

More companies today are sending out questionnaires asking buyers to evaluate their purchasing experience. As with other achievements, make sure your salespeople are aware of all the positive responses from their customers, and the company's appreciation of these responses, as well as the occasional negative ones.

Help your salespeople to develop this motive if they do not already have it. Make them aware of the tremendous wealth of satisfaction that results from outstanding service to customers. While some customers seem perpetually dissatisfied, most are very appreciative of good service. Many will express their appreciation generously.

Letters of gratitude from customers should be displayed in sales offices or models, with copies in the corporate office where visitors and other employees can see them.

Let your team know that you have special appreciation for salespeople who can perform the triple play of outstanding sales, consistent loyalty to the company, and top-flight service to customers.

8) VICTORY

The desire to be the best is another strong motive for success. Most top salespeople are competitive to some extent, even though it may not consume them. Competition is a healthy element in the environment of a successful sales team, and you should use it as a motivational tool. In addition to competition with others is the desire to exceed one's own prior accomplishments.

Since your purpose in fostering competition is to motivate, you must be especially careful that it does not backfire by accidentally de-motivating your salespeople. When you design competitions for your salespeople, remember two points:

1) Make sure that everyone is playing on a level field. Don't penalize those salespeople who have the tougher situations. "Handicap" the competition by factoring in a "degree of difficulty." Competition can be measured by comparing the percentage of individual goals achieved, or with some other equalizing factor so that everyone has the same chance to win.

2) The purpose of the competition is to create winners, not losers. Reward the winners without forcing the rest of your team to feel inadequate about their performance, especially if they did a good job. Your goal with the contest was, after all, to help everyone maximize their own *individual* performance. We will also discuss this idea further in the next chapter.

Some salespeople do not like to compete because they have rarely experienced the thrill of personal victory. If you want to promote a more competitive atmosphere among salespeople who seem reluctant to compete, create situations where people can take turns winning. We're not saying to stack the deck in favor of losers, but simply not to stack the deck *against* anyone. Vary your criteria for victory so that everyone gets to be rewarded for improved performance, or for those special efforts which produce results that surpass expectations. If you allow salespeople to achieve victory against their own past performance or management expectations, they may then become more confident competing against each other, as long as the playing field is level and there is no disgrace in losing.

9) PRESTIGE

Prestige can be a motive for success just as monetary rewards can. To be *known* as a success — to have a *reputation* — can be very rewarding. Make sure all of your successful salespeople get the prestige they deserve. Wall plaques and business cards which reflect special successes are two ways to enhance prestige.

Cultivate the individual reputations of your salespeople throughout the company for achievements they accomplish or skills they develop. Allow salespeople to be known by their individual strengths and victories rather than by their weaknesses and failures. People who are known as "successes" are more likely to be successful. Naturally, the prestige of success must be legitimately earned to have real meaning. You should not pretend that failure is success. However, when salespeople are successful, be sure that they are enriched by the prestige which accompanies success, especially if you know that this prestige is one of their motives for pursuing excellence.

10) RESPECT FOR THEIR LEADER

This motive for success should not be underestimated. By winning your salespeople's respect and loyalty, you will also give them additional motivation to achieve excellence. It is much easier for people to make those extra sacrifices that produce success when they respect their leader. As we said in Chapter Two, your leadership sets the tone. As you lead by example and provide a support system to help your salespeople solve problems and achieve success, their respect and loyalty become one more source of energy they can draw upon. Your commitment to your salespeople will be rewarded by their commitment to you in return. When you help them succeed, they are more willing to help you achieve success of your own. This shared commitment is one of the factors that turns a group of salespeople into a winning team.

* * *

You may have noticed that one motive for success is missing from our list — *fear*. The power of fear as a motive has been frequently studied and widely debated. There may be times in your management career when the only source of motivation you have left for a particular employee is, "Improve or you're fired." It is true that there have been many instances when this "motivational technique" produced a breakthrough after all other attempts had failed. However, the purpose of this chapter is to explain how to create an *environment* for motivation. Fear does not accomplish this.

Summary

An environment for motivation is built upon a foundation of respect, trust, support and communication. As a manager, you must think of motivation as a long-term commitment, not a series of short-term, adrenaline-producing bursts. A doctor would not wait until a patient is in a coma to give him a vitamin. For a patient in good health, however, vitamins can make him feel even better. Motivational speeches and pep rallies can be much more effective in an overall *environment of motivation*. They are of little use in an environment of cynicism and neglect. Salespeople need a spokesperson to convey their ideas to upper management. They look to you, their sales director, for this kind of support as much as for problem solving. They must not perceive you as a helpless puppet of upper management. They must trust in you as part of their team, defending their position when you believe they are right, and counseling them patiently when you feel they are wrong.

Many of the principles we have been discussing throughout the first nine chapters relate to a motivational environment. The quality of the support system you provide your salespeople will be the primary factor in your success as a motivator.

Find out what motivates your salespeople as individuals and as a team. Discuss motivation and motivational programs as a group during meetings, and one-on-one during your site visits. It is tragic when an ill-conceived motivational program only serves to de-motivate the team instead. Keep the channels of communication open with respect to motivation. As we said before, your goal in managing, as in selling, is to meet your "customers'" needs. Your salespeople are now your customers, at the same time that you are their manager, boss and leader.

In this chapter we discussed ten different kinds of "motives" for success expressed by many new home salespeople. We then discussed ways that you can increase their motivation by helping them to fulfill their motives.

1) Money.
2) Quality of life.
3) Respect and Appreciation.
4) Confidence of others.
5) Confidence in the company.
6) Belief in their work.
7) Service to customers.
8) Victory.
9) Prestige.
10) Respect for their leader.

Once an environment for motivation is achieved, specific programs to further motivate salespeople for short-term goals can be more successful. Our next chapter will discuss ways to use compensation, contests and incentives to provide special motivation for specific objectives.

COMPENSATION, CONTESTS AND INCENTIVES

Compensation for salespeople is a controversial topic in the home-building industry. There are a variety of theories about the fairest way to compensate, and what forms of compensation provide the best motivation. It is not our goal in this chapter to resolve this controversy. Nor is it to standardize the industry's pay system. Many different approaches to compensation have been successful in our business. We will share some of these approaches in an effort to provide a "menu" of strategies to choose from. If you and your salespeople are happy with your current system, then there is no reason to change it. However, if you are considering a change in your overall approach to sales compensation, or if you are re-evaluating your approach from the standpoint of motivation, we hope that the strategies discussed here will provide you some alternatives.

There are likely to be some ideas in this chapter that may seem way off base for your management philosophy. Considering the variety, this is almost inevitable. To provide a broad range of ideas as impartially as possible, we will try to resist the temptation to advocate a specific approach.

One final word of caution: we will occasionally use illustrations that include dollar amounts as examples. These numbers are used only to clarify the illustration, not to suggest a pay scale. Sales income varies widely from one company to the next, as well as from region to region. Please do not consider any of our numbers to be "typical" or "recommended." We have used them for mathematical purposes only, showing how they could fit together as pieces of a total compensation package. We are not promoting high pay scales or low ones, and we will not try to compare them to the compensation of employees in other departments within a company.

We have intentionally included this chapter in our section on Motivation rather than our section on Management. Our purpose is therefore not to suggest the perfect way to compensate salespeople, but rather to explore some of the considerations for developing a compensation package which can help *motivate* your sales team.

As we discussed in the last chapter, you should feel free to discuss your company's approach to compensation openly with your salespeople. While personal compensation issues should be discussed privately, general issues may be discussed with your group as a whole. One example of an appropriate group topic would be your company's overall approach to sales compensation. Another would, of course, be contests or other compensation incentives that apply to the entire team.

Remember, if your salespeople believe your compensation program is inadequate or unfair, it will not motivate them. If you expect to have top performers, you must pay wages comparable to what other top performers are earning in your area. As sales director, you may need to keep upper management focused on the motivational implications of sales compensation. If your program does not motivate your salespeople, you need to discuss this with your supervisor or builder, and propose alternatives for their consideration. At the same time, you must also help your salespeople understand the positive reasoning behind your compensation system, using it as a motivational tool to whatever extent is possible. Make sure they understand why your company believes that its approach is the best, fairest and most motivational of any program it could have chosen.

As in all other aspects of management, communication is vital to the success of your sales compensation program. If it appears that you are reluctant to talk about it, it could be assumed that you are ashamed of it. If you explain it clearly, support it enthusiastically, and are willing to address criticism with well-though-out confidence, your program will be more successful.

Not everyone can be the highest-paying company in the industry, and a high pay scale does not guarantee high motivation. *Fairness* is the key. Make sure that your pay system rewards accomplishment as well as "luck."

Let us look first at several general approaches to long-term compensation. Then we will discuss examples of additional programs designed to achieve specific short-term goals.

LONG-TERM COMPENSATION

By long-term compensation, we mean a pay program designed to give a fair reward to a salesperson for a full year, or for the life of a community.

It is very important to plan the long-term compensation for each salesperson to assure that it is reasonable. Not everyone has to be paid on the same scale. In fact, having the flexibility for an associate to choose is a motivator in itself. What is important is that everyone is compensated with *fairness*. Based on *reasonable* sales expectations and your planned compensation package, estimate the income for each salesperson over the next twelve months.

If you estimate that one salesperson will receive a windfall, ask yourself two questions: Will that salesperson *earn* what they will be paid? Will their income be so far out of proportion with everyone else (or with industry standards for a salesperson of their skill and experience) that it could cause a morale problem for the rest of your team, or an unfair financial burden to the company?

It can be discouraging for salespeople on difficult communities to watch those on easier ones earn more money. Some personal counseling from you may be required. Explain to your salespeople that earning cycles are a part of our business. For example, in a five-year cycle, a salesperson may spend one year "paying their dues," one year "raking it in," and have three "normal" years along the way. The cycle does not work in the same order for everyone. The lean year and the fat year may fall anywhere in the cycle. Even the idea of the five-year cycle is not foolproof, because there are so many potential variations. The point is to help each of your salespeople think long-term. During their boom times, help them keep their skills sharp and prepare for lower expectations in the future. In the slow part of the cycle, help them stay focused on doing their best to keep developing those skills that will pay bigger dividends in the future. As their manager, it is your job to help keep your team balanced by moderating the cycle of each employee as best you can.

When a salesperson does pay their dues with a diligent commitment, do your best to reward their loyalty before it's too late by adjusting their compensation or providing them a lucrative community.

If you have to move a person from a windfall into a position with less potential, make sure that it is not perceived as punishment for earning too much. Help them understand that great markets or easy communities don't last forever, and that you are still committed to providing them with a good income as long as they meet their goals.

It is important that your compensation strategy reward all salespeople who meet the company's goals and maintain its standards. Beyond that, try to minimize the long-term impact of bad luck as best you can. Bad luck is very demoralizing for salespeople. If they do the best that anyone could have done and do not receive adequate compensation, you will run the risk of losing good people.

Discuss each person's pay package with them privately. As with customers, do your best to patiently address their objections, explain your point of view and help them to see the total picture. If you believe that a salesperson's pay package is unfair, take their case to upper management (or your builder) without setting management up to look bad to the salesperson if they deny the request.

Some companies use the same basic compensation strategy for all of the salespeople, while others offer each salesperson a choice of packages, depending upon which will provide the best motivation. If you give your people a choice, be sure all choices are equally fair.

Here is an overview of the most popular methods of new home sales compensation, with a few ideas to consider for each:

DRAW AGAINST COMMISSION

This method is well known and requires little explanation. The primary advantage of this method is that the salesperson is protected at the beginning while he is getting his momentum started. The disadvantage is becoming indebted to the company, a situation that can demotivate some associates.

The draw also may not provide the salesperson with any cash flow during market downturns or delays in construction later on when the commissions earned have advanced beyond the limits of the original draw. This problem can be partially solved by providing the salesperson with a new draw against the next wave of commissions.

Of course, this method of compensation puts the company at risk if a salesperson leaves with an outstanding draw that exceeds commissions earned.

SALARY AND COMMISSION

Some builders and salespeople prefer this method because it offers more stability. The advantage to the salesperson is that the salary is permanent and the salesperson does not "go into the hole." The disadvantage is that maximum income potential is often lower. A top producer may earn more money on straight commission because the builder is willing to pay a higher commission in return for not being at risk with the salary. Salary plus commission is often used by builders who want to protect the range of the salesperson's income at both the high and low ends. For example, a company might decide that it wants to pay $60,000 for selling 50 homes a year at $140,000. The company will pay a base salary of $20,000. The base salary has nothing to do with selling. It compensates for all of the other responsibilities of the new home sales profession. The commission portion of the package is then determined by dividing the remaining $40,000 by 50 homes, producing a commission of $800 per home. Perhaps that same builder would have been willing to pay 1% of the selling price to a straight commission salesperson (with a modest draw), for a potential of $70,000. However, if market conditions or construction delays reduced sales to 25, then the salaried salesperson would earn $40,000, while the commission person would earn $35,000.

Many companies believe they should not base their sales compensation solely on a per cent of the sale price, because some salespeople may wind up being overpaid while others are underpaid. Before setting the compensation they might consider the following factors:

- A realistic sales projection based upon sales volume of competitors.
- The number of salespeople at a community. (Do not assume that more salespeople will always mean more sales. A salesperson can quickly become demoralized and unproductive when he realizes there will never be enough sales to go around, no matter how hard he tries. Even winners in this kind of environment can feel guilty starving out "losers" who are giving their best effort.)
- Sales income in the surrounding marketplace.
- The individual salesperson's track record. (Are they a superstar, a sales-

person with a fairly strong background, or a rookie?)
- Will the salesperson have to pay for his or her own assistant? (Some salespeople prefer to take financial responsibility for their assistants in order to structure the assistant's compensation to their mutual advantage, stay flexible and promote personal loyalty.)
- Will the salesperson be an independent contractor or an employee with company benefits?

SALARY AND COMMISSION AND BONUS

This type of compensation package works on the same principle as the last one, except that part of the projected compensation potential is in the form of a bonus. Like other programs, this should be carefully planned and completely budgeted at the beginning of the year. Both you and your salespeople deserve a reasonable expectation of their earnings in advance so that they can plan their lives and you can plan your sales budget.

The bonus portion of this plan can be paid in a number of ways. It could be paid upon achievement of periodic goals (such as reaching a planned number of settlements or net contracts each quarter). It could be an increase in commission after a certain number of sales. Or it could be a discretionary amount which you would budget for special contests or incentive programs as the year progresses. Examples of these special motivational programs will be discussed shortly.

INSTALLMENT COMMISSIONS

Some builders are moving in the direction of commissions paid upon completion of certain milestones within the sale. This is another way of providing cash flow to salespeople, while also motivating them at points in the sale prior to settlement. For example, if the total commission is $1000, payment of the commission may be dispersed as follows: $300 at ratification of the contract; $300 at loan approval (or release of contingency on the sale of a prior home); and $400 at settlement. If commissions are advanced on a home which does not settle, then the advance portion is deducted from the next pay check. This form of compensation can be used in place of a draw. It can also be used in conjunction with a salary.

Since we are discussing compensation as a *motivational* tool, we will not discuss company benefits in this book.

Let's look now at ways you can supplement your long-term compensation plan with short-term programs designed to provide additional rewards for accomplishing special goals.

CONTESTS AND SPECIAL INCENTIVES

When we discussed the package of "salary and commission and bonus," we mentioned the option of budgeting a discretionary bonus fund at the beginning of the year. For example, if you feel that special incentive programs throughout the year will help your salespeople stay motivated and focused more consistently, you could budget $10,000 of each salesperson's projected income to be tied to these special programs. You may want to divide it up into $2500 each quarter, leaving yourself the flexibility to decide what kind of incentive program would be most helpful when the time comes.

Special incentive programs can support your training efforts as well as your motivational efforts. You can reward salespeople for developing new skills or accomplishing new tasks just as you can reward them for selling additional homes. Here are a few types of special contests and incentives companies have used to provide motivation for specific short-term objectives.

CONTESTS TO ACHIEVE SHORT-TERM SALES GOALS

This is the most familiar form of sales contest. A goal for sales and/or settlements is established for a relatively short period of time. A bonus is awarded if the goal is reached.

As we said earlier, if you create this type of contest in the form of a competition, make sure everyone has the same opportunity to win. If everyone starts off with an equal chance, the motivation for victory will be greater. You could have everyone competing against their own individual goal, with the person achieving the highest percentage of goal being the winner.

If you do not want your contest to be competitive, you could award each person individually for meeting their own goal, and then give the entire team an additional bonus if they achieve a total team goal.

TEAM COMPETITION

Another form of competition would be to divide your salespeople into teams that compete against each other. Bonuses would be awarded based upon the total performance of each team.

This type of competition can work especially well in companies where salespeople are encouraged to refer customers to each other. Teams would be determined based upon their referral potential. Each salesperson now has two motivations — the bonus and their teammates' success.

In some cases you may be able to divide the teams in such a way that the total sales goals for each team are exactly the same, which means that the teams can compete in terms of real numbers that are easier to track.

CUSTOMER SATISFACTION

As customer satisfaction continues to become the object of greater focus, more builders are offering part of their sales compensation as a reward for high ratings on customer surveys. For example, on surveys in which customers are asked to rate the salesperson on a scale of 1 ot 5, if a salesperson's average response is 4.5, the salesperson would receive a $1000 bonus. With $4000 of their annual income at risk, the focus on excellent service can result in less buyer's remorse and more referrals.

SALESPERSON OF THE MONTH

A "Salesperson of the Month" contest enables you to combine a number of goals into a single bonus. It also provides a way for you to reinforce your commitment to maintaining and rewarding high standards among your team. It allows you to reward the *total* efforts and achievements of your people, instead of just sales volume.

One way you could structure a "Salesperson of the Month" contest is to determine a series of categories which are consistent with top priorities that you are trying to achieve. The categories could remain the same for the entire year, or they could change as your needs change. Just be sure that the criteria and scoring system are the same for everyone. This is not the type of contest where you would vary the criteria for different salespeople in order to build individual strengths.

For example, you could rate each of your salespeople on a scale of 1 to 5 in categories such as the following:

- Per cent of sales goal achieved. (This score could exceed 5 for surpassing the sales goal if it is important enough. Otherwise you could set 5 as your cap for making or exceeding the goal. The same reasoning would also apply to the next category.)
- Per cent of settlement goal achieved.
- Customer service rating (derived from scores on customer survey forms).
- Maintenance of model homes and sales office.
- Prospecting efforts.
- Follow up.
- Other special initiatives taken to solve problems, increase sales, assist the marketing effort or improve company systems.

The salesperson with the best total score would win the award for the month.

For some of the categories, scores would be determined on a purely mathematical basis (sales, settlements, customer service, perhaps even model maintenance if there is a standardized rating form). However, other categories will require a subjective judgment call. For the subjective categories, consider allowing the salespeople to rate themselves in addition to your own rating. Discuss your rating with theirs, and use the average of the two numbers for the final score. This type scoring system establishes one more format for coaching and counseling your salespeople. It also conveys an atmosphere of trust.

PERFORMANCE EVALUATIONS

The approach discussed for a "Salesperson of the Month" award could also be used for including bonuses in your periodic Performance Evaluations with salespeople. Unlike "Salesperson of the Month" contests, the criteria for bonuses with Performance Evaluations can vary from one salesperson to the next, as long as everyone's criteria are equally fair.

Suppose you review a Performance Evaluation with each salesperson once a quarter, and you want to allocate $4000 of their annual pay package to these evaluations. At each review you would establish the criteria for the next review, and how the amount of the $1000 quarterly bonus would be determined. You could again allow salespeople to rate their own progress and average their score with yours.

SPECIAL OBJECTIVES

Part of your discretionary incentive budget can be spent on specific objectives which arise as the year progresses. Challenges can arise suddenly, and this approach allows you to react quickly. You may want to encourage your entire team to develop a particular skill or grow in a new way. A contest can help your salespeople focus more seriously on the new objective, especially if it is an objective which provokes mixed feelings.

Be careful with these types of incentives. Some employers believe that it is wrong to "pay a bonus to get salespeople to do what they are supposed to be doing every day." This, of course, is not the point of the bonus. The purpose is to demonstrate the company's commitment to helping its sales team achieve excellence through initiative. These bonuses usually should not be large amounts. The monetary reward in these situations is often more symbolic. It simply helps you to formalize your program, measure progress and reward exeptional achievement.

Here are several ideas which have been used successfully as motivational tools, along with a few words of caution for each. You may feel that some of them are inappropriate as goals, but you may find the principle useful for another objective of your own. You might even use different programs for your various communities, and you may use them at different times. Just make sure everyone understands that over the course of the year they will all be given equal opportunities.

• *Negotiating Bonuses*

In markets where price negotiation is the prevailing custom, and where everyone understands that home prices are negotiated individually, some builders give their salespeople a percentage of any money obtained above a bottom line sales price. The danger with this program is that it might encourage salespeople to give different "deals" to different customers, which is not always the best public relations strategy. In some markets, however, this is considered the standard way to buy and sell a new home.

• Bonuses for Selling Options

Since many builders earn a higher profit margin on options than on the base home, they encourage salespeople to sell options by paying a higher commission percentage on options. The danger here is that the builder could be perceived as "peddling" excessive options which buyers do not need and cannot afford. Be careful that this type of incentive does not result in high-pressure selling tactics for extracting additional dollars from reluctant customers.

• Difficult Homesites, Unpopular Models, Inventory Homes, and Other Sales Challenges

Companies sometimes use incentives to provide an extra motivation (or reward) for selling tougher homes and homesites. The goals here are to reduce builder carrying costs, and also to sell off less desirable properties more quickly, before they become all that is left. You need to be careful that this type of incentive does not cause sales challenges to seem greater than they really are. There can also be differences of opinion over when or why a home deserves a bonus.

• Bonuses for Excellent Shopping Reports

Bonuses can make a salesperson's sales evaluation by a mystery shopper financially rewarding as well as a valuable learning tool. The risk is that the salesperson who does not earn a bonus may develop a more antagonistic feeling toward the shopper's judgment. This is why we recommend all shopping reports be taped. The recorded presentation, as well as the written report, can be analyzed by the salesperson and sales manager.

• *Rewards for Specific Parts of the Selling Process Where You Want a Special Focus*

This type of bonus can help motivate salespeople to implement the principles taught in sales training programs. If your goal is to demonstrate more models, get more of your qualified customers to the homesites, or increase your sales team's commitment to follow up or prospecting, you could provide a small bonus for progress achieved. Naturally, you do not want to convey the message that executing normal parts of the selling process deserves a bonus. However, if you are asking your salespeople to try a new technique or to focus exceptional energy in a particular area, the bonus simply says, "We want to help you take this next step." The method you choose to measure these types of extra efforts may involve an "honor system" for reporting achievements. As we said before, expressing this kind of trust in your salespeople has motivational value of its own.

If you are concerned that these types of incentives could send a wrong message (or risk backfiring on you), do not use them. We mentioned them here because they have been used successfully by others. You may want to budget a small amount for bonuses which support those parts of your training that you feel are difficult to implement, but which could raise your team to a new level with an organized effort.

A FEW MORE THOUGHTS

Bonuses, contests and incentive programs can sometimes offer a greater mathematical challenge for builders who are represented by outside Realtors than for those with in-house sales teams. If the builder does not feel that he should participate in bonus programs beyond the basic commission to the Realtor, and if bonuses cannot be negotiated into the commission, then the mathematical challenge transfers to the Realtor. However, with careful planning of total commission dollars available, and clear explanations to salespeople, these types of incentives for special excellence can be a valuable motivational tool for Realtors as well as builders.

* * *

Spontaneous, unexpected bonuses for exceptional effort can have tremendous motivational impact. Even small amounts, such as $100, can provide a lot of gratification to a salesperson who takes that special initiative which pays off. It proves that the company appreciates the effort. The salesperson went beyond the call of duty, and the company did the same.

* * *

Remember the value of recognition in ways other than money. A letter of thanks from the president can give a salesperson the kind of satisfaction which lasts a long time. Announcements in meetings are another way to show appreciation.

Some companies produce their own newsletter that is sent out monthly to all employees, highlighting special achievements of individuals as well as those of the company.

Other kinds of non-monetary rewards can provide additional motivation. Extra time off, participation on a prestigious corporate committee, a ticket to a self-improvement seminar, or a higher degree of decision-making authority can be enriching rewards for salespeople. Remember to design your rewards with the "motives" of your team in mind. Knowing each of your salespeople through relationship building will help you know when and how to motivate them, and which incentives to implement.

SUMMARY

In new home sales, unlike salaried jobs, the purpose of compensation is to motivate as well as reward. Compensation packages for salespeople should be planned and budgeted very thoroughly in advance so that they are fair as well as motivational. As sales director, you may need to educate other managers who adhere to cliches such as, "Salespeople earn enough already," or, "We're not paying extra for people to do their job."

There are valid reasons for designing compensation strategies for sales-people more creatively than those of other employees.

New home sales demands a unique kind of energy and perseverance that is impossible to sustain at its highest level every day of the year. Contests and incentive programs can help improve performance by focusing a higher level of intensity on special goals.

Discuss your compensation strategies with your salespeople so that you can be assured your programs are having the desired effect. Contests that backfire are an extremely disheartening experience for managers as well as salespeople.

Pick and choose your special incentive programs. Don't have too many, and don't make them complicated. Remember that your goal with these programs is not to intrigue or fascinate your salespeople, but to increase their skills and success.

The effectiveness of your compensation program will be determined by how *fairly* you pay as well as by how *much* you pay. While luck will always be an element in new home sales earnings, you should do every-thing possible to assure that *accomplishment* is the primary factor.

Handling Slumps And Burnout On Your Sales Team

Slumps

Even the best salespeople are vulnerable to slumps. They need your help to make these slumps less frequent. When they do fall into a slump, they may need your help to pick themselves up. In this chapter we will use the term "slump" to refer to a *personal sales slowdown,* as opposed to a decline in the market as a whole. In a slump, a salesperson frequently cannot explain exactly why his or her sales have declined. They don't know where the slump came from, or how long it will last. What can you do to help?

Once you and your team accept the fact that slumps are normal, then you can discuss the issue openly and honestly. This will help you take measures to prevent them, and also shorten them when they occur.

Where do slumps come from? They can have a variety of causes. Here are some of them:

- Feeling physically tired.
- Feeling mentally tired of the profession.
- Feeling mentally tired of the particular community.
- Feeling tired of the repetition of selling, and therefore taking shortcuts in the selling process.
- Losing touch with the competitive market.
- Feeling discouraged, frustrated or helpless.

• Moving from an "easy" community to a difficult one.
• Feeling lonely at the job site, especially on a slow community.
• Feeling a lack of fulfillment.
• Taking a wrong overall approach to the selling process.
• Making specific mistakes in the selling process.
• Forgetting what made them successful in the past.
• Forgetting what made their homes successful in the past.

Some of these causes can be easily eliminated, while others may be more difficult. Some can even develop into burnout. There may be times when it is difficult to distinguish whether your salesperson's problem is a slump or burnout. Unless you are certain that the problem is burnout, begin with the assumption that it is a slump. Burnout is a more difficult challenge, and will be discussed later.

As a manager you want to help your salespeople prevent slumps before they occur. Many of the principles of leadership, support, training and motivation discussed in previous chapters will offer the fringe benefit of cutting down on slumps.

Once again, communication is a top priority. Your message to your team should be, "If you believe something is wrong, let me know at once so that we can nip it in the bud together. It will not put your job at risk to tell me you are feeling negative. It will become a much bigger problem if we don't address it soon enough."

The more time you spend with your salespeople, the quicker you will pick up signs that things are not right.

Your salespeople must realize that, as their coach, you are not there to hassle them when they are in a slump, but to help them. If you believe that any of the causes listed above (or any other problems) could be affecting their performance, you should join forces with them to neutralize the problem and get them back on track.

One way to take a proactive approach to slumps while salespeople are performing well is to help them understand what it is that makes them successful. As we said earlier with training and coaching, take time during the successful periods to discuss what your salespeople are doing right. Help them to "bottle" their secrets of success for a rainy day. When a slump arrives, if salespeople can remember how they have succeeded in the past, they can revitalize themselves more easily. Encourage your salespeople to keep a record of their successes as they occur.

There are several ways they can keep this record. One way is simply to keep a running journal of each day's events, focusing on the successes of that day. This journal could include successful sales interactions (whether they resulted in a sales agreement or not), other successful sales activities such as prospecting efforts or follow up calls which paid off, problems they solved, or ideas they had for new ways to handle objections.

Another way to preserve their successes is with a tape recorder. We always say that the best time for a salesperson to greet a customer is right after he has just made a sale. That is when his confidence is at its peak. What if he could preserve that feeling just a little longer? Suppose after each sale he could capture the feeling of that moment on tape. Your salespeople can put their feelings into words which can be played back and relived each time they need a boost.

A third method for recording successes is by keeping a chart which summarizes highlights of all their sales at their current communities. This chart includes five columns which would be filled in every time they write a purchase agreement: the lot number; the customer's name; why the customer chose your community over all the other available alternatives; what the salesperson did that was special to help make the sale; and the exact way the salesperson closed the sale when that final moment arrived. A chart like this can help them track patterns in customer hot buttons as well as in their own sales-winning strategies and techniques. We are familiar with many top performers who record successes on a computer to refer back to.

Remembering their successes can keep their skills sharp while it keeps their confidence and energy at a high level.

It is important for salespeople not to become paranoid during a slump. While this chapter is attempting to pinpoint causes and solutions for slumps, sometimes slumps simply come and go and we never do figure out what happened.

One of the mysterious truths in new home sales is this: Even if a salesperson does everything right, it doesn't always work. This makes selling different from other skills such as mathematics. If a salesperson is absolutely certain that he is doing everything right, then he should just keep doing it, and wait for it to start working again. Don't assume that salespeople must change their technique in order to get out of a slump.

However, sometimes a change in the selling method can produce new excitement for a salesperson, especially when a slump has resulted from the boredom of repetition. A change in behavior may produce a change in attitude.

Talk the situation through with your salespeople. Engage in role-playing sessions. Work with them on weekends.

Are they doing something wrong? More importantly, have they stopped doing something which had previously been part of their success formula?

Be helpful without being critical. Compassion is important in slumps because the salesperson's confidence may already be lower than normal, and your job is to boost it back up again. While you have to take a no-nonsense approach whenever an employee is not producing, you are still their coach and their support system, not their critic. Help them to keep a positive attitude about themselves, their company and their profession.

Encourage your salespeople to speak frankly if they believe they have an explanation for the problem. Have they lost confidence in their company? Have they lost interest in their community? Do they feel they would be more effective at a different community? Do they have a hard time relating to the product line or the clientele? Do they feel that they need some time off? Are there any books, tapes or seminars which might help them?

You will still need to make sure that your solution to their problem is compatible with company policy and fair to your other salespeople, but at least with open communication you will have a better chance of addressing the real problem. It only adds to everyone's frustration when your solution for a slump is not relevant to the actual challenge a salesperson is facing.

What about the competition? Are they cutting prices to liquidate inventory? Are they offering some other overwhelming advantage to your customers? Is it something you can combat, or will you have to just tough it out? Have other communities in your market also slowed down? If so, why? Ask your salesperson to research these issues. You may want to research them yourself.

Be aware of your competition, but help your salespeople to stay focused on what it is about them and their homes that has caused people to buy up until now. Salespeople must not exaggerate the trauma of losing an occasional customer to someone else. That is a normal part of competing. Focus on the *patterns* of buyer response.

When salespeople are in a slump, help them to think long term. They need to remember what it was like before the slump. They must also envision what it will be like when the slump is over. In the big scheme of things, a slump is only a brief moment in time, during which old skills are revitalized and sharpened and new skills are developed. Entering a slump can be startling. Enduring one can be discouraging. But emerging from a slump is tremendously gratifying.

Here are a few specific selling ideas to help your salespeople emerge from their slumps more quickly.

Emotion is an important part of a homebuyer's motivation. One way that a buyer's emotions are stimulated is by the enthusiasm of the salesperson. Focusing on this selling priority can be even more critical when a salesperson is in a slump. During a slump it can sometimes take tremendous *will* to act enthusiastic. But it is important for salespeople to force themselves. It really is true that we can make ourselves *feel* more excited when we *act* more excited. What's more, enthusiasm is contagious. If our customer captures our enthusiasm, we will in turn capture theirs, and the cycle snowballs.

Remind your salespeople that every customer offers them a fresh opportunity to break out of their slump. The customer doesn't know that the salesperson is in a slump. Tell your salespeople to think of each customer as the one who may end their slump, and to take that customer as far as they can in the selling process. If the salesperson has become gun-shy as the result of a string of failures, remind him that every customer who walks in the door really does *expect* him to try to sell them a home. The salesperson should simply keep going from one stage of the selling process to the next until the customer stops them. Only the customer should stop the selling process, never the salesperson.

During a slump, the salesperson should stay focused on creating *transitions* from one stage of the sale to the next by creating *anticipation* for the next stage to come. If salespeople can stay focused on moving one stage farther than they already are, it will help them to persevere in the face of discouragement.

Closing is another area in which salespeople can become gun-shy during a slump. Help your salespeople to remember once again that the customer expects them to close, once they have *earned the right.* When the salesperson has given the information which a customer needs in order to make an informed decision, and when the customer has picked out a favorite home and homesite, then the salesperson has "earned the right to close." If the customer says no, that is not a failure. It simply means that the salesperson took the opportunity as far as they could that day. The next step is follow up.

When salespeople reach the closing stage in the selling process, then they should go ahead and ask for the sale, even if the buyer does not seem to be giving strong buying signals. Salespeople should not get too hung up on *buying signals* during a slump. If the buyer is not acting enthusiastic, that could simply be a personality trait. Perhaps the buyer is simply not motivated to give strong, emotional buying signals at that point. The truest buying signal is the ability to *make decisions*. Getting buyers to make decisions must remain one of the salesperson's primary focal points.

If salespeople can act enthusiastic, stay focused on reaching one more stage in the selling process, keep the customer on a decision-making track, and then ask for the sale with confidence when the time comes, they can maximize their selling opportunities and emerge successfully from their slump. If they can be encouraged and coached by your support in the process, their success will return even more quickly.

BURNOUT

Although slumps and burnout have several features in common, burnout is much more serious. While many of the causes for slumps listed earlier may also be causes of burnout, the effects are usually more severe in burnout. Sometimes the damage is irreparable, so that neither you nor your company can offer a solution that works. But this is not always the case. Burnout can sometimes be cured. How will you know the difference? What can you do to cure it? What will you do if you can't?

As with slumps, the first thing you can do is look for ways to help your salespeople avoid burnout. If any of your salespeople are overly tired, or are bored with their work, or feel discouraged, frustrated or unfulfilled, encourage them to talk with you about it. Be sure you do not allow their honesty to backfire on them. You must continue to evaluate their value as associates based upon their performance, and not on private conversations about their challenges. These conversations may, however, help the two of you to arrive at a plan for improving their performance.

Here are some of the symptoms of burnout which can help you distinguish it from a slump. However, as you review this list, you may still find yourself faced with the puzzle of whether these characteristics are really symptoms of burnout or simply the personality traits of a particular salesperson. Ask yourself this question: Did the salesperson manifest the same characteristics before, when their productivity was higher, or have these characteristics increased as productivity has declined?

• A constant attitude of pessimisim.
• Chronic complaining.
• Lack of initiative in overcoming obstacles.
• Making excuses instead of seeking solutions or trying to improve.
• A sense of helplessness.
• Causing disciplinary problems.
• Treating co-workers or customers poorly.
• Creating a negative impact upon other salespeople.

If you see these types of problems increasing as productivity declines, and if your attempts to address these problems with the salesperson prove futile, then the situation is probably more serious than simply a slump.

Burnout can be heartbreaking, because sometimes it is hopeless. Drawing upon our earlier analogy of a car battery, sometimes it seems as though you have successfully jump-started a battery and restored it to its former energy, only to find out that the battery is dead again the next morning. However, if you know that you have a burnout problem, begin by addressing it with a positive attitude. Assume that salespeople can make a comeback, but be willing to face up to it if they can't.

In dealing with burnout, it is valid to make a distinction between a salesperson whom you have just hired and one who has given your company years of faithful, productive service.

Someday you may hire a salesperson based on their excellent track record and an outstanding interview, only to realize soon after they begin working for you that they are burned out. Make an effort to help them. However, if you can't get them on track in a reasonable amount of time, then it is best for the sake of the company to admit that you made a hiring mistake and replace them with someone better. With burnout, you do not have the same obligation to a new associate that you have to one who has burned themselves out in faithful service to your company. The difficult reality is that eventually you may even have to replace your long-term salesperson. However, you should consider several options for helping them revitalize their careers, as long as it does not create other problems for your company or your team.

Talk to them frankly about their situation. The primary issue is their productivity. Their demeanor is only an issue if it is disruptive. Do they believe they are burned out? If you believe they are, but they say they are not, discuss the evidence for why you think they may be in trouble.

Ask them what they need in order to improve. If their request is not one you can grant (such as lower prices or product revisions), then tell them you must reach another solution. Your goal is still to help them, in return for their past performance and loyalty, if there is any way possible. Can any of the following options offer a solution? Are they feasible within your company?

• An extended vacation.
• A different community.
• An upbeat sales partner who could offer a revitalizing influence.
• A different position in the company, such as research, marketing, production or customer service (the last could be risky for a burned out salesperson, but can still be considered for the right person).

While you are trying to resolve their situation, keep them focused on priorities we discussed for slumps. They need to exert the will to *act* enthusiastic, with the hope of a positive effect on both the customer and themselves. Keep them focused on getting through the stages of the selling process, in an effort to revitalize them by revitalizing their success. Help them to regain a positive attitude about themselves and their profession. Remind them of their own past successes, and of the tremendous good which they have accomplished for so many people through their work.

At the same time you must be honest with them about your responsibility not to allow anyone on your team to become a liability to the company. If termination is a possibility, they have a right to know it.

Unfortunately, your efforts to prevent or cure burnout among your salespeople will sometimes fail. When you have provided the best leadership, support, training, coaching and motivation that you can, do not feel guilty about it. You have provided high quality sales management. The rest is up to the each of the individuals on your team.

SUMMARY

The priorities and techniques of management discussed throughout this book will help you to cut down on the problem of slumps and burnout on your team. However, you must not feel that it is your responsibility to prevent slumps and burnout single-handedly. There is no way you can. Every person on your team is living their own life in a different way. There are many factors, on and off the job, which can cause slumps and burnout. Most of these factors are beyond your control. Here is what you *can* do:

1) Provide the kind of consistent support system described throughout this book.
2) Look for the symptoms of slumps and burnout as described in this chapter.
3) Encourage honest, open conversation with salespeople who show these symptoms. Ask their ideas for a solution, and tell yours.
4) Realize that slumps are normal, and that encouragement will usually help a salesperson out of a slump more effectively than criticism. However, include constructive criticism when it is helpful or necessary.
5) Help them recall why they have been successful in the past, and why other customers have bought homes at their community.
6) Be honest with them if their job is in jeopardy.

In trying to help a salesperson who is burned out, you will not always be successful. Long-term associates with a successful track record present you with a dilemma: your loyalty to them vs. your loyalty to the company. Do not surprise them with a dismissal. Try to work out a program for revitalizing them which is mutually acceptable to the salesperson and the company. Several ideas were suggested in this chapter. The salesperson must understand, however, that when an employee becomes a consistent liability to a company, their past record (for which they were compensated, by the way) can no longer be the predominant factor. You must maintain your performance standards and stick to your commitment, even if it means losing a member of your team.

Salespeople will appreciate the commitment you demonstrate to them during a slump — "when the chips are down." It is one of the ways to prove you are an exceptional leader.

PART FOUR

CONCLUSION

MANAGING NEW HOME SALESPEOPLE: IS THIS THE LIFE FOR YOU?

At six-thirty on a Friday evening Jill and Sally sat across the desk from each other in Sally's office, reflecting on their careers as sales directors for the same company. This was one of those times when the last day of the month fell on a Friday. The building was empty except for Jill and Sally, who had just finished putting out the last fires on the final settlements for the month. They had exceeded their company goal for the month by two settlements, and were five ahead for the year to date. Sally was relaxed. They had been discussing the success of their teams and their company, but then suddenly Jill got quiet. She seemed distracted by her own thoughts.

"What's going on up there?" Sally asked, motioning toward Jill's forehead.

Jill stared out the window for a few seconds, as though she hadn't heard the question. Then she said, "You know, Sally, I'm thinking of going back into sales."

"No kidding," Sally answered. "I hope that's not a final decision. I've sensed that you were happier in sales, but you know, Jill, you've been a good sales manager. You really have."

"I guess I've done okay," Jill replied. "But it's been a lot different than I thought it would be. It's just one hassle after another. I was expecting more freedom. I thought I'd make a bigger difference. It seems like all I do is sit in meetings, fill out reports, talk on the phone, handle other people's problems, and watch everybody in the office kiss up to each other. It just seems like the air was cleaner out in the field. At the end of each day I knew I'd given it my best shot, and usually it was pretty satisfying. In this job I'm not even sure what I've accomplished. Are you?"

"I guess it seems different to me," Sally answered. "I have to admit, I love the job. I know what you mean about the field. But then I still think of myself as a field person."

"I know you do," Jill said. "And I can't figure out how you've been able to pull it off. We both have the same job, but somehow you're always able to get out of the office while I keep getting chained to my desk."

"The desk is tough to walk away from," Sally said. "But I've noticed it never follows me down the hall. As far as accomplishment goes, I guess I look to my sales team for that. They're successful, motivated, and they love the company. I'll give them most of the credit for that, but I'm going to claim a little for myself. I've done my best for them, and I feel like it's really paid off."

"You've certainly made a commitment to your people," Jill conceded. "You're a true leader, and I think everybody sees that. They're willing to bend over backwards for you. And I know how tough it's been for you when you've had to fire people. I guess I'm just not into training and coaching and motivating and counseling the way you are. Personnel problems drive me nuts. As a teenager I hated babysitting, if that has anything to do with anything. What I like is being out there with the live action every day, just getting it done right one day at a time — finishing one thing and moving on to the next."

They both sat quietly for a while before Sally broke the silence. "It sounds like you've made up your mind. I wish I could persuade you to stay. You've been a good partner. There really is a lot of satisfaction in this job, once you get the hang of it. The responsibility is exciting. We actually do have a lot of influence over important decisions, as long as we back up what we say. It's even better when we can get the sales-people involved. I guess the best part of all, though, is helping other people succeed."

Jill smiled. "We actually do have pretty much in common. I think we even deserve to pat ourselves on the back a little! We're smart and resourceful. We're two of the company's best problem solvers. We're both good listeners, even if we like listening to different kinds of people. We think ahead, and we never give up. Except maybe this once. But it's not really giving up. It's just doing what I do best, the same as you."

Jill and Sally are both right. They both understand themselves, and each knows where her contribution lies. For Sally, new home sales management is a true calling. If you feel that it is also the direction for you, we hope this book will help you to reach the peak of the mountain you are climbing and, once there, to enjoy the magnificent view you have earned.

Sample Of A Sales Training Program Which Can Be Taught In House

Adapted from

NEW HOME SALES TRAINING

by

Richard Tiller

The purpose of this Appendix is to provide an example of an in-house sales training program.

The six-session program is presented in a way that you, as a sales director, can prepare and lead each session with as little effort as possible. This program does not require you to be a charismatic speaker. The format is fairly casual, and the presentation is low-key — non-threatening for you as well as for your salespeople.

The format offers a variety of opportunities for your salespeople to participate in your meetings without being "put on the spot." While the format encourages interaction, it is natural for a group to take a little time to warm up to a new program. For that reason the first two sessions place a greater emphasis on your presentation than on participation. As the weeks progress, you will find that the rhythm of the program shifts toward increased participation from your salespeople. Since this is the natural trend, we have tried to adapt this program to fit that trend. By the time you get into your third session — "Overcoming Objections and Creating Value" — you should be getting significant contributions from members of your group. If it happens earlier, that is even better.

An in-house sales training program, where you are the leader and all of your salespeople can contribute, will provide three distinct benefits for you and your department:

1) It will improve the skills and productivity of your salespeople.
2) It will increase the vitality of the sales department.
3) It will strengthen your position as a leader.

This program is designed to maximize all three of these benefits, not just the first. Throughout each of the six sessions we have tried to remain sensitive to group dynamics, and to your position of leadership. In addition to structuring the meetings informally, we offer suggestions for your consideration throughout each of your presentations.

In order for the program to be taken seriously, it needs to be well organized. But within the structure of the program, your group meetings must also offer the opportunities of a free-wheeling, interactive think tank. Combining structure with interaction will help make the meetings productive as well as enjoyable.

Your goal in this training format is to maximize the benefits of group dynamics. Ideally, when you have completed this program, your salespeople will have learned more from each other than from you. This ending is the best one you could possibly have, because when you have finished with your program, the group dynamics which remain will be healthy, progressive and stimulating. Your salespeople will still learn plenty from you throughout the program, and they will thank you for creating the brainstorming environment instead of trying to forcefeed techniques that they don't buy into.

This program attempts to use group discussion to apply successful selling principles. While we have included examples to illustrate principles throughout this program, you may frequently prefer to use examples of your own. Whenever possible, encourage your salespeople to provide their examples, too.

PREPARING FOR YOUR TRAINING MEETINGS

This Appendix is designed to make your preparation for these six seminars as easy as possible. We have presented each of the sessions in the form of a "script," with our own comments to you running throughout. It's somewhat like a play with "stage directions." The presentation appears in regular bold type, while the background thoughts are in italics. The reason we have used this format is that we believe this is the easiest one to adapt to a variety of possible training situations.

For example, if you prefer working from an outline, you can condense what we have written into that format. You can also modify what we have written to meet your particular needs and circumstances. You can lead the meetings yourself, or have your salespeople take turns leading them.

Parts of this program may be copied and passed out to salespeople in advance of the meetings. For all of these reasons we believe that the format we have chosen is the most universally adaptable.

Our "stage directions" are written in a "writing style," while the presentation is written in a "speaking style." Parts of the "stage direction" are repetitious from one session to the next. Again, this is so the leadership of the sessions can be rotated if necessary.

The program covers a broad range of topics, from the initial greeting through the final close. Since our approach must be somewhat generic, you will want to customize it to provide your own flavor and accomplish your own agenda. You will find many parts of each seminar where you will want to address issues that are unique to your department in your own way. Be sure you use the material we have provided in whatever way is best for you.

Each presentation is simple and straightforward. It is casual, but still a no-nonsense approach. We have tried to avoid sales training gimmicks that we felt could be awkward for you or your salespeople.

You can give your presentation sitting or standing. Your group can be seated in rows, in a circle, or around a table. The latter two formats are better if your group is small enough.

While you do not need any special speaking skills to conduct this program, there are a few basic habits that will help you increase the quality of your presentation: eye contact, voice modulation, motion and enthusiasm.

As you read through the material for each seminar prior to the meeting:

1) Plan in advance how much time you want to spend on various parts of the presentation, and which points you want to highlight.

2) Decide what points you want to add or delete.

3) Plan ways you can apply the principles you present to specific challenges your salespeople are facing at their individual job sites.

4) Use your knowledge of these challenges, combined with your knowledge of the strengths and weaknesses of each of your salespeople, to develop ways to promote group interaction. The more involved your salespeople are, the better they will like your program.

Naturally you do not want to embarrass or antagonize anyone in this type of environment by preying on their weaknesses in front of others. One of your goals in this program is motivation, and one source of motivation is self-esteem. However, you do want to take advantage of opportunities to exalt people's strengths, and to encourage them to use their strengths to help others in the group. Again, you want them to learn from each other. When you have a salesperson who is especially strong or inspired in dealing with a particular challenge you are discussing, encourage that person to contribute. At the same time you must be careful not to cause embarrassment by implying favoritism, or that the person is superior to others in the group.

As you prepare for each seminar, it is equally important that your salespeople have an opportunity to prepare. The week before each meeting, give them a brief outline of what you will be discussing. They should prepare to contribute in areas where they have had successes and can offer insight. They should also use the seminars as opportunities to discuss challenges they are facing that would be valuable topics for others in the group.

Salespeople should be especially encouraged to contribute comments that are relevant to your topic when they have a strategy or technique which is succeeding. In general, discussions about what people are doing right are more productive than discussions about what they are doing wrong. One of the greatest benefits of this type of group program is the opportunity to share with one another which approaches *do* work. When discussions are focused on what people are doing wrong, make sure they remain solution-oriented, and not merely critiques.

One thing is certain in new home sales: there are many right ways to sell. When you see many new home salespeople succeed in completely different ways, you have no choice but to be open-minded. There are, to be sure, certain principles of new home sales which nearly all salespeople agree are essential. Yet it is equally true that every salesperson's individual gifts are different, and that every project has its own unique "rhythm." Part of the true genius of selling is figuring out your own community's unique rhythm and aligning it with your own unique selling gifts. (This theme will appear in the first seminar.) You do not want your salespeople to walk away from your training with "your way" (or our way) of selling new homes, but rather with a menu of successful approaches from which they can choose, depending upon which particular challenge they are facing on any given day. Once this progressive attitude becomes established in your training seminars, it can extend into the whole culture of your department. Perhaps it is already there. If it is, then your training program will be that much better.

One of our criteria for including material in this program is that the material must have already received positive feedback from our own clients in sales training programs which we have personally conducted. We used this standard in order to avoid subjecting you to an approach that has not been proven.

We hope that you and your team will find this program useful, enjoyable and profitable.

GENERATING MOMENTUM

GAINING A COMPETITIVE ADVANTAGE THROUGH POSITIONING

To the Manager

Your first meeting will set the tone for your entire program. The purpose of this program is not to give your salespeople a shot of adrenaline, but to discuss techniques and strategies which will help them to sell more homes — starting today. They need to expect a positive return on their investment of time immediately, and you will begin discussing their results at your next meeting. They should also expect the positive results to be long-term.

Today's meeting will provide an overview of some of the key dynamics in the selling process. This session builds the foundation for the next five, in which you will explore how these dynamics relate to each stage of the process.

It is important for this first meeting to begin on a positive note. One of your continuing objectives is encouraging them to participate and to teach each other. Since they are a group who knows each other, you can start this first meeting by inviting them to talk about what they are doing right — not bragging, just analyzing their successes. You will find this discussion will lead you very naturally into the subject of momentum, which is the primary topic of your first hour.

The Presentation

Let's start out this week by talking about what we're doing right. So often we beat ourselves up over all the things we do wrong. While it's good to always be trying to improve, some-

times we can benefit far more if we think about what it is we're doing best. And we need to spend time now and then talking with each other about what we're doing right, so that we can keep learning from each other. So in that spirit:

What do you think you've done best in the past month?

What is something you did recently that was the difference between making a sale and not making it?

Your answer can be a generalization or a specific anecdote.

- - -

This is the type of topic where if your salespeople are shy or reluctant to come forward, it is okay to call on people. You may refer to a specific situation which you think someone handled well, and start the discussion off with that example. Then you can encourage them to think of others.

- - -

This is a valuable exercise to go through as a group, but it is also a good exercise to go through on your own. Keep a diary in which you write down every time you think you did something especially well — something unusually effective, or successful or brilliant. Or every time you heard of someone else doing something you thought was great. Doing this will help you focus on the good things you and others are doing — to think them through and analyze them — so that you can make them a consistent part of your program. And when you get into a slump, these notes will help you remember how good you really are.

- - -

As this discussion progresses over the next few minutes, take advantage of every opportunity to give positive reinforcement to constructive comments which are helpful to the group.

Once this discussion is completed, you will then begin to move into another key area — problem-solving.

- - -

Now let's turn the coin over and look at the other side. I want you to think about what you believe are the biggest challenges, or problems, facing you at your community, and write them on a sheet of paper with your name. Keep the paper in front of you and write down anything that pops into your mind throughout the course of this morning's meeting.

We will not be able to address these issues this morning, but one of our goals for this program should be to address them as a group before our six weeks are over. While I will try to work with you to address them in the field, I also want to be able to use the combined brainpower of everyone here to tackle the toughest ones. At the end of today's meeting, please leave your list with me and I will look over all of them before our next meeting.

But while we're all here together, are there any issues which you think are most critical that you would like to bring up verbally so that others in the group can be thinking about possible solutions right away?

- - -

After setting a positive tone for the program with your discussion of what they are doing right, you are now letting them know that this program is for their benefit, to help meet their challenges as well as sharpen their skills.

Take several minutes for this overview of difficult issues which your people would like to see tackled. Show that you are committed to helping them develop strategies for their challenges.

You can now move into the heart of your presentation by tying your first two discussions in with your main theme for this week — MOMENTUM.

At this point we recommend you begin using an easel or blackboard to write down key words, phrases and points that you want to highlight and keep track of throughout each seminar. Our stage directions will not include how and when to use the easel. It would be at your discretion.

- - -

In both sides of this coin — what you are doing best, and what is toughest for you in today's market — one of the main issues we're

dealing with is the subject of *MOMENTUM.*
* What things can keep your momentum going?
* What things can threaten it?

The whole quest of new home sales boils down to our ability to get momentum started, and then keep it going.

Momentum is the single most powerful force in new home sales. Therefore, the most powerful approach you can have to new home sales is a selling strategy that stays focused on momentum. Momentum is what we will talk about this morning, and then it will be the major theme that ties together the rest of our meetings. If you can establish momentum, you will make sales. If you can't establish momentum, you won't make sales.

Momentum occurs on 2 levels:
1) It carries over from one sale to the next.

We've all heard the cliche, "The easiest time to make a sale is right after you've just made one." When we can get momentum going, customers suddenly seem to become easier to work with. And when customers can see momentum at a community, it is easier for them to get emotionally involved.

2) The same principle of momentum also occurs within the sale — from one stage to the next.

The hardest thing about momentum is getting it started. Once you do get it started, it is crucial to keep it going, and not let it die.

- - -

One key to momentum is found in the concept of "aggressive selling." As you look through this next section of your presentation, it will be more effective if you can give examples from your own experience, or from other experiences that you know of. The concepts you will be discussing are:
1) "Aborting your own mission during the selling process"
2) "Hard selling"
3) "Aggressive selling"
Hypothetical examples are sometimes best for illustrating certain principles. For other principles, real examples can make your point more effectively. This is one of those topics where real

examples are better. If your background includes new home sales, try to recall any relevant examples from your selling days. Otherwise, go for second-hand experiences, or ask your salespeople if they can provide illustrations.

- - -

When you stop and think about it, one of the greatest ironies in new home sales is that more than 50% of the time it is actually the salesperson and not the customer who stops the selling transaction — who winds down the momentum of the sale. They "abort their own mission" and bring the selling process to a halt. The reason they do this is not incompetence or laziness. The reasons are usually much more complex, and may include:
1) "Curb qualifying" — deciding as we see people getting out of their car and walking up the sidewalk that they are not buyers who will be interested in our homes.
2) Something we feel from the customer — "vibes" — real or imagined.
3) Our energy level that day.
4) Our mood, or level of confidence, that day.
5) Our level of expectations that day. (We all have days when we fall victim to our own cynicism.)
6) Something will seem to send us the message, "I've gone far enough with this customer. I can pick it up again at a future time." Or, "The next customer will be even better."
7) We don't want to slip into "hard selling."
All of these issues, and perhaps many others, can be very real reasons for "aborting our mission" — deciding that it is time to stop the selling transaction with a particular customer. The last one is especially difficult: we really don't want to slip into hard selling, because in new home sales hard selling is rarely effective.
In order to keep from "aborting our own mission" — in order for us not to be the one who threatens the momentum of the selling transaction — we need to understand the difference between "hard selling," which usually fails, and "aggressive selling," which is a much more successful approach.
"Hard selling" is attempting to defeat the buyer in a battle of wills. It is unsuccessful because it is *threatening*, not to mention

obnoxious. It is selfish, and usually avoids the all-important goal of successful selling — *identifying and fulfilling the buyer's needs.* Buyers have enough threatening stimuli to intimidate them without adding a hard-sell salesperson on top of it all.

"Aggressive selling" is much different from "hard selling." "Aggressive selling" does not have to be threatening at all.

"Aggressive selling" is simply *continuing through the stages of the selling process until the buyer causes you to stop.* In "aggressive selling," only the buyer can stop the selling process, never the salesperson. "Aggressive selling" is simply focusing on how to keep from stopping the sale transaction ourselves. It focuses on sustaining momentum. It can even be called "benevolent aggressiveness."

So how do you know when you're being too aggressive? How do you know when you've gone too far? When you really stop and think about it, in new home sales, it is almost impossible to go "too far." You can only go "far enough." The customer will make sure you don't go too far. You don't have to worry about it. You can stop taking responsibility for going too far, and turn that responsibility over to the customer. As soon as you've gone far enough, they will let you know. If they don't, then it's simple: just keep going.

Think of your customers as you would think of a traffic light. When you come to a light it is either green, red or yellow, and that tells you what to do next.

In new home sales a green light would be like a customer saying, "Would you please accompany me through the models so that I can learn more of your features and benefits?" This rarely happens.

A red light would be like a customer saying, "Thank you for the brochure and sales pitch. We would now like to tour your model homes alone. Please do not accompany us, or you will blow any chance you have of making a sale." This also rarely happens.

In new home sales, we usually get yellow lights, because most of the time customers are still at the point where they are indecisive and non-committal. The odd thing is that in new home sales we often treat yellow lights as red, while in driving a car we treat yellow lights as green. When a light turns yellow just as we approach an intersection, we get a burst of adrenalin and usually speed up.

Why can't we treat new home sales the same way? The principle actually is the same. And this is the principle of "aggressive selling."

- - -

The purpose of your presentation up to this point has been to lay a foundation for a Strategy to Achieve Momentum. *From now until your first break you will introduce this strategy and explain how it works.*

- - -

In order to sell aggressively we need to have an organized game plan that will help us to:
1) Get the momentum started as quickly as possible.
2) Keep it going once we have it.

Getting momentum started is one of the hardest parts of the selling process. Many salespeople find it more difficult than closing. In fact, if you can develop a good *Strategy to Achieve Momentum* that carries all the way through the selling process, the close becomes much easier.

How do we bring this whole idea of momentum to life in the selling process? How do we really focus on momentum, and how can we develop a strategy that gets our momentum started and then keeps it going until the buyer stops us? That's what we're going to talk about now.

The point of having a *Strategy to Achieve Momentum* is to have a game plan for getting your sale started and then keeping it going. To accomplish this you need to have more than just a series of steps to go through. You need to have a series of goals. So the stages of your selling strategy need to be goals, not just steps.

To get your momentum started you need to arouse the customer's interest. And to keep the momentum going you have to get from one stage of your strategy to the next. The goal of each stage of your strategy therefore needs to be getting to the next stage. Throughout the selling process your focus stays on getting to the next stage, until you either reach the closing stage, or until the customer tells you that you've gone as far as you can go. This, in a nutshell, is the mentality behind successful, aggressive selling that stays focused on closing without being hard sell. Again, the important point is that only the customer can stop the sale.

So that you can see how this strategy fits together as a whole, I'll run through a brief overview. As I'm describing the eight stages of this *Strategy to Achieve Momentum,* one thing you'll notice is that none of the stages ever stops. Each stage leads into the next stage and then continues on throughout the rest of the process. That is how momentum accumulates. You don't have a series of stops and starts. You only have goals which continue to accumulate until you complete the close or until the customer stops you.

– – –

This is a situation where using an easel will increase the impact of your presentation. The eight stages of the Strategy to Achieve Momentum *are shown in capitalized italics, and should be combined into a single list on your easel.*

– – –

The first goal in your strategy — the first thing you try to accomplish when the customer walks through your door — is to *ESTABLISH RAPPORT* with them. Again, this is not a stage that stops before you start the next stage. But it is the first thing that you are concerned with, and all the other stages hinge on it. The goal of establishing rapport then continues throughout the selling process. We will talk about this stage in detail next week.

The second goal is to *SELL YOUR "CONCEPT."* We will talk about Concept Selling today after the break. Even though it's the second stage of the process, I want to talk about it first so that you can be thinking about it between now and next week. Next week, when we talk about the front end of the sale I will want to talk about Concept Selling again as it relates to your specific communities. So as we talk about it in the second hour today, think about what your own selling concept is at your project.

The third goal is to *BEGIN IDENTIFYING YOUR CUSTOMERS' NEEDS,* and then your fourth goal is to *BEGIN FOCUSING ON HOW YOU CAN FULFILL THOSE NEEDS.* Need fulfillment is critical to your selling success, so these 2 stages also start early and continue through to the end.

This takes us through the first 4 of your 8 goals, which may sound like you should be half way through your sale by now. Actually at this point you are probably still in the first 10 minutes of getting to know your buyer. In a selling strategy which focuses on momentum it is important to lay the foundation for this momentum early.

To get your momentum started as quickly as possible, and to get the maximum impact out of the model viewing, there are a number of things you want to accomplish before the customer sees your models. By the time they do walk into your models, you want to be sure they are seeing the models your way — through your eyes.

So the time you spend with the customer before they see your models is actually quite critical. Ideally you would like to find a way to get all the way to stage 4 of the *Strategy to Achieve Momentum* during your first conversation with the buyer. This may sound ambitious, but we will explore the possibilities of this in our meeting next week when we discuss what we will be calling "The First Ten Minutes" of the selling process.

Once you have established rapport, explained your concept, and have begun to learn and address some of your customer's needs, your next two goals are to:

5) *GET THEM TO PICK OUT A FAVORITE MODEL.*
6) *GET THEM TO PICK OUT A FAVORITE HOMESITE.*

Remember, your goal is not simply to show models and show homesites. There's no momentum in merely showing. You keep the momentum rolling by getting the customer to *choose* a favorite model, and then a favorite homesite, so that you can 7) *CREATE URGENCY (fear of loss)*, and finally 8) *CLOSE FOR THE SALE.* We will cover these last four goals in detail in the later meetings.

When you create your selling strategy, it should include 4 objectives:

1) *Focus*
Your strategy must cause your customer to focus on who you are and what you are offering.

2) *Competitive Advantage*
Your customer must understand why your home is better for them than the other alternatives that are available.

3) *Involvement*
Your strategy must be designed to create interest and excitement for your customers in order to get them emotionally involved in both the home and the buying process. Your strategy must have a dynamic energy.

4) *Control*
Your strategy must enable you to gain as much control as possible over the selling environment.

After the break, we will talk about how concept selling helps you to begin to accomplish these objectives.

- - -

At this point you should be about one hour into your schedule. Your break should last 10 minutes, leaving you 50 minutes for the rest of today's session. You have 2 topics remaining to cover in that time. You might want to divide your time for these two topics approximately as follows:
1) Introduction to Concept Selling — 40 minutes
2) Maximizing your personal gifts in selling — 10 minutes

CONCEPT SELLING

Before the break we finished up an overview of the *Strategy to Achieve Momentum* by talking about 4 objectives of your selling strategy:
1) Creating Focus
2) Establishing a Competitive Advantage
3) Creating Involvement
4) Gaining Control

When the customer walks into your sales office, your first immediate challenge is getting them to focus. Sometimes even getting them to pay attention to you is a triumph. Getting them to focus can often seem insurmountable.

There are legitimate reasons why getting them to focus can be difficult.

1) Perhaps they have already seen 5 or 10 other communities, and things are starting to run together.

2) The customer may be experiencing "battle fatigue" from his encounters with previous salespeople, and is now looking for ways to shortcut the process — to get in and out with minimum interaction.

3) Perhaps they don't know exactly what they want yet, or even if they really want to buy at all.

Maybe you're lucky, and you're one of the customer's first stops. The problem then becomes getting them to remember you later on after fatique and confusion begin to set in.

To get them to begin to focus quickly on what you are selling, and then to remember it after they've left, you need to develop a "Hook" which you can use early in your presentation, soon after you set about establishing rapport. (Again, we'll have more time to talk about rapport next week.)

- - -

Think of examples of hooks from your experience, or ask for examples from your salespeople. Two examples you could use are:

1) An exciting beginning to a TV show or movie is sometimes used to draw the viewer quickly into the program, and to give a quick sense of its flavor. The James Bond movies were an especially good example of this.

2) A book cover or inside flap of the jacket often try to draw you to that one book of the many available on the shelf.

- - -

One way many salespeople start out their presentation is by giving customers a brief description of the homes. The danger of this approach is that so many salespeople do it the same way. The sales pitch begins to run together with other sales pitches because it sounds like them. For the customer this kind of monotony makes it even harder for us to establish momentum. You have to start out by creating a difference in the buyer's mind immediately.

Just like in the James Bond movies [or whatever other example you used], you create interest and begin to establish momentum with a hook — an attention-getter.

In new home sales, here is how to establish momentum in your first ten minutes:

SELL YOUR CONCEPT FIRST, AND YOUR PRODUCT SECOND. Your concept is your hook.

- - -

You will now move into an explanation of "Concept Selling." Concept Selling is more than just a technique. It is a sales mentality.

You may find this to be the most difficult of all the principles you will be covering, so it will help to be especially prepared for this section. It is not that Concept Selling is complex. But for people who have never thought of selling in these terms, Concept Selling may at first seem difficult to apply. However, the results we have received from clients who have applied this principle have been consistently excellent.

We have structured this portion of the session in outline form in order to help keep your presentation organized. There are a number of points to be covered under Concept Selling, and many examples, all in a short period of time. Encourage your salespeople to ask as many questions as they need in order to be able to apply Concept Selling to their communities.

Because Concept Selling is innately competitive, this section also has motivational overtones. In some cases you may need to sell your salespeople on their concepts so that they, in turn, can sell these concepts to customers.

Concept Selling is not the same as a "unique selling proposition." It is broader in scope, and is intended to help establish your marketing position and your competitive advantages in the customer's mind. These are the issues which will now be developed in your presentation.

Remember, we have provided your presentation of this section in outline form in order to simplify it. Your approach will be more conversational.

- - -

1) What is a "Concept?" Your "concept" is *a concise statement of your product's unique significance: why your product is important in the marketplace.*

To begin thinking about the concept at your particular community, here are six questions you can ask yourself:

a) Why was your product (or community) designed in the first place?

b) Who was it designed for?

c) What is special about it?

d) In one concise statement, what is your product's competitive advantage? In what way is it the best?

e) What puts it in a category apart from all the others?

f) If you had to create a slogan for your community, what would it be?

2) In Concept Selling, you first tell your customer "WHY" your product is; then you tell him "WHAT" it is.

a) It is the "why" questions in life that create interest, even more so than the "what" questions.

b) People find "why" questions intriguing, so that "why" questions help create involvement.

c) In all areas of life, when people can answer the "why" questions they feel fulfilled. When they can't, they feel frustrated.

d) We've all heard the riddle, "What is the ultimate question in life?" The answer is "Why?"

e) Telling the customer why your product exists gives it more meaning, more significance, more intelligence, and, most importantly, more value. Value is what we're selling today more than anything else.

    1. To *sell* value, we must first *define* value for our customers in our own terms. We will discuss the whole subject of value in detail in the third week. But for now we can set the stage for selling value when we sell our concept.

3) With Concept Selling, you put yourself in your very own category in the customer's mind. You're in a different category from everyone else.

a) This is the way you want your customer to think about you. Not as one of the mass, but apart from the mass, better than the mass.

b) You are carving out your own space in the buyer's mind by carving out your own territory in the marketplace.

4) With Concept Selling, you are getting the customer to see your product your way, through your eyes, in your terms, rather than in the terms that he has heard from previous salespeople.

a) In a jury trial, attorneys use an "opening statement" to establish their "position" in the jury's mind before any evidence is given. Each attorney is hoping the jury will evaluate the evidence from his client's point of view. Our challenge in sales is very similar.

5) In Concept Selling, you are making your "Positioning Statement."

a) Positioning is often thought of as a "marketing" concept.

b) Concept Selling brings this marketing concept into the selling arena.

c) You are "positioning" your product in your initial interaction with the buyer. This is critical in determining how the customer will view your product in contrast to the others that are available.

d) You are making an "impact statement" early — taking your "best shot" as quickly as you can.

    1. Again, you are stating for the customer, as concisely as possible, why your home is "best" — why you did it the way you did it.

    2. Your "Positioning Statement" is just that — it states your position — what you stand for.

e) In your positioning statement, you are also laying the foundation for what will ultimately become the all-important question in the selling process — *why* the customer should make the decision at this point in his life to buy your home over all of the other alternatives which are available to him (including staying where he is now).

6) In showing why you are the best, and why your position in the marketplace is the correct one, Concept Selling is innately competitive.

a) A competitive approach is essential, because we're in a very competitive business.

b) The customer needs to know — intellectually and emotionally — why you are the best. While emotional selling is important, and while you must seek to get your customer to love your homes, they will not buy a home purely because they love it. They must also believe that the home is best for them.

7) When you sell concept first and product second, you are able to begin your presentation by creating your own "value territory" — your own unique credibility.

a) Think about this: When you sell product first, what you are really selling is price, and selling price only works when you're the cheapest in the marketplace.

    1. If you are, in fact, the cheapest in the marketplace, then of course you do want to sell price. But even then, you will still have to convince at least some of your buyers that you are also giving them the best value.

b) When you focus your sales pitch primarily on square footage and features included, sooner or later, in the buyer's mind, everything is going to come back to 2 questions about price:

    1. Are you the cheapest?

2. If you're not the cheapest, are you at least the cheapest per square foot?

c) When you sell your concept, you are starting out by telling your customers that value is far more than just, "Who's got the lowest price?"

d) With Concept Selling you are defining value as "the best total package," and you are telling why your approach to value is better than anyone else's.

8) If you really stop and think about it, people actually do buy "concepts" more than they buy "products."

a) Think of the car industry, where people will accept many "unsatisfactory" features in the product in order to get the concept they want.

1. We will talk about this in more detail when we discuss "Overcoming Objections" in Session III.

b) You can also see the importance of concepts in TV advertising, where you have only a few seconds to make a powerful initial impact.

1. Most ads use concept selling rather than product selling to achieve maximum impact in minimum time.

2. The purpose of the ad is to "set up" the sale, just as you are using your first few minutes with the customer to set up your sale.

9) Perhaps most importantly, as all the sales pitches that customers hear begin to run together, your concept is what keeps your pitch from sounding the same as everyone else's.

a) The important thing to remember about your concept is to use it quickly and powerfully. It is your "hook," not just another routine part of your sales pitch.

Once we have established our market position and our competitive advantage in the customer's mind, and have gotten them to begin focusing on our homes from the right perspective, we can then begin selling the specific benefits of our homes with greater impact.

Next week we will talk about how this element of your selling

strategy fits in with all the others. We will talk about:
a) How you work it in among your first qualifying questions.
b) How it fits into your efforts to establish rapport.
c) How it becomes a consistent theme throughout the rest of the sale.

- - -

At this point you are probably nearing the end of your second hour. Whatever time you have remaining should be spent discussing examples of concepts. You will want your salespeople to think about this issue between now and next week. If any of your salespeople already have ideas about what their particular selling concept might be, that is great. You can begin discussing them this week, in order to give the others something to think about.

Concept Selling is a good brainstorming topic, whether as a group or one-on-one between you and your salespeople individually. Concepts are usually developed better in a conversational environment than in isolation. Ideas are tossed around which ultimately evolve into an articulate concept.

To help provide some ideas for types of concepts which might evolve, I have listed a few examples of concepts below for you to review prior to your presentation.

1) A home that puts the space where you really use it (that spends your money in places where you would spend it, and doesn't waste it in places where you wouldn't).

a) "You're spending $100 per square foot for this home. We designed it with the idea of making every one of those square feet have the highest possible value."

b) "We designed this home as though every square foot had a price tag on it that said $100."

2) A home that's designed for the way people really live — the best family/kitchen area of any home under $300,000.

3) The best total value of any home in our price range. We define value as the total combination of architectural design, square footage, and location [or however else you might define it — lot size, trees, total living environment, amenities, dollars per square foot, standard features included, etc.].

4) A home designed to enhance the spirits and improve the state of mind of today's buyer.
5) A home designed for today's revised concept of value [then you define it].
6) The right balance of aesthetics and function.
7) The largest home in our market for under $300,000.
8) The best combination of _____, _____ and _____ [whatever items apply to your project] of any home priced under $_____.

Or, your concept may be something thematic about the product which offers an unusually powerful benefit:
9) A townhome (or condominium) that lives (feels) like a single family home.
10) Townhomes with more privacy than most single-family homes.
11) Homes designed to give an estate feeling in a close-in location with lots of community amenities as an added bonus.

Most homes and communities were originally designed with some sort of concept in mind. There were meetings with corporate officers, marketing and production people, engineers and architects with specific goals and priorities. Your job as manager is to make sure these priorities are conveyed to your salespeople as that part of their selling arsenal called the "Concept."
To help you set the tone for the next 5 weeks, you may want to conclude this session on an inspirational note. Encourage your salespeople to maximize their personal selling gifts.

- - -

To finish up this first week, here's one thing you can be thinking about: What are your most important gifts as a salesperson?

We often do a lot of soul-searching about our weaknesses, and that's good because we should always be trying to improve. It's a wonderful accomplishment to turn a weakness into a strength, although most of the time it's great if we can just bring a weakness up to average. But what is it that really makes us successful? What are those special gifts we have that enable us to sell? What it is that makes customers like us, respect us, and trust us enough to

buy from us? And what are those special skills we already have which enable us to convey to our customer that we have what they want?

Is your gift:
Personality?
Warmth?
Intelligence?
Charisma?
Enthusiasm?
Credibility?
Articulateness?
Energy?
Perseverance?
Self-discipline?
Creativity?
An ability to help others create their own visions?
A servant's heart?
A love for your product?

The list is endless, because everyone's gifts are unique.

While improving our weaknesses is a good discipline, we must remember that it is our gifts that really make us sell.

If we can figure out what our gifts are, and use those gifts to their maximum potential, then we can achieve our greatest success.

Think of your personal gifts outside the selling world. They might be the same as your gifts in the selling world.

Then think of specific ways you can apply your gifts to your own selling process.

Will your gifts be most helpful in the rapport-building stage, or in model demonstration, or when you're showing lots, or when you're explaining financing? Different gifts sometimes make you especially powerful in one particular stage of the selling process. If this is true in your case, you might want to gear your strategy around that phase.

Next week we will talk about the first phase of the selling process — the time when you're getting to know the customer. We'll be calling that phase "The First Ten Minutes."

THE FIRST TEN MINUTES

To the Manager

Last week was an overview, and in that first session you may have been the one doing most of the talking. Frequently the first session is like that, so don't worry. It gave you a chance to acquaint your salespeople with the type of program this is, and it gave them time to think about some of the principal dynamics of selling that you will be covering as a group.

This week the tone begins to shift to a more discussion-oriented, problem-solving, workshop type of atmosphere. You should begin using every opportunity to draw your salespeople into the discussion, especially those who feel comfortable sharing a constructive opinion that will be of value to others.

If you find that you have one or two people who want to dominate a disproportionate amount of your meeting, you might need to cut them off without sounding unappreciative of their participation. You could say, "Thank you, but we need to move on in order to get done in two hours. I'll be happy to stay around afterward to talk about anything that you think needs more time than we were able to give in the meeting."

Session Two deals with the initial interaction between the salesperson and the customer. If you have a model home, and your customers are routed through a sales office before they see the model, then this session will cover the period of time your salesperson spends with the customer before the customer sees the model. If there is no model, or if the salesperson is located in the model with no separate sales office area, then you could perhaps consider this session as the "meet-greet-qualify" portion of the transaction.

If you have one or more salespeople who are particularly strong in this area, you may want to talk to them before the meeting to discuss some of the topics for the meeting, to pick their brains, or to encourage them to "help you out" in the meeting.

The Presentation

In new home sales there are 3 primary selling "arenas:"
1) The sales office
2) The model homes
3) The homesites
    One of the decisions we always face in selling is how much time and effort to invest with a particular customer in each of these arenas.
1) Should we spend much time with them before they see the models?
2) Should we go with them to see the models?
3) Should we take them to a homesite?
    Sometimes we try to figure out the answer to these questions by asking ourselves, "What does the customer want?"
    While we may be asking this question with good intentions, we already know that the true answer usually is, "The customer wants to be left alone." Then we conclude, "If I leave them alone they will be more comfortable, and they will like me more, and that will make it easier for me to sell them a home."
    But deep inside, we know that most of the time leaving the customer alone really won't help us to sell them a home.
    The problem with asking, "What does the customer want?" is that, while it sounds very enlightened, we wind up digging ourselves into a hole where we have no control at all.
    So are we really asking the right question?
    The customer knows that we are salespeople, and they respect us for doing our jobs as long as we are professional, caring, respectful and non-threatening.
    The real question is not, "What does the customer want?" but rather, "What course of action will produce the best result?"
    Or you could think of the question this way: "What selling opportunities can I gain in each of these three arenas? What opportunities could I lose if I do not take the initiative?" These are the questions we will be asking when we discuss "Model Demonstration" in Session 4 and "Showing Homesites" in Session 5, but it's also an issue which faces us when we first greet the customer. "What will happen if I only give them a brochure and a price list

and let them look? Do they really have sufficient motivation, or comfort, confidence, or knowledge to initiate a sales transaction?"

The questions that we will try to resolve this morning are:
1) How much can we accomplish in our initial conversation with the customer?
2) How can we create a greater impact in "The First Ten Minutes?"
3) How can we begin to control the selling environment in The First Ten Minutes by generating momentum?

"Controlling the selling environment" is one of those expressions that people often throw around without explaining what it means. *You are controlling the selling environment when the customer wants to go farther. So we must focus on ways of getting the customer to want to go farther.*
How much could we possibly hope to accomplish in our First Ten Minutes in an ideal world?
If everything went perfectly, it could be possible for us to begin to achieve 7 goals which can help us establish momentum. This is what we will spend our time this morning discussing.

– – –

Once again your easel will be useful here.

– – –

1) Establish rapport.
2) Establish a difference.
3) Establish a position.
4) Establish momentum.
5) Begin relating to the buyer's needs.
6) Gain control of the selling environment.
7) Set up the model viewing.

Before we discuss these 7 goals, let me issue 2 "disclaimers" about the principles we will be discussing.
1) I'm not making a pitch for you to change your current approach, especially if it's working. Generally, in new home sales, it's fair to say, "If it works, it's good." Another way of saying it is,

"If it ain't broke, don't fix it."
2) I'm not pretending that it's realistic to expect to accomplish all of these goals with every customer. We want to be able to take every road we come to in selling as far as that road will go. So what we're talking about here is a roadmap, and the 7 goals are the benchmarks we could come to along the way.

- - -

You will now be making the transition from your general introductory remarks into the specifics of the 7 goals. Any of these 7 goals can take an entire meeting in itself, so in order to get through all 7 in the remaining time, you will have to manage your time carefully. If you feel that you are getting into topics which you believe are especially important to the effectiveness of your salespeople, you may want to extend this session to 2 meetings. If you limit it to one, you might consider dividing your 120 minutes up as follows:
Introductory remarks — 10 min.
1) Establish Rapport — 15 min.
2) Establish a Difference — 15 min.
3) Establish a Position (including review of Concept Selling) — 20 min.
Break — 10 min.
4) Start Momentum (including qualifying) — 20 min.
5) Begin Relating to the Buyer's Needs — 10 min.
6) Gain Control of the Selling Environment — 10 min.
7) Set up the Model Viewing — 10 min. (If you run out of time before you get to this last goal, you can postpone it until Session 4 — "Demonstrating Models.")

At this point you begin your discussion of the 7 goals with "Establishing Rapport." Many of your points concerning the other 6 goals will also relate to establishing rapport, so at this stage you are really just introducing the topic. You will then be developing it further with your second goal — "Establishing a Difference" — and you will continue to build upon it from there throughout the rest of the meeting.
In this section you want to elicit ideas from your salespeople more than dictate. Most of your salespeople probably already have

well-thought-out ideas on the subject of establishing rapport, and effective techniques to go with those ideas. This is a good time to draw your salespeople into the discussion by asking questions. Here are several suggestions for the types of questions you could ask:

1) Does anyone have a set routine where you greet each customer exactly the same way, or do you vary it each time?

Most salespeople will say they vary it every time. If this is the case, you can then ask:

2) What determines the approach that you take? How do you decide what to say?

Occasionally a salesperson will say they start out every conversation the same. This is okay, too, if it works for them. Some people find comfort in routine. This is not to say that their whole presentation is a routine, or that they think spontaneity is bad. They just believe that at certain points in their interaction they have found a technique that works most of the time, and so they have one less thing to worry about. There is nothing wrong with that.

Another way you might word your leading question to the group is:

3) Does anyone have a special way they like to break the ice with their customers? Do you feel that there is a way you can create "instant warmth" with your customers?

When your salespeople respond to these questions, you can then draw them out further with such questions as, "What do you say next?" or, "What would you do if they say ...?" What you are beginning to do here, of course, is to role play. This approach to role-playing is often much more effective than saying, "Okay, let's role play," especially if your group is not accustomed to role playing. They will slip into this routine quite comfortably, and a very productive exchange of ideas and techniques can be generated.

Let this part of the session be a free flow, with everyone feeling comfortable talking about the subject, about themselves and about each other. After all, that's what establishing rapport is all about anyway.

There are still several points you want to be sure to work into your discussion at whatever moment you think is appropriate. We *will return to the presentation format to cover these points, even though your presentation will probably be unfolding differently.*

- - -

I) ESTABLISH RAPPORT

Any type of personality can establish rapport. Characteristics like warmth or charisma can be one path to rapport, but so can expertise and credibility. Don't think of a shy personality as an obstacle to establishing rapport. Shyness can have its own kind of appeal for many customers.

Naturally, not every kind of salesperson can establish rapport with every kind of customer, and sometimes it takes longer than others.

It's important not to get hung up too much on the idea of rapport. Establishing rapport is an important tool in selling homes, and it should be an objective in the forefront of your mind at all times. But it is not everything, and it should not be an end in itself. If you find yourself having difficulty establishing rapport with a particular customer, sometimes you need to simply relax and give it up for a while. Just go on about the business of asking questions concerning needs (which we will discuss in a few minutes) and fulfilling the other objectives in your selling mission.

One characteristic of many top salespeople is single-mindedness of purpose — the ability to stay focused on the ultimate mission. This ability can relate as much to establishing rapport as to any other aspect of selling.

Sometimes salespeople can get so wrapped around the axle on the idea of establishing rapport that they lose sight of all of the other objectives of their mission. Rapport becomes everything. It becomes an end in itself, and the whole focus of the selling process is lost in the meantime.

Work on developing your relationship with the buyer: getting to know them, and letting them get to know you. But don't get discouraged if rapport is not established to your satisfaction in the first ten minutes. It may still come later. You may simply have a customer who is, by nature, more guarded at the outset. It's not that they have less warmth; they just wait longer to show it, or show it more cautiously.

Sometimes we get frustrated at how difficult it is to draw some customers out. They don't seem to respond to anything we say.

- - -

This is another place where you may want to get a discussion started, depending upon how your timetable is running. If time allows for a discussion, you may want to ask:

- - -

Does anyone have a preset game plan for how they try to draw customers out who seem reluctant to talk, or do you feel that it's better at this point to just give them the most important information and let them see the models?"

- - -

If you choose to ask a question like this, be sure you remain open-minded and encourage a variety of answers. When members of your group offer to contribute to your conversation, it is important not to "punish" them by making them feel that their answers are wrong. If you, or everyone else in the room, disagrees with an answer, be sure you disagree respectfully, and, if possible, leave their approach as one possible option.

Following are several points you can make about "drawing customers out." You can go ahead and make these points up front, or you can work them into the responses of your salespeople.

- - -

Questions about where your customers are living now sometimes make good icebreakers.

When you have customers who don't want to talk about themselves, one thing you might try is talking a little about yourself. Some people are reluctant to open themselves up first. They feel too vulnerable.

Remember, in developing rapport with a customer, it is just as important for them to get to know you as it is for you to get to know them. Sometimes we are so focused on "qualifying" customers or "learning their needs" that these goals get in the way of getting to know them. This is the flip side of what we were talking about earlier.

While we don't want to become obsessed with developing rapport without accomplishing our selling mission, we also don't want to become so absorbed in our selling mission that we forget about the importance of establishing rapport. We need to balance rapport with the business at hand. Achieving either one of these goals can often help us to achieve the other.

So let them get to know you. Let them know a little about your background, why you chose that builder to work for, why you like working at that community. Don't go on and on, or they will simply regard you as self-absorbed. But at the same time don't be too guarded, or it may cause them to be more guarded. Your ability to set the tone will affect your ability to control the selling environment.

Here's another thing to think about when you have a customer who is reluctant to communicate. Be sure that whenever they do say something, even if what they're saying is irrelevant to the business at hand, you respond favorably and warmly. Make them feel that anything they say is important, and that you appreciate every little bit of communication that they give you.

Sometimes we are focused so intensely on our presentation or our qualifying mission that when a customer does speak we pass up the opportunity to respond. Whatever they say, be sure to respond appreciatively, even if they disagree with you.

Here's an important principle about developing rapport with customers: *If you want to make customers feel good about you, make them feel good about themselves.* We tend to feel good about people who make us feel good about ourselves. It's part of the way the human ego works. This doesn't mean obvious flattery. It simply means our behavior toward the customer should be "appreciative."

- - -

Here you might want to develop your own analogy or ask your salespeople to give you an example of how they have seen this work. If you want to take the lead with an analogy, it could be something like this:

- - -

Suppose you are talking to a couple. You seem to have the wife's interest, but the husband is just standing there looking out the window. Then, out of the clear blue, he says, "What kind of a tree is that?" You may be irritated that he is showing you he couldn't care less about what you've been saying all this time, but instead you realize that the best strategy is to take time out from your presentation and honor his question. If you don't know anything about trees, you could say, "You know, I'm not sure what kind of a tree that is, but it is sort of an interesting looking tree. What was it about that tree that caught your attention?"

At this point, it might actually help your selling effort more to indulge the customer's question about the tree than to dismiss his question and go on with your pitch. The point is that he has done what you wanted him to do: he has spoken to you. You want to make him feel glad that he spoke to you, and you want him to feel comfortable speaking to you again. So you have to "reward" him for speaking to you. In psychological lingo, you want to give him a positive reinforcement so that he will repeat the behavior. The principle here is, *If you want to create a pattern of behavior, reward the behavior when it occurs at random.*

With customers who seem more aloof, you also want to start out with less threatening questions. Ask about where they live now, or what they know about your area, rather than how motivated or qualified they are to buy a new home.

– – –

For many salespeople this is a critical topic. If it stimulates a conversation, let the conversation flow. After all, the same principle you have been discussing is the one which you are trying to accomplish with your own salespeople in these meetings. You want them to open up and contribute: to teach and learn from one anoth-

er, and to increase the group dynamics of your department for the long haul.

Once this topic has run its course, you will be ready to move on to goal #2 of the First Ten Minutes:

- - -

II) ESTABLISH A DIFFERENCE

One of your earliest objectives in getting to know your customers — and letting them get to know you — is to establish a difference in their mind between you and all of your competitors.

Buyers frequently accumulate frustration during their search for a new home. They might start out fresh and full of optimism, but as they go through their search, it's possible for them to become grumpy. Some of this grumpiness may be caused by the kinds of relationships they have developed with other salespeople along the way. This frustration often translates into fear, hostility and disorientation. In this situation, your first big challenge may be simply to get the customer to *focus* on what you are saying.

You can begin to establish focus — and create interest — by setting yourself apart from the competition in 3 ways:

1) A difference of SELF — you as a person.

What we're talking about here is demeanor. The customer needs to see you as the "oasis in the desert." You need to make them comfortable with the kind of person you are as quickly as possible. They will become more comfortable if they can see these characteristics in you as a person:

   a) Gentleness.
   b) Calmness.
   c) Dignity.
   d) Confidence.
   e) Credibility.
   f) The ability to personalize your conversation, as opposed to giving them a routine that sounds like a routine.
   g) They need to see you as a counselor more than as a salesperson.

This issue of being a counselor is an especially important one.

A position of counselor is stronger than a position of salesperson. The reason for this is that the customer *needs* a counselor more than they need a salesperson, even though they generally believe that you need them more than they need you. This belief puts the salesperson in a natural position of weakness, and makes it harder to gain control of the selling environment.

But if you can position yourself as a counselor, who is there to explain things and perform services, then you create a situation where the customer needs you more than they would otherwise.

The next way you want to "establish a difference" in your customer's mind is:

2) Difference of BUILDER

- - -

This is another one of those issues on which you could now spend a great deal of time, if you haven't already. What you will be talking about is your builder's image and its position in the marketplace. What is it that sets your company apart from the rest?

You might want to address this issue in your own terms, or you might want to make it a discussion topic for the group by asking such questions as:
a) How do convey our corporate identity to your customers?
b) What do you tell customers are the benefits of buying from us?
c) What do you believe is special about our company?
d) What do you believe is our position in the marketplace?

Spend as much time as you need in order to get everyone on the same wavelength with this extremely critical sales issue.

Once you have completed the discussion on your company's difference, you can finish up with the following technical pointers:

- - -

When you ask customers how much they know about us, consider wording your question like this: "Are you familiar with our company?"

Sometimes questions like "Have you ever heard of us?" or "How much do you know about us?" can be awkward. They can either appear to question the customer's level of sophistication, or they can lead to a potentially awkward answer.

When you tell them about us, put it in the form of third-party endorsements — how you are perceived: "Our company is known for ..."

3) Difference of Product

You've established a difference in the customer's mind concerning yourself and your company. To complete the goal of "Establishing a Difference" you will need to show the customer why your product is different. This brings us to our third goal — "Establishing a Position."

- - -

III) ESTABLISH A POSITION

Establishing a position means two things:
A) Making the customer understand your position in the marketplace.
B) Establishing a position of strength in the selling environment.

Let's look at each of these in detail.

When we talk about "making the customer understand our position in the marketplace," we are talking about what it is that makes us special. We're explaining, in a sentence or two, not just why customers *should* buy from us but, more importantly, why customers *do* buy from us. This point is especially important. We often dwell on the sales that we feel we lost. But the truth is we won't sell to every prospect, no matter how good we are. Our homes are not designed to sell to every prospect, even if they were ready, willing and able to buy.

The important thing is why we *do* sell. You might find it helpful to keep a list of every buyer you sell to, by lot, showing why they bought, and what special steps you took that you feel helped you make the sale. This kind of information is just as important as the demographic marketing information that we are sometimes much more careful about keeping records for.

The idea of establishing our position in the marketplace gets back to the idea of Concept Selling that we were discussing last week.

- - -

At this point you want to spend whatever time you need reviewing Concept Selling, and then discussing it as it relates to your various communities. Hopefully, in the last week your salespeople have had a chance to think about their concepts and to develop a concise concept statement. You can spend this time talking about what benefits this approach may offer, and what success salespeople have had with it so far.

- - -

Another dimension of Concept Selling that is important in establishing your position is *creating your value statement.* How has your builder defined value at your particular community? In what way are you offering a better value than anyone else in your marketplace?

When you determine the way in which you can say your value is superior, then this becomes, for your particular community, your definition of value.

It is very important that this value statement be clear in the customer's mind before they see your model. Otherwise they could be viewing your model in terms of someone else's definition of value, which, of course would put you at a disadvantage. You need to give yourself the "home court advantage" by getting them to see your model from the standpoint of your unique definition of value. This is competitive selling in its highest form.

When you present your value statement, it is important to give any evidence available which can support your claim:
1) A successful sales rate.
2) Third-party endorsements.
3) Good response from the Realtor community.
4) Industry recognition.

The other important element of "establishing your position" is "establishing your position of strength." One way of establishing a position of strength is what we discussed earlier: positioning yourself as a counselor, not as a salesperson. You have more control as a counselor because you place yourself in a more credible position for learning the customer's true needs and then fulfilling them.

How do you set yourself up as a counselor? You begin when you make your value statement. Instead of just qualifying and selling, you are explaining principles of the marketplace and of the homebuilding business which help the customer to understand the strange, confusing world they've ventured into. You are explaining to them what the general needs of the homebuying public are, and how you've set about fulfilling these needs for others. You're helping them to learn what needs they should be considering, as well as the needs they've already determined they have.

Once you have set the tone of counselor with your value statement, you then maintain that tone as you continue to develop rapport. Look for opportunities to *explain* things to your customers — not only principles of the industry, but also:
1) The buying process.
2) Principles of construction and engineering.
3) How communities and homes are planned and designed.
4) Obtaining a loan.
5) Tax benefits.
6) The principle of "leveraging" in homeowner investment.
7) How builders make their profit (if you feel this is relevant — sometimes it can be because many buyers believe builders make a larger profit on each home than they really do).

The list can go on and on. The point is that the more of a counseling service you can provide, the more credibility you can build. Naturally, you don't want your explanations to become tedious or overworked. You are simply trying to build a position of alliance rather than adversity.

Another way of establishing a position of strength is through confidence. Not arrogance. Just a quiet confidence that you know your homes are the best, and you know why. You want to sell your customer a home, but you don't have to. The home sales will take care of themselves. Your goal is to offer the best service in the process.

Along with confidence comes enthusiasm. You love your homes and community, you love your builder, you love your job, and you love your customers. If the customer can sense a genuine atmosphere of this kind of enthusiasm, your position will be stronger. Confidence and enthusiasm are both contagious, just as insecurity and pessimism can be contagious.

These issues lead us into our next goal for the First Ten Minutes:

- - -

IV) ESTABLISH MOMENTUM

Confidence and enthusiasm play a large role in what we call "Emotional Selling." This is another one of those terms that is often thrown around, but rarely defined. Taking away all the mystique, basically *emotional selling starts with enthusiasm and grows into involvement.*

As trite as it sounds, the fact is that enthusiasm is contagious. We can all remember times when we became interested in something that we never would have considered on our own, just because someone else was excited about it. Often we must face the challenge of how to generate enthusiasm in someone else.

- - -

Analogies can often be helpful in bringing principles to life. Consider this analogy for generating enthusiasm:

- - -

Sometimes we feel like we want to light a fire inside our customers, but we just don't know how. It's like trying to set fire to a pile of sticks when we don't have any matches, and we don't have time to rub two sticks together. Then we notice that close by there is another pile of sticks which is already burning. What we need to do is pick up our pile of sticks and move it over next to the burning pile. Very quickly the sparks from the burning pile will set the other pile on fire.

Sometimes this is the way to light the fire in our customers.

Don't try to start the fire from scratch with contrived questions and involvement gimmicks — it rarely works. Let the sparks from your own fire shower down on them and see if a spark ignites.

Another important tool in getting momentum started is *qualifying,* because this is how you begin to learn your customers' needs. Fulfilling needs is a critical part of establishing momentum. It is also important in controlling the selling environment, which will be our sixth goal.

There are 3 main questions we are trying to answer for ourselves when we qualify our customers:

1) Are we selling what the customer is looking for?

We want to learn their primary needs so that this knowledge can help us to direct our selling presentation.

2) How motivated is the customer?

3) Is the customer able to buy if they want to?

Timing is an important element in qualifying. By timing, we basically mean which questions to ask and when to ask them.

Most customers feel more comfortable "trading information" than answering a barrage of rapid-fire questions. Mixing questions with information can help you establish a rhythm which is comfortable for the customer, and which can help you to establish rapport while you stay focused on your mission. This conversational approach is, for most salespeople, more effective for eliciting information than the "machine-gun" approach of continuous questioning, which the customer may find annoying and threatening.

Let's spend a few minutes talking about the various qualifying questions we use. Since we're also talking about timing, I want to find out which questions you use most often, and which ones you are most likely to ask first.

- - -

This is a good subject to open up for discussion. It gives your salespeople an opportunity to compare notes on which qualifying questions are most important to them. This often results in a productive exchange of ideas, since most salespeople have one or two questions which are slightly different — at least in wording, and perhaps in content.

You will still want to guide the discussion, however, and to do this you should classify your questions by category. You can use your easel for this purpose in order to create a complete "menu" for your salespeople. You might even want to distribute a copy of these questions later as a handout.

We will now return to the presentation format, although at this point you are simply inserting these comments, if necessary, into the group discussions.

- - -

Let's organize our questions in terms of categories:

1) Questions which determine the customer's level of urgency.
 a) **"How soon are you planning to move?" ("Are you looking for a new home this year?")**
 b) **"How long have you been looking for a new home?"**
 c) **"Have you seen anything so far which you've liked?"**

2) Questions about their current living situation.
 a) **"Where do you live now?"**
 b) **"Do you own or rent the place where you live now?" ("Will you have to sell the place where you're living now?")**
 Notice that I referred to their "place" rather than their "home."
 c) **"How do you like the place where you're living now?"**
 In this last question you're opening up a new — and critical — frontier: discontent with their current home. This is an area which is especially important for a salesperson to delve into as quickly as possible, because it opens up the issue of their needs.

 It is very risky to ask a person point-blank what their needs are, for 2 reasons.
 1. It could open up a situation where you are putting yourself in the position of playing Santa Claus: getting them to tell you their complete list of fantasies, and then disappointing them when you cannot fulfill their wish list.
 2. Your customers may not yet have truly figured out what their needs are. They may not have gotten to the point where they can clearly distinguish between real needs and fleeting wants.

Listening is great, but selling is a combination of listening and leading. In determining and fulfilling needs, you need to keep in mind that:

    a. You really do want to know their needs; but —

    b. You also want to sell them on the fact that your home is better suited to their needs than the other available alternatives, if this is at all possible.

So now we're back to our question of, "How do you like the place where you're living now?"

Let's talk about some other ideas for opening up the issue of their discontent with their current home. Again, you're not looking for a laundry list of everything they wish they could have if money were no object. You want to learn what their "primary" needs are:

1) What are their top priorities for a new home?

2) What is the primary motivation that made them walk into your sales office in the first place?

If you ask them those very questions, they may not answer you honestly. What you can do is ask the question in the context of their current home. We'll call this category:

3) Questions which determine the customer's primary needs.

The question about the customer's primary motivations is a crucial one, so here are 5 different ways of wording that question:

    a) "What is it that's made you think about moving?"

    b) "What's your number one priority for your next home?

    c) "What is the main thing you need in a home that you don't already have?"

    d) "What is it about your next home that you would most like to improve?"

    e) "What are you looking for that is different from what you have now?"

You might also want to find out how their expectations are being met by other homes they have seen so far. This could also help you to find out what their current frame of mind is. To get this information you can follow up one of the above questions with a question like this:

f) "How is your search coming? Are you seeing things that you like?"

Your goal in this whole line of questioning is threefold:
1. To learn their needs and hot buttons.
2. To get them to *express* a discontent for their current home.
   a. You can refer back to this discontent later on if you need to reawaken it in order to create urgency.
3. To find out what their expectations are today in light of their experiences in the marketplace up to this point.
   a. This may give you some insight into where they are in their search, and what your chances are of really satisfying them.

Another important category of qualifying questions is:
4) Financial qualifying

- - -

Again, this is a good topic to open up for discussion, since sales-people have so many different ways of determining whether their customers are financially qualified.

One suggestion for salespeople who find financial questions espe-cially awkward in the first ten minutes is to give the buyer a half-minute thumbnail sketch of typical qualifying requirements for that community (minimum cash required and range of monthly payments), and to conclude by saying, "And most people who live here earn in the fifty to sixty thousand dollar range. How do those numbers sound to you? (Are those the kinds of numbers you were hoping to hear?)"

This approach is not necessarily conclusive, but usually it will accomplish what the salesperson is looking for at this early stage — namely, is this customer even in the ballpark? It also gives the cus-tomer a sense of whether he will feel as though he "belongs" in the community, since to many customers "qualifying" and "affording" can mean two entirely different things.

- - -

5) Location
   a) "Where do you work?"
   b) "Are you familiar with this location?"

6) Home size

   a) "How many are in your family?" (You could also ask, "How many bedrooms are you looking for?" However, customers will sometimes ask for one more bedroom than they really need.)

   b) The question, "What size home are you looking for?" should also be used cautiously, since often your customer's ideal is a larger home for less money than what you are selling. If this is the case, you could find yourself back-peddling.

   What ways do you use to determine what size home the customer is looking for? Do you believe this question is even necessary?

- - -

This is another issue where, instead of dictating a strategy, let the discussion take its own course so that your salespeople can be exposed to a variety of ideas.

Then conclude by asking if there are other qualifying questions that the group has not covered? If time permits, you might also ask if there are other qualifying issues which they would like to discuss as a group before you move on to Goal 5.

- - -

V) BEGIN RELATING TO THE CUSTOMER'S NEEDS

This goal is usually associated with model demonstration, and it also relates to showing homesites and closing. However, there are sometimes opportunities to begin making headway toward this goal before the customer sees the models.

Naturally, the ideal situation is when the customer begins opening up right away with needs that you know you can fulfill. In this case you should give them your good news right away.

Your goal here is to arouse their interest and begin to get them involved with your homes before they even see your models. That way you will already have gotten your momentum started before they view your homes. They will be approaching your homes more optimistically, and evaluating them more open-mindedly.

In the case where the customer is less open about their needs in the beginning, you will need to take a little more initiative in leading them in the direction of need fulfillment. There are several ways you can do this:

1) We talked a few minutes ago about ways to zero in on the level of their dissatisfaction with their current home. If this approach does not lead you far enough, you can:

2) Show how you have fulfilled the needs of others.
   Here you are fulfilling your counselor role again.
   We talked earlier about keeping a list of all of your previous customers and why they bought. This practice comes in very handy now. (It is also helpful if the time comes for you to turn your community over to someone else and move on to a different one.)
   Here are several examples of how this can work:
   "Customers often tell us that we use our space better for the way they really live."
   "People tell us our kitchens are more workable than any others they've seen."
   "People tell us that quality really is important to them, and that's a primary reason they bought here."
   "One comment we get again and again is that our neighborhood really has a feeling of community about it, and that's so important to most of our buyers."
   By showing how you have fulfilled the needs of others you are accomplishing several things:
   a) You are showing your customers what needs most people in their situation have, which may help them to clarify their own needs and goals.
   b) You are also giving third-party endorsements to your homes.
   c) You are showing how your well-researched approach can improve your customers' investment value by providing a broader appeal in the future resale market.

You have to keep fulfilling needs in order to keep your momentum going. Sometimes this is easy. Other times you need to help your customers to create (or perhaps reshape) their needs. If you find you must go down this more difficult road, you can start out

with this approach: "One reason this community has been so popular is ..."

There is nothing as effective as third-party endorsements to help
bring the advantages of your situation into focus and build your
position of strength.

3) A third way you can lead your customers down the road to need
fulfillment is to talk about your own needs. Sometimes, when it is
relevant, this approach can provide several benefits:

   a) It can help you to establish rapport and common ground.

   b) Sometimes talking about yourself and your needs can make
the customer more comfortable talking about theirs.

   c) It can help them to view you as a vulnerable human being,
just like them. It makes you less threatening.

You might include details about your own home, if it relates to
the situation at hand. Or you might simply state your own desire
for some feature of your product: "This is something I wish I had."

You can see by now that all of these goals we have been discussing for your First Ten Minutes with the customer are closely
related. And they all help to set up Goal #6:

VI) GAIN CONTROL OF THE SELLING ENVIRONMENT

We have been talking last week and this week about momentum.

Momentum and control are closely linked. When you gain
momentum, you gain control. When you lose momentum, you lose
control.

Today we have been talking about ways to get your momentum
started.

In the selling environment there is a natural, perhaps subconscious, battle between you and the customer for control of the selling environment. There is nothing sinister about this. You want control because that is the way you accomplish your mission. The
customer wants control because he feels threatened and vulnerable.

The customer basically has control of the selling environment
the moment he walks in the door. The reason is that he doesn't
have to buy your home, and he can walk out at any time.

You cannot take this control away from him by force or intimidation. That will only make your position weaker. This is one of the risky things about a hard-sell approach. There is always that occasional gifted salesperson who can make a hard-sell approach sound acceptable. But for most of us, hard-sell tactics only make a position of strength more difficult to obtain.

In order for you to gain control of the selling environment, the customer must give it to you. Your goal is therefore to make the customer want to give it to you. And the only reason they will want to give you control is if they believe it is in their best interest.

There are ways to make this transfer of control more comfortable for the buyer, and we have been discussing a number of them today.

1) Confidence and enthusiasm.
2) Positioning yourself as a counselor and an expert.
3) Positioning your company and your project as successful.
4) Establishing your credibility with a strong value statement and a strong positioning statement — Concept Selling.

But ultimately, the secret to controlling the selling environment is to be constantly solving the customer's problems — fulfilling their needs. This is the one goal which the buyer and the seller have in common. The customer will yield control if his needs are being met. As long as you are solving his problems and fulfilling his needs — in other words, as long as the customer is benefitting from the experience — there is no reason for him to have control.

If you are solving the customer's problems and fulfilling his needs, he may even feel that he is controlling the selling environment because he's getting what he wants. But you are also getting what you want: you are getting your customer more involved in your homes. You are getting the customer to want to go farther. As we said earlier, you are controlling the selling environment when the customer wants to go farther.

We will be talking a lot more about fulfilling needs in future weeks. In fact, this topic relates to all of our remaining topics:
• Overcoming Objections
• Creating Value
• Showing Models

- **Showing Homesites**
- **Creating Urgency**
- **Closing**

Need fulfillment is a topic that won't ever go away in selling — and shouldn't. For today the important point is that in some cases there is actually the opportunity to begin to focus on needs, start momentum and gain control in our first conversation with the customer. While this will not always be possible, it can still always be a goal of our selling strategy.

The final goal of our First Ten Minutes is one which we can explore in greater detail when we have more time at the beginning of the session on Demonstrating Models — our fourth meeting. This final goal is:

- - -

VII) SET UP THE MODEL VIEWING

At this point, if you are able to squeeze all of this into one session, you will have very little time or energy left to discuss this final goal. Even if you stretch this session into two weeks, you may find that this last goal will serve a better purpose two weeks from now when you start up your session on "Demonstrating Models." For this reason we have included it in your presentation in Session 4.

You will be detouring into "Overcoming Objections and Creating Value" in your next session. The reason for this is that some of the issues in the session on "Objections and Value" relate to issues discussed today, and others will need to be covered before your sessions on "Models" and "Homesites" in order to keep those sessions from getting sidetracked. For now, you can conclude today's session with a brief overview of your seventh goal.

- - -

The issues about this last goal that I would like you to think about between now and the session on Demonstrating Models are:

1) How to use your First Ten Minutes to whet the customer's appetite for seeing your models — and seeing them from your point of view.

2) How you will make it comfortable for you to go through the models with them if you believe your customer will benefit from a demonstration.

We will also talk about this last issue of going through the model with the customer in some detail: what opportunies will we gain by going with them and what opportunities will we lose by letting them go alone?

In the meantime, the topic of our next meeting will be "Overcoming Objections and Creating Value." We will be discussing some principles, but I also want us to have the opportunity to put these principles into action. So bring along any objections you feel are really costing you sales at your community, and we will brainstorm as many of them as the time permits.

Overcoming Objectives
Creating Value

To the Manager

*If there has been any inhibition among salespeople toward partic-
ipating in the program, it should be gone by now. They now understand that one of the primary benefits of this type of training program is the interactive element.*

*Interaction is especially important in this session. In addition to
discussing general principles of overcoming objections, you want to
bring your training program into the real world by dealing with
tough objections which customers are raising at your individual
communities.*

*There are four advantages to your salespeople bringing up their
objections in this session:*

*1) They can use their specific situations to apply principles learned
today.*

*2) You have an opportunity as manager to function as a true support
system in the context of the training program.*

*3) Your salespeople can use the detached opinions of their peers to
help add an objective dimension to their problem-solving. You can
mobilize the combined experience and brainpower of your sales
team for the good of everyone.*

*4) If you keep the atmosphere of the meeting constructive and posi-
tive, you can help your salespeople deal more effectively, and more
confidently, with their challenges, so that they can begin to increase
their sales immediately.*

*In this session you may find yourself jumping around from one
topic to the next as salespeople bring up specific issues they want to
address. It will help (not hurt) the mood and momentum of your
meeting if you can address issues as they arise. The other alternative
is to ask your people to "hold on until we get to that topic." While
there may be a few instances when you will want to take the latter*

approach, too much of that will create an atmosphere of distraction, and perhaps even cynicism, in the meeting. For this reason you will want to look over all of the material in this session in advance.

As with Session Two, you might decide that it would be better to expand this session to two weeks. From this point on, we will not be suggesting how you should schedule the segments of your meetings, because they can vary so much with the types of issues your group will need to address.

An important theme throughout this session is the salesperson's position of strength in the face of objections, and this is where you should start.

The Presentation

When we talk about solving objections, we're really dealing with three different questions. Two of them are involve mental, or psychological issues, and the third is technical. The three questions are:

1) What goes on inside our mind when an objection occurs?
2) What goes on inside the customer's mind when an objection occurs?
3) How do we solve the specific objection which has been raised?

Let's look at these 3 questions one at a time, and then see how they all fit together.

*** WHAT IS GOING ON INSIDE OUR MIND WHEN AN OBJECTION OCCURS?

We all know from our own experience that dealing with objections depends as much on our perspective and our attitude as it does on our finesse. When we're on a roll, objections don't affect us the same way they do when we're down. Somehow the more confident we are, the better our skills seem to be. When we can approach objections from a position of strength, we seem to be able to get through them.

We also know that whether or not we make a sale does not necessarily depend on our overcoming all the customer's objections. Sometimes we may have the perfect answer to every objection, and still not make a sale. And sometimes we might leave five objections unresolved, and yet somehow make the sale.

So what should our perspective be? How should we think about objections?

In order to deal with objections from a position of strength, we must understand that we don't have to offer perfection in order to make a sale. No one else is offering perfection either, and the customer's current home is obviously not their ideal.

To keep a healthy perspective toward objections, we need to remember two important principles of human nature. We take these two principles for granted outside of the selling arena. All we have to do is remember that selling is part of the real world, and that these principles apply inside our arena as well as outside of it.

I) The first principle is that *nobody ever gets everything they really want. And they don't honestly expect to.*

For one thing, most people cannot afford what they really want. If they could, they would want something more. That's just human nature. Sooner or later most people go through a struggle with that truth. As salespeople, we have to go through that struggle with them. This struggle can be traumatic for many customers, and it can produce anger. We may temporarily have to weather the storms of that anger. We may even be the targets of it. This is what people mean when they say that a new home salesperson is sometimes an "emotional punching bag." But all of this is normal, and it doesn't stop our industry from selling homes.

II) The second principle of human nature is that *people really do have a high tolerance for imperfection in things that they really want.*

Another way of saying it is that *people will accept a lot of what they don't want in order to get what they do want. Or, people will accept what something is not in order to get what it is.* We see this not only in our attitude toward our possessions, but even in the way we approach relationships. We are much more tolerant of flaws in our friends or loved ones than in our enemies. We are much more willing to put up with imperfection or inconvenience when the "total package" is the one we really want.

We are so close to the housing industry that sometimes it can be difficult for us to see this principle at work in our selling. But if we look at the car industry we can see it very plainly. To get the car they want, people are willing to spend enormous amounts of money and still settle for such shortcomings as poor gas mileage, poor storage space, poor legroom, and high maintenance demands.

When you think about it, the reason that people are willing to make these sacrifices is that what they are really buying is a concept, not just a bunch of features. People do buy features, but they buy them as they relate to the concept, especially in more expensive, more complicated products such as cars and homes.

What all this means is that when we sell new homes, we need to keep the buyer's focus — and our own focus — on why people *do* buy new homes rather than why they don't. A *positive mentality* focuses on what you *are*. A *negative mentality* focuses on what you *are not*.

When we answer the question, "What is going on inside our mind when an objection occurs?" we must realize that fearlessness is one important part of our position of strength.

*** WHAT IS GOING ON INSIDE THE CUSTOMER'S MIND WHEN AN OBJECTION OCCURS?

There are at least six reasons why customers raise objections, and part of resolving these objections involves understanding their motivation. Let's take a few moments to look at these six reasons for objections. If you can think of any others, bring them up and we'll add them to the list.

1) The most obvious reason for an objection is that the customer simply doesn't want what you're selling, or can't afford it.

When this happens you just need to shrug it off. After all, this is why we qualify people. Don't let it affect your next interaction. You are playing a numbers game where your product was never intended to please everyone. That does not mean your product is deficient, or that you did anything wrong.

This kind of objection offers no opportunity. But don't forget that every customer is still a potential referral source. You can always say to them, "I'm sorry we weren't able to have you as a customer. If you know anyone else who might be interested in our homes, I'd love it if you could send them our way."

Unlike this first type of objection, all of the other types do offer an opportunity for selling.

2) Sometimes people raise objections because they're not sure what they do want.

How do we recognize this type of objection? They frequently seem uncertain, unfocused, misguided, uninformed, or just plain peculiar. Often we can use these types of objections to probe the customer's needs and help them to develop a focus. But as we help the buyer to develop this focus, we must still defend our product and show why it is best for the customer, if we can.

For example, a customer may be planning to buy in the price range of your detached homes, but feels that he is entitled to a larger lot for the price. As a counselor you explain several facts to him:

a) Today the trend in many markets is toward smaller lots because buyers are realizing that is the way to get the most home for their money.

b) Many people start out wanting a larger lot, but as they go through the searching process they realize that a large lot is actually lower on their list of priorities than they originally thought it was.

c) Many people who buy homes on larger lots wind up wishing they had not spent the money for the larger lot because they don't use it as much as they thought they would. Meanwhile the maintenance has become a greater burden than they imagined.

d) In many markets, the fact is that the average small-lot community is more successful than the average large lot community. This proves that the "Great American Dream" has been reevaluated.

- - -

When you give examples of these types of principles, make them as relevant as possible to the salespeople in your group. The above example would obviously not be the one to pick if half of your salespeople are selling large-lot communities. In that case, your argument would be that at your community buyers are getting everything. With this argument you also could make a case for the resale potential of the large-lot community in the face of the increasing scarcity of land and the trend toward smaller lots.

- - -

Another example of this type of objection would be the customer who "wants it all" on the inside of the home. They want to stay in a modest price range but have a larger foyer or dining room. In this case your argument is that the smartest solution in their search for the best value is to get the home which gives the most space in those parts of the home where they spend the most time.

I am classifying these customers as people who "aren't sure what they want" because they have not yet reconciled their priorities to the realities of the marketplace. Many people start out wanting it all, and then make their decisions of what's really most important as they go along.

Sometimes buyers in this category are even more obvious. They show their uncertainty by saying, "We'll know what we're looking for when we see it." In this case the "objection" is not so much to your product as it is an objection to the selling process.

Again, the opportunity in this type of objection is for focus and probing. You can ask, "Have you seen anything so far that you've liked?" Or, "What is the main thing you're looking for that you don't have in your current home?"

Two thoughts to keep in mind when you use this kind of objection for focus and probing are:

a) *Adopt your counselor demeanor* in order to build credibility and establish rapport.

b) *Reinforce your position.* You had the choice to offer your home the way you are offering it, or to offer it some other way. The customer needs to understand:

1. why you made the choice you made, and

2. why other people have agreed that you made the right choice.

- - -

As you proceed through these categories of objections and suggestions for dealing with them, keep the spirit of the meeting open to comments from the salespeople: Do they have any other examples or suggestions? You are now into the types of situations that have all sorts of variations and applications, and you don't want to miss any opportunities to deal with the issues your salespeople faced in real life over the last weekend.

- - -

3) A third reason people raise objections is that some particular issue is causing them to be afraid. There may even be more than one thing they're afraid of.

This type of objection is usually easy to spot. The objection demonstrates the fear.

While customers are not always honest about their objections, that is a different subject than what we're talking about now.

In dealing with fear objections you have 3 tools:

a) Anecdotes and third-party endorsements to show how other people have dealt with the objection.

b) Reason — a rational statement which makes good sense but which the customer may not have considered in their fear.

c) Patience and caring — showing that you can relate to their concern and want to try to work through it with them. It is important when you take this approach that you not let your sympathy erode your position of strength.

One example of an objection based on fear is pessimism about the economy, or about the customer's own job future during a recession. In an economic slowdown, you need to help the customer evaluate how great the job risk really is. Some people are suffering such anxiety over this situation that you might wind up making the judgment call that they would not be likely to make it all the way to settlement. Obviously, you're not going to make much of a living selling to people who really are about to lose their jobs. But most people will have to admit that they are in a very low-risk category, and their worries are based more on the mood around them than on an honest evaluation of their personal situation. In this case, you can bring all three of the principles we just mentioned into play. You could present your case this way:

"If you think there's a real danger of losing your job, then you shouldn't buy. You would never be comfortable with the decision, and I wouldn't be comfortable knowing that I'd been a part of it. But many of the people who've bought here are thinking, 'You know, I'm really one of the lucky ones. Nobody's ever 100% safe, but I'm as safe as most. And this is a great opportunity to take advantage of this economic situation because so many other people are afraid to.' And they're right. It's because the economy is slow that interest rates are so low and prices have stabilized at the same time. The economy always goes in cycles, and when this one starts to turn, most people believe prices and rates will go up simultaneously."

Here you've brought all three of our principles into play: reason, caring and third-party testimonies. You're not telling them as a salesperson why they should buy. You're telling them as a counselor how other people in their situation have reasoned through the decision. And you've protected your position of strength. You've implied that you want them to buy from you, but you don't need them to. This approach is always critical to maintaining a position of strength. You're not worrying about selling your homes. You know your homes will sell. You just want to make sure that they sell to people who are sure they're doing the right thing. This is how you bring your counselor identity and your salesperson identity together in a confident demeanor that will raise your customer's comfort level.

Fear objections are not necessarily caused by external circumstances. Sometimes they can be caused by issues relating to your homes.

Not many homes back up to interstate highways. But a lot of homes do back up to two-lane roads, and sooner or later they all sell. If a customer raises an objection of fear concerning a two-lane road, find out exactly what the fear is.

If the fear is noise, it is usually best to address the objection at the actual lot you are trying to sell. If the home is completed, that is best. If another home along the same street is completed but unoccupied, discuss the problem inside that home. Show how little the noise is when you're inside with the windows closed the way they normally will be.

Explain that the noise is only an issue during rush hour, when they are in the traffic themselves making part of the noise (if this is true for their situation). Explain that the noise is minimal at night and on weekends, and invite them to check it out for themselves.

Explain that people who live in the homes nearby don't notice the noise, and invite them to ask other homeowners along the same street what it's really like, if that is possible.

Compare the decibel noise of the passing cars to the level of other familiar sounds which the buyer considers a normal part of life, if this information is available.

The fact is that most homeowners who back up to roads stop noticing the noise within several days of when they move in.

For some reason, people feel more threatened by roads behind their homes than by roads in front of their homes, even though the road in front is usually closer. Explain to the customer that most buyers have no objection to buying a home which faces a two-lane road.

Finally, explain that people who have already bought similar homesites in your community have thought through all of these factors. They realized that a home backing up to a two-lane road really offers a pretty normal living situation in terms of overall noise level. (If you don't have any other homes sold on similar lots in your community, then the fact still remains that millions of people in this country live in homes in similar situations elsewhere.)

Of course, using this approach to the objection of noise will not guarantee that you can resolve the objection and make the sale. Any adverse condition will always eliminate a portion of your potential market. It might mean that your lot will take two or three times longer to sell than better lots in your community, and this assumption needs to be built into your projections.

Realistically, your goal in using reason, caring and third-party endorsements to deal with an objection is *not to change the mind of the customer who is adamantly opposed to your situation, but to increase the comfort level of the person who is on the fence and*

likes your home better than any other except for the objection.
Many of the objections that you have to deal with are major objections for only some people. They may be minor objections to others, while some of your market will be indifferent. The important thing is to remember that not everyone is thinking the thoughts which your greatest objectors speak.

Back to the road example. The objection may be privacy more than noise. In this case your argument would be that the reason others have bought homes backing up to the road is, when they really stopped and thought about it, backing up to the road is more private than backing up to another home. When you back up to another home, those neighbors know who you are and can watch you all the time. When you back up to a road, it's strangers that are driving by, and they must keep their attention on the road anyway. If they see you at all, it won't be for long.

If the objection to the road is the safety of their children, you must be very careful, because the issue of sensitivity comes into play. You don't want to brush this objection off, for fear of sounding like you don't care about the welfare of children. The fact is that backing up to roads is a very legitimate objection for people with small children, and you might need to concede that portion of the market for those homes which back to the street. You might test the strength of their objection by saying, "You're right, that's a good point. If I were in your situation I would probably fence in the back. How would you feel if that road were in the front of your home?"

If they respond, "Well that wouldn't be so bad," (or, "That would be more normal"), then they have opened up a door for you where you can point out that having the road in back is better because it's easier to fence in a back yard than a front yard.

But if they respond, "I would never live with a road like this in either the front or the back," then you might want to back off and consider this one of those objections that you cannot overcome.

With each of these objections, the principles we have been discussing are these:

a) Remember that the objection is not equally important to everyone.

b) Tell why other people have found it acceptable.

c) Compare the objectionable situation to some other situation which the customer considers normal, such as the road in front, another home in the rear, or other types of noise.

In order to overcome objections of fear, you use reason, caring and third-party endorsements in order to:
a) Help to put the objection into a different perspective for your customer.
b) Show why you made the choices you made in the design and marketing of your homes.
c) Show why other people have found the situation acceptable.

In overcoming objections, one important principle to keep in mind in order to protect your position of strength is this: *There are no accidents. Every decision your company made was for a purpose. You had a choice to do what you did, and you did it because you thought it was best.*
This is perhaps a variation on the cliche that "the best defense is a good offense." You had a choice to buy (or develop) homesites backing up to the road or not buy them. You bought them because you know that some people like them. The proof is the enormous number of people throughout the country who do buy them.
Another example of a fear objection is homesites which back up to a flood plain. All of the same principles that we discussed before also apply here. The homes are not *in* the flood plain. They back up to the flood plain. If your jurisdiction prohibits building homes on flood plains, then your customers have the best of both worlds. The jurisdiction is protecting the customer by designating the risky areas as flood plains and only allowing homes to be built outside of those areas. At the same time, it allows the flood plain area to remain natural. In many areas, builders charge premiums for homes which back up to flood plains. We had the choice of buying those lots or not buying them, and we chose to buy them because of the appeal which they hold for so many buyers.

- - -

You have been discussing some critical principles for dealing with objections, and this part of the session may open up a variety of discussions on how to overcome other objections. If this happens, you may want to go ahead and digress for awhile so that these issues can be discussed by the group, and the principles just discussed can be applied, or modified, immediately. But you still have three types of objections left to go.

- - -

4) The fourth reason that people raise objections is that they want to make sure they are doing the right thing.

In some ways this motive is similar to objections of fear. And the methods of dealing with them are similar — reason, caring and third-party endorsements. But this type of objection is different from fear because the customers are usually a little farther along in the buying process, and they are looking primarily for reassurance. This motive can be a little more subtle. You have already determined that they do want to buy, and you sense that the buyer has reached the point where they are asking you to convince them.

Sometimes you will be able to resolve this type of objection simply with facts, or by relating the experiences of others.

One example of this type of objection may be "buying in a down market." You can counter this objection with historical evidence. It is an undeniable fact, proven again and again, that people who buy in buyers' markets do better than people who buy in sellers' markets.

Perhaps the customer wants to be reassured that it's okay to buy a home that hasn't been built yet. You can explain that this is the way most new homes are sold, and they are sold this way for 2 reasons:

a) If the home can be occupied when it is completed, it can be sold for less money because there are no carrying costs.

b) A buyer can "customize" (with standard options) a home which hasn't been completed, allowing it to fulfill more of their needs and better express their personal identity.

As far as risk is concerned, warranties, jurisdictions and consumer organizations often protect new home buyers more than resale buyers.

Another area where customers want reassurance is in believing they got the "best" deal they could from you. Later in this session we will talk about negotiating, so I would like to put that subject off until then. But when we get there, you will see that the same principles of handling objections apply to negotiating as well.

- - -

As you continue through your sessions, sometimes you will find it may help the energy level of your meetings if you create a sense of anticipation for upcoming topics that you know are important to your salespeople. This not only gives them something to look forward to, but it will give them a little time to organize their own thoughts.

- - -

5) The fifth reason people raise objections is what we might simply call problems in their personality.

Sometimes these situations involve a judgment call. Does the customer seem genuinely threatening — physically, emotionally, or legally? Do you just know that they will be a problem for everybody forever? Are they a bona fide kook? Are they people who are simply incapable of making major decisions in their lives? Have they revealed any patterns of behavior to you that tell you not to pursue them?

There are those rare cases when you're better off without the sale. More often, the personality problems are less serious. They're mainly annoying. These kinds of people are frequently lonely. Showing patience and caring will often give you a decided advantage in dealing with this type of customer, because most salespeople you are competing against probably do not have that level of patience. Perhaps this customer has been run out of every other sales office in town. With this type of customer, patience and tolerance may be the force that gets your momentum going. You simply have to decide, on a case by case basis, whether it's worth it.

6) The last reason people raise objections is the one we really need to dig into. This is the objection where the customer genuinely and rationally does not like a particular feature, but likes your home as a whole.

This type of objection brings us back to the two principles of human behavior that we discussed in the beginning when we talked about what goes on inside our mind:

a) People don't really get, or expect to get, everything they want.

b) People have a high tolerance for imperfection in things that they really like.

We've been dealing with the question, "What goes on inside the customer's mind when an objection occurs?" In the arena of buying and selling, there is a battle going on for control of the selling environment. Sometimes this battle is conscious. People who use "winning by intimidation" tactics, for example, are consciously waging a battle for control of the selling environment. More often the battle is subconscious. The typical customer is not waging this battle consciously, or with any sinister motives. The battle is simply natural. In this case, battle is perhaps even too strong a word. But we'll use the word "battle" to make a point.

The customer wants the selling transaction to occur in a "territory" where he is comfortable. Not a geographic territory, but a psychological territory: a territory in which the customer can control the progress and direction of the transaction. During the give-and-take between you and the customer, you will see the customer try (not deliberately, but instinctively) to move the transaction into his territory. Sometimes it's by simply trying to escape from yours. You can see this happening when the customer:

a) Wants "to see the models alone. "

b) Says he "only has a few minutes."

c) Comes in alone and leaves the spouse in the car.

d) Says he's "looking for a friend who may be moving into the area."

All of these are tactics customers use to maintain their control by "escaping" from your control — your selling "territory."

If a customer wants to continue the interaction with you, then they must use more subtle ways of moving the interaction into their territory. Again, they're not rubbing their hands together plotting this strategy. It's something they do naturally in order to reduce their anxiety and strengthen their control over the situation. But what they are doing is putting you in a defensive position.

Because you aware that this is going on, you must immediately counteract this effort by moving the transaction back into your territory.

Let's look at this whole situation a little more closely. You have a customer who is raising objections to particular features of your homes. But you already know that he likes your homes overall.

So the customer is interested. You know he's interested. He knows that you know he's interested. He does not yet have a high comfort level with the whole situation, and he feels threatened. He wants to move the transaction into a safer territory where he has more control. In order to do this, he will frequently use one of two "tactics." Again I'm using the word "tactic" in the innocent sense. The customer is not necessarily conniving. He's simply reacting.

Let me mention these two tactics in general first, and then we'll go into each of them in detail.

a) One tactic is for customers to attempt to move the transaction into the territory of "their ideal world," the world where only they can rule.

In this situation your mission is to quickly move the transaction out of "their ideal world," where they are dealing, into "the real world," which is the world where you are dealing.

b) The second tactic is where they zero in on a particular component of your product — perhaps a component in which you are truly weak — and put you on the defense by making your weakest link the issue. In this situation we can call their territory "components of your product." We then call your territory "your product as a whole." This is the territory where you want to be dealing.

Sooner or later they will have to choose between your total product and the total product of all the other available alternatives in the real world, including where they are living now. In the real world, there is no "mix and match."

This issue brings us into the third question we raised at the beginning of the session:

*** HOW DO WE SOLVE THE SPECIFIC OBJECTION WHICH HAS BEEN RAISED?

We've already dealt with a number of examples of specific objections. But now we're talking about solving objections for customers who are seriously interested in your homes, but have one or two stumbling blocks. You need to get past these objections in order to keep your momentum going toward the close. So what do you do when your biggest problem is that your product doesn't live up to the customer's ideal?

First, let's ask this question: What is an objection really?

Usually an objection is *an unfavorable comparison in the customer's mind between his ideal and what you are actually offering.* When you have to overcome the problem of your product not matching the customer's ideal, you need to keep the buyer focused on reality. No one else's home will match their ideal either. In the real world they have three choices:

1) Your new home.
2) Where they live now.
3) The other *real* alternatives.

As a counselor, one thing you can help them to do is refine (or redefine) their ideal. Suppose your customer is looking for an affordable townhome with a spacious separate dining room. The home you are offering has a family kitchen and a living/dining combination. The first thing you must do is get them to reevaluate their ideal.

"You know, when you get under $_____ in price, a spacious separate dining room is going to do you more harm than good. It will hurt the main two rooms on the first floor that you care the most about, and it will kill the openness on the first floor. All this for a room that most people use less than any other room in the home."

You don't want to insult your buyer's level of affluence by saying something that comes out sounding like, "A person with your income has no business thinking about separate dining rooms." You will wind up insulting yourself as well, because it will sound like you're also saying, "We really don't give you that much home in this price range."

Talk in terms of trade-offs, not sacrifices.

We talked earlier about selling smaller lots. You're helping them to reevaluate their ideal by saying, "If you're not really going to use the lot that much, and you could use the same money to get more in your home or to get a better location, don't you think that would give you a better overall value?"

You might even want to take a more mathematical approach if your true numbers can justify it. The mathematical approach might sound something like this:

"You're talking about the difference between the quarter-acre lot that we have vs. the third-acre lot that's one of your desires. That's basically 12 extra feet in the front, 12 extra feet in the back, and 5 extra feet on either side. Those kinds of dimensions will really not affect either the usability or the privacy of the lot. But with that same money you can get 300 square feet more inside the home, which will affect the way you live every day of your life. That's why we made the lots a little smaller and put that money into the home instead. We really believed it was a smarter way to spend your money. And that's why so many people have bought them — they tell us we're the best value around."

Perhaps your customer wants a walkout basement on a single family home, and you don't have any.

Your answer could be, "Walkout basements aren't really in as much demand in single family homes as they are in townhomes. People like the access to the rear yard from the main level, and inground basements often have flatter, more usable lots. A lot of people in the single family market just don't think the extra money for a walkout is worth it."

In dealing with the customer's ideal world, remember that anecdotes and third-party endorsements are normally more convincing than one-on-one arguments.

Use research and documentation to support your position whenever possible. This research can come from publications, from research companies, or from your company's own research, especially from surveys done with your previous buyers. You can also use this kind of research to show the resale potential of your homes.

Use your own experience. Use objections as an opportunity to reassert your position as an expert and counselor.

Personal, first-person anecdotes are often helpful in breaking down barriers. They can also have a unique type of credibility. You can talk about times when you went through the same struggle your customer now faces, and how you got through it.

Sometimes it has a special impact when you can talk about times when you were wrong.

* "I used to feel the same way until..."

* "When I bought my home it was so important to me to have a [large lot, separate dining room, walkout basement, etc]. Now that I've been there a few years, I realize what a mistake that was for me. I wish I'd gotten [whatever feature you're trying to sell] instead."

Whenever possible, use the argument that your company thought through the homeowning process one step further than everyone else, and that's the reason you designed your homes the way you did. As we said earlier, "There are no accidents. Every decision you made had a purpose."

Many of these principles we've been talking about for dealing with the customer's "ideal world" also come into play in the other territorial struggle we mentioned earlier — where the customer's territory is called "individual components of your product."

- - -

In parts of this session we have suggested that you repeat some points which you made earlier. We have done this because:

1) The points are critical.

2) We felt that it was worthwhile to reiterate the principle every time we used an example of it.

3) We wanted to make the principles a part of your sales team's total mental process. In overcoming objections, the mental process is more important than the technical expertise.

If you, or your group, begin to find the repetitions tedious or irritating, or if your group ventures into an area that is a more productive use of time, leave out the repetitions and pursue the opportunities.

- - -

As we said earlier, when the customer attacks your Achilles' heel, your goal is to bring the transaction back into the territory of your product as a whole. Since they can't have their favorite part of your home combined with their favorite part of someone else's, they must ultimately choose one of the three options mentioned earlier:

1) All of your home.
2) All of someone else's home.
3) All of where they are living now.

If the customer attacks one element of your home as deficient, remember, as we said earlier, to talk in terms of tradeoffs, not sacrifices. The theme of this type of approach is, *We traded away something less important in order to give you something more important, so we improved the value of your total package.*

If you are selling a starter townhome with a small bedroom #3, you can justify your position by saying, "We call this room a third bedroom because three bedrooms is what's easiest for the market to understand. But we also realize that in our market most of our buyers really won't be using that room as a bedroom. We knew we would not be selling many homes to families of 4, so we designed a better use of space for families of 3 or less. We knew that the "extra room" would probably be used as a study, hobby room or guest room, so we made it a little smaller in order to make the master bedroom suite a little larger. Most people in our market feel that's a better use of space, because it puts most of their space where they spend most of their time, and still makes the price a terrific value. It's a shame when builders try to keep a home affordable by shrinking the master bedroom, bath or closets."

The same position works for the objection of a small foyer. "We wanted to put your money into rooms you live in, not rooms you walk through in order to get to the rooms you live in."

Or you could say it this way: "We knew when we designed this home that you would be paying $80 a square foot to own it. So we designed it as though every single square foot in the entire home had a price tag on it that says $80. Would you want to spend $18,000 for a foyer or a dining room, or would you rather have that same money go into the spaces where you really live? Our goal here was to make every square foot worth what you pay for it."

If there is no way to rationalize or justify a weak component, then don't beat the dead horse. Keep reinforcing your total package. Remember to keep a competitive perspective, because while you may not match their ideal, chances are no one else can either. To be the winner, you don't have to give them everything they need; you only have to give them more than anyone else. Since this is obviously a subjective issue, your mission is to prove to them how you *are* giving them more than anyone else. Like the example of the attorney we mentioned in the first week, you are showing them that your definition of value is better than anyone else's.

One final point about objections:

Sometimes you have an objection that just won't go away, and it has your whole transaction stuck in quicksand. If you can't resolve the objection, and can't go any farther without resolving it, sometimes you have nothing to lose by asking the question, "If I could solve your problem [specifically describing back to them the objection they have raised], would you buy this home?"

Sometimes the objection is something you can solve if you know the sale hangs in the balance, and if you need the sale badly enough. Most of the time you cannot solve the problem, so the question is a bluff. But sometimes you don't have any other option, because you need to know if the objection is a bluff. More often than not you will find that it is, and this is the best way to find out for sure.

If the customer's answer to your question is, "Yes, if you could solve that one problem, we would buy your home," then at least you know, and you can redirect your strategy accordingly.

You might then say, "Well, if you can just hold on to that thought, let's come back to it at the end if everything else looks okay." What you're hoping in this situation is that the objection will diminish as they get more involved with the home as a whole. Or it may be that the objection is worth resolving on the builder's end, if this is possible.

- - -

Before moving on to "Creating Value," stop and see if there are any other objections your salespeople would like to address as a group, or if there are other thoughts about objections they would like to discuss. Generally your salespeople will look forward to this session and the session on closing more than the other four. It is critical to your program as a whole that they come out of these two sessions with their expectations met, and their problems solved to the best of the team's ability.

- -

CREATING VALUE

Last week, when we were talking about establishing impact in the First Ten Minutes, we said part of this impact comes from making your value statement early. This helps you establish your value credibility. Now we want to build on that idea by talking about how we define value at our communities.

What is our value advantage?

- - -

It is impossible for us to write a script for this portion of the session since it will be different for every group.

Before leading this session, you as the manager should prepare a discussion of what you believe is your company's approach to value. You might also want your salespeople to prepare for this portion of the meeting by stating, in one or two sentences, their unique definition of value for their community and product. This is one place in your training program where it is important that every one of your salespeople participate. The length of this portion of your session will therefore be partly determined by two factors:

1) How many salespeople are in your meeting.

2) How many different approaches to value you have.

In your company, your approach to value may be a corporate theme — similar at all your projects — or it may vary considerably from one community to the next. The latter case may be especially true if your company specializes in "niche" products.

To help provide some guidelines for this portion of the session, here are a few questions you or your salespeople may want to consider:

1) Are you positioned at the bottom of your market in either price or price per square foot?

If so, your value statement may be fairly easy to articulate. Your biggest challenge may be to prove that you also include the level of quality that your particular market demands, without "squandering money" on features that most of your market does not regard as having perceived value.

2) Do you have a value advantage by virtue of having more items included as standard that most of your competitors feature only as options?

In this case your value statement may sound like this:
"We believe that if more than 50% of our customers want a feature to be included we should make it standard. If less than 50% want it then we should offer it as a 'choice.' (You might prefer the word "choice" to the word "option" because it has a connotation of freedom.) The reason we price our homes this way instead of making everything optional is this: If we know our customers want a feature, we can include that feature much less expensively by guaranteeing our subcontractor that they can install the item in every home. We feel that we can give a much better value that way than if we sell the item with the higher markup of an option."
Again you are a counselor, not a salesperson. You are explaining to the customer how the system works, and how they can get the most for their money.

3) Are you above the market in price per square foot because of more expensive construction costs — that is, a more architecturally complex home?

In this case your value statement might be that you believe value includes more than just square footage. It is the total quality of life which the home offers. You would then explain the value of volume ceilings, extra light and architectural details in improving the *emotional as well as functional value of a home.*

You can also sell two long-term benefits of higher construction costs:

a) As the buyer lives in a home over the years, they become more affluent. Including more quality features in the home at the time they buy it will allow them to enjoy the home more when they become more affluent, instead of "outgrowing" it as soon as their tastes and needs begin to change.

b) These same features will allow a home to have greater potential for appreciation, because they have those features which appeal to a clientele more affluent than the one who originally purchases it.

Your buyer needs to understand that although they may need to earn, for example, $70,000 per year to buy the home, when they resell it in 5 years they may need for the home to appeal to someone who earns $100,000. Will the less expensive homes that you are competing against have the potential to appeal to that more affluent market as well as yours will, or will their investment potential be limited by their deficiencies?

4) Are you above the market in price because you offer a more expensive total package — architectural design, lot size or features, location, community amenities, etc.?

In this case you would expand upon the theme in #3 above. You take a more sophisticated approach to value. You believe that value is the sum total of home, lot, location and lifestyle.

As you discussed in your meeting last week, your positioning statement is vital to your credibility and your competitive advantage. Spend as much time as it takes to make sure every one of your salespeople believes in their value position. For those who don't, it is very important to the success of their community that you as the manager can provide a solution to this vulnerability. Salespeople who do not believe in their value will find it very difficult to establish a position of strength in this area. They don't have to be the cheapest. They only have to understand, and be able to communicate, the way in which their value is superior.

Once you have completed your discussion of the value statement, you can move on to other ways of creating value.

- - -

As we discussed in the first week with Concept Selling, value is competitive. At some point before your customers can make their final decision to buy, they must be convinced that what you are offering is *the best*, at least the best for them. The idea of you being the best, and one of your available selection being "the best of the best," is an important part of creating urgency. So when you sell value, remember that although you never knock the competition, you are selling the fact that your approach to value is better, and smarter, than anyone else's.

You can also sell value in the form of your own expertise. Customers really do attach value to your expertise, and this is one of the ways in which you can establish an advantage over your competitors. So many salespeople in our industry have only a limited knowledge of construction, land development, engineering and even many of the business aspects of the industry. Your ability to show that you have superior knowledge will help you develop a counselor relationship that truly does convey value to the customer. At the same time it increases their comfort level with buying your home.

- - -

Another subject that you will want to cover in your discussion of value is the issue of negotiating. As with value, your discussion will vary with your corporate strategy toward discounting.

If your strategy is to discount heavily, then your salespeople are probably already equipped to execute that strategy.

Often the situation which salespeople find more difficult, and which most seem to be in, is the one where there are competitors in their market who can offer larger discounts than they can. That is the challenge that we will address here. You will want to modify our comments as necessary for your corporate strategy.

This is another topic you may want to open up for a lengthy discussion, if time permits. For many salespeople this is one of the most sensitive and frustrating challenges they face. If there are some who have developed their own effective strategy for dealing with it, encourage them to share their approach in this group setting. Many salespeople, however, look to their managers for insight on how they are to deal with this challenge. Here are some approaches you could suggest:

- - -

In today's market, one of the greatest challenges we face in trying to sell value comes when we are selling against competitors who are giving larger discounts than we are. The issue of discounting has gotten tangled up with the issue of value. Our job is to untangle that mess. The best position for us to take in this situation is again that of a counselor. This is another case where a "counselor relationship" can allow us to regain a position of strength, while a "salesperson relationship" would not.

When a customer hits us with the argument that a competitor is giving a larger discount, there are several points we must make. And we must make these points from an "objective" position. As the customer's counselor, we must be the one who explains to the customer how the housing market really works. To do this "objectively" we need to include ourselves in that evaluation.

1) We must explain to the customer that *a discount is not a deal. It is a pricing strategy.* All sellers decide what their actual selling price must be, and then create a strategy for getting to that price.

At one end of the scale, some builders set their "list price" as low as they possibly can, and then stand firm with that price.

- - -

Depending upon your company's pricing strategies, and your salespeople's understanding of these strategies, you may want to offer support for certain pricing positions. Your salespeople might want to articulate your position when they explain pricing strategies to their customers. They might also choose to articulate opposing positions in their role as "counselor." We will defend each of the positions in our notes to you, and you can decide how you want the positions explained in your sales offices.

The advantage of the "low list price" approach is that it assures buyers they are all getting as good a deal as everyone else. When they talk among themselves after they move in, no one will feel ripped off. This strategy is all above board. It also allows you to show lower prices in your advertising and on your price list.

- - -

At the other end are the sellers who build enormous negotiating room into the price of their home.

- - -

The advantage of this method is that it provides a closing tool which can give the buyer a feeling of "conquest," and allow the salesperson one more way to make customers feel that "they are in the right place at the right time."

Oddly enough, many builders who have large negotiating strategies are surprised to find that the thrill which the buyer receives from a big discount fades very quickly, often leaving the buyer with feelings of ambivalence. ("Why did I really get such a good deal?" or "I wonder how many people got an even better deal than I did?")

Sometimes the customer who buys the big discount is not really as sold on the home as the customer who pays the list price. With buyers waiting four months or more for their homes to be completed, the big discount strategy can sometimes solve one problem only to cause another.

- - -

Then there are builders who are all along the spectrum in between.

- - -

The advantage of being in between is that you can combine the best of both worlds. You can adjust your strategy to market conditions, and even to your salesperson, in order to create the optimum balance between the list price and the negotiating flexibility for each of your communities.

- - -

You must then explain to the customer that what they must do is strip away all of the pricing strategies and determine who is really giving them the best total value. You must counsel them not to compare discount with discount, but bottom line with bottom line. That is how the truly savvy buyer determines which builder is really giving the best deal.

2) Another point that you must make to your customers objectively is that *all sellers sell a home for as much as they possibly can.* That includes you, and you admit that. That is an undeniable fact in a free market economy. You are then in a position to explain to the customer that if your competitor is offering a $20,000 discount, he is doing it for only one reason: He knows that if he only offered $19,000 off he couldn't sell.

Your purpose in explaining this to the customer is because they could be thinking that the competitor's $20,000 discount will be the buyer's profit. In fact, some salespeople who offer big discounts even say, "By the time the ink on your contract is dry, you will have increased your net worth by $20,000." Your job is to neutralize this appealing incentive.

3) Finally you explain to the customer that as they evaluate the various strategies, they should keep their primary focus on the most important issue — which home will most improve their lives. You must get your customers to project their minds into the future and envision their life in the new home. The instant they walk away from the settlement table, the deal will be a part of their past and their new home will be their real world and their future.

Sometimes you are negotiating price because of a particular liability in your product. Perhaps a particular home has one insurmountable flaw. Or you may be trying to get rid of one especially bad lot.

When the purpose of your negotiation is to compensate for a bad feature, and there is no getting around the fact that the feature is bad, consider explaining that you are not charging for that feature. While this approach would not work for every objection, in some cases, and with some customers, it might be a way of justifying your price.

For example, suppose you have a power pole (or some other encroachment) located in an easement which is actually on the property. It is not only an eyesore, but it inhibits the use of the back yard. You have decided the problem is so bad it is worth a $20,000 discount. You know the home will not sell to someone for whom a great backyard and a great view are top priorities. So you are biding your time until you get a customer who is looking for the most house for the most money, and for whom the lot is not critical. For this person, you may justify your pricing this way:

"This may be exactly the type of situation you're looking for. This homesite has a power pole in back of it, which for some people may be a problem. We figured we'd sell this home to someone looking for a terrific home in a terrific neighborhood for a terrific price. It would be someone who didn't consider the back yard a priority. Except for the pole, the homesite and the view are really both pretty decent. But we still decided to give a $20,000 discount to sell it more quickly. The value of this lot is about $40,000, so actually what we're doing is giving you the back yard for free."

For some customers this might satisfy their need for justice to be done, and give them more gratification than simply saying, "We're giving a $20,000 discount on this home." You have justified the size of the discount rather than making it seem arbitrary. If they think your discount is arbitrary, they may be motivated to seek a bigger discount.

We will talk a little more about negotiating when we talk about showing lots, and then again in the last week on closing. I wanted to touch on it today because the customer sometimes presents negotiation as a form of objection.

In general, when a customer tries to bargain, they have three deep-rooted needs:

1) They need to know they got the best deal possible.

One thing you sometimes need to explain to them, even though it should seem obvious, is that you really want to give them the best deal possible — it is in your best interest.

With some customers, there's nothing wrong with coming right out and saying, "Believe me, I want to give you the best deal possible just as much as you want me to. I'm a commission salesperson. If you walk out the door, I don't get paid. With as much as you love that home, there's no way I would let you walk out that door without giving you my best deal. My company pays me to give you the best deal."

That's just common sense, but it never occurs to many customers. They simply see you as an adversary.

Sometimes when customers seem skeptical that you're giving them the best deal you can, you need to help them focus on reality by asking them, "How will you know when you got the best deal?"

Often, they will not know how to answer that question, but it will cause them to think the whole issue through. Whatever way they do finally answer the question will tell you how to sell them.

There's a lot of truth to the cliche, "If you listen carefully enough, your customers will tell you how to sell them a home."

2) The second need customers have when they negotiate is to achieve a sense of victory.

However, as with getting the best deal, they often don't know a victory when they see one. Your goal is to make them realize that true victory is achieved when they get the best home which offers the best value for them. And this, of course, is the ultimate focus of the whole selling process that we've been talking about.

3) Finally, they need to be satisfied that they could not have "made more money" with someone else's deal.

As we discussed earlier, everyone sells their homes for as much as they can. Whatever discount the customer gets, they need to be willing to give away again when they resell.

At the beginning of this session we made the point that nobody ever gets everything they want, and they really don't expect to. This principle applies to negotiation, too. If we give them everything they demand, then that's not negotiation any more. That's simply a gift. A negotiation, in the true sense of the word, is successful when:

1) The buyer and the seller both believe the deal makes sense for them.

2) They both believe the deal is fair.
3) The buyer is convinced of the value of the home.

- - -

If time permits, you can take this opportunity to discuss particular issues of negotiation with your salespeople, adapting your comments to your corporate (or community) strategy.

Continue to reinforce the message that even though you don't offer the biggest discounts, it does not put you in a position of weakness. It simply requires your salespeople to get the customer to reevaluate their preconceptions. This is the same strategy we used to deal with objections.

Having laid this foundation, you are now able to move into the specifics of selling which involve model demonstration and selling the individual homesites — the subjects of your next two sessions.

DEMONSTRATING MODELS

To the Manager

Many salespeople feel uncomfortable with the idea of demonstrating models. One of your objectives in this session is to make these salespeople more comfortable with demonstration. Then you can set about discussing ways to make everyone's demonstrations more successful.

Let those salespeople whom you know are most effective at demonstrating have an opportunity to share their attitudes and techniques with others during this session.

The Presentation

When you get into the subject of Model Demonstration there are so many approaches that do work. What I want to talk about today is as many of those ways as we can fit into two hours.

In our second meeting we talked about the fact that there are three primary selling arenas: the sales office, the model homes and the homesites. In that meeting the questions we raised were, "What opportunities exist in that selling arena, and what strategies can we develop which will maximize those opportunities?" At that time we were talking about the sales office. This week we'll be raising the same questions in connection with the second arena — the model homes. One of the questions some of us struggle with most is, "When do we show models, and when do we let the customers go by themselves?" Do you show every model to every customer who walks through the door? Of course not. That's why we qualify people at the beginning. So how do you determine when you should demonstrate models, and which ones you should show?

- - -

The next few paragraphs will be repeating points which you made at the beginning of Session 2 — The First Ten Minutes. You *may want to revise these remarks as you deem appropriate. The message is a crucial one, so it is worth restating in some form.*

- - -

Sometimes we decide by asking the question, "Do I think the customer wants me to show them the models?" We talked about this idea a little in our meeting on The First Ten Minutes.

If we ask the customer whether they want us to go along, they will usually say, "No." But in this particular situation, the question, "Is it what the buyer wants?" is really not the best question.

We already know that given a choice, they would not want us to go. Given a choice, many customers would rather not ever talk to a salesperson at all. They would rather have a price list, a set of open models, and a button to push if they want further assistance. That does not mean we run and hide every time we see a customer coming, even though we know that's what they want.

When we see a customer coming, the real question we ask is, "How can we make our first conversation with the customer as enjoyable and productive as possible?" This is the same question we should be asking when we get to the point where the customer is ready to see the models. Again, as in the First Ten Minutes, we need to ask the question, "What opportunities for selling exist in this selling arena, and what strategies can we develop to maximize those opportunities?"

Here's a slightly different way of asking the same question, but it helps to emphasize the kind of stakes we are playing for with this decision. "What opportunities for making a sale will we gain if we do a demonstration? And what opportunities will we lose if we don't?" Sometimes that second question is even more important than the first. There are a number of selling opportunities that are unique to the model demonstration. If we don't take advantage of those opportunities, we often don't get the chance to pick them up any place else.

The answer to these questions is a case-by-case judgment call. Sometimes when we ask the question, "What are the opportunities?" the answer is zero. Obviously, if the customer makes it clear that they are truly not in the market, or do not qualify, then we have to assume the opportunities are zero. There would literally be nothing to gain by demonstrating models, other than perhaps prac-tice or feedback. But if we honestly believe that for a particular customer there are opportunities, then we have to be armed with the best possible strategy for maximizing those opportunities. So now let's talk about how to maximize the opportunities.

- - -

It may seem as though we have overworked this idea of whether to show models, and that you really don't need to spend this much time on such an obvious issue. If that is the case with your group, then you can easily condense our remarks down to a minute or two. But for many salespeople, and managers, the whole idea of mental attitude toward model demonstration is the single most important issue in the entire topic. If that is your situation, then it is important for the mental approach to be solid before the technical approach begins.

To make sure you are not going down an irrelevant path, you might ask your group at this point what they find to be the most dif-ficult part of model demonstration. Is it getting the demonstration started? Is it keeping it interesting and meaningful once they are into it? Is it giving the demonstration a sense of direction where it is real-ly leading toward a sale?

- - -

When we left off in our session on The First Ten Minutes, our final goal was "setting up the model demonstration."

Once you have decided that you do want to go with the cus-tomer to the models, does anyone have a particular technique that you use to make it comfortable to go along with the customer?

- - -

There is a wide range of feelings on this subject. While some salespeople find this particular moment in the selling process to be the most intimidating of all, others find it very easy. Those who find it easy might give a response that sounds like, "What's all the fuss about?" This is good, because it may help others to realize that they could be overreacting to the situation.

*Some salespeople like to ask the customer's permission. This can
be risky. As we discussed earlier, the customer, if given the choice,
might say no.*

*Other salespeople let customers start through the models alone,
and then catch up with them later. They feel this gives customers time
to "decompress" before resuming the interaction. But the salesperson
who chooses this approach needs to be sure that he is not using it
because he has an underlying hangup about demonstrating models.*

*Whatever technique a salesperson suggests, even if it sounds
bizarre, it is important that you respect his or her approach if it really works. You may ask the salesperson to explain why he does it that
way, or why he thinks it works better than other approaches. These
explanations may be helpful to the group .*

*As the manager, you need to be open to any new ideas about
model demonstration. Your goal is still not to promote a single particular approach, but to give your salespeople a "menu" of successful approaches to choose from. They may want to experiment with
several until they find the one that works best for them. They also
need to be attuned to the fact that different approaches might work
better on different customers.*

*After the salespeople have discussed the approaches they have
been successful with, you can then add the following ideas, if they
have not already been covered.*

- - -

**Some salespeople set up the model demonstration by creating a
need for them to go along.**
**1) To help the customer understand features — what's standard
and what's optional.**
2) To help clarify a point they made during the First Ten Minutes.
**3) To explain the superior approach that you said you have taken
toward value.**

**They might make a point to the customer during the First Ten
Minutes and then say, "I'll show you what I mean when we see the
models."**

**Other salespeople set it up by saying, "I'll go into the first model
with you and get you started by explaining a few things that people
often find confusing."**

Some use this approach: "Let me show you what we have here. As we're walking through, please point out things that you like and don't like so we can figure out which of our homes might work best for you." This technique helps get the customer on to a decision-making track as they are seeing your home.

Many salespeople don't do anything fancy at all to set it up. They simply tell the customer they're going with them. Their point is that most people will do something if the expert tells them to, as long as it's reasonable. People who do it this way claim it's very easy, although this kind of approach is not for everyone.

- - -

As you go through these approaches, you might ask your salespeople if anyone in the group does it that way, and find out what the results have been.

Naturally the approach your salespeople take will be affected by the location of their sales office. If they have a regular model, or set of models, and the sales office is in a garage or trailer which requires some sort of journey to get from the office to the models, the approach is a little more complicated than if they are already in the model with their office. The approach we have been using assumes they are in a sales office separate from the model.

Perhaps their office is located in the living room, dining room or library, so they greet the customer from their "office" as the customer walks in the front door of the home. Or perhaps the office is in a bedroom upstairs or the basement downstairs, so that the salesperson has to arrive on the main level in order to greet the customer. In these cases the transition is much more natural, and the model demonstration becomes partly incorporated into the strategy of the First Ten Minutes. The primary principles of the selling process remain the same, while the specific rhythm of the sequence will vary.

Once you have completed your discussion of the variety of successful approaches toward making the transition to the model demonstration, you are ready to move on to your next point, which is a critical one.

- - -

Once you are out of the sales office environment and approaching the model home, the most important ingredient of a successful model demonstration is a sense of purpose. Salespeople who go through the model as though it were a tour, simply pointing out features, are often the ones who feel most awkward about it. They believe that their customers could get through this portion of the selling process just fine without them. And they are right. They feel that their presence is pointless. And they are right about that, too.

What their presentation is missing is a *theme.* If your model demonstration has a theme, then it has a sense of purpose. You are no longer there just to point out features, but to tie those features, and their benefits, into a larger pattern. At this point you are finally achieving your goal of getting them to see your model from your perspective.

The model demonstration is where you bring your concept to life. Your concept is the theme of your model demonstration. The demonstration is also where you prove your value statement. The purpose of your demonstration is not to describe the home, but to explain why it is best. This approach helps to create urgency and generate momentum.

It is no wonder that the "guided tour" approach makes salespeople feel self-conscious, and customers uncomfortable. There is no vitality to it — no apparent direction. But once you are following a strategy which is directed toward a specific theme, then there is a point to it all. And the point is the same one you were making during the First Ten Minutes as you explained your concept. Now when you show the features, these features become the proof of your concept, the examples which prove your value statement.

The model demonstration is frequently the first opportunity you have to spark the customer's imagination. When I talk about "sparking the customer's imagination," I don't mean the gimmick where you say, "Imagine yourself living in this home at Christmas." Contrived sales techniques sound to the customer like contrived sales techniques.

There are more down-to-earth ways of bringing your homes to life. One way is through our old friend — the third-party endorsement. An example would be, "Here's what some people have done [with this room / space / feature / type of homesite]."

Or you could speak from your own personal perspective. "Here's what I would do if I could have this home..."

You can even speak in the second person without making it sound contrived. "One thing you could do is..."

To spark a customer's imagination, your goal is to get them involved without making them feel awkward.

- - -

You are now into another area where you want to generate new ideas — "Creating Customer Involvement."

Two questions you can ask your group are:
1) Do you have any special ways that you try to get customers involved?

The other question is something of a tangent from your immediate topic, but that can be okay, because you can still relate it back to the subject of involvement and rapport:
2) When you demonstrate a home, do you have a particular routine, or do you vary it each time? If you vary it, what questions are you using to direct your path?

Both ways have their benefits. A routine could mean that your salesperson has found an approach which always seems to work. A variety could mean that your salesperson is good at establishing rapport and adapting quickly to different situations.

This second question could also evolve into some informal role playing where you can pursue several hypothetical scenarios.

- - -

Part of creating involvement is creating enthusiasm. When we talked about creating enthusiasm in the First Ten Minutes, we used the analogy of lighting one fire with the sparks of another. The same principle applies here. Your demonstration must use your own enthusiasm to help generate theirs. This doesn't necessarily have to involve "showmanship" if that is not your flair. But it does have to involve *animation.*

Animation truly does help to create involvement. You know this yourself when you listen to speakers. If they are animated, it affects you in 3 ways:

1) They hold your attention better.
2) You become more involved.
3) You also learn more.

A speaker can be extremely intelligent and have excellent material. But if they speak in a lifeless monotone, it is hard to follow. The same intelligent material delivered by an animated speaker will not only interest you more, but it will also teach you more. This does not mean that you have to have a flamboyant personality in order to convey your message. Whatever type of personality you have, you can still be yourself. You must simply be yourself in an animated way.

Animation does not mean theatrics. But it does mean developing certain good delivery skills, just as a speaker must in order for his message to have maximum impact. The speaker can still be himself. He must simply be himself with certain skills. The skills which will help you to be animated, and which will help your model demonstration to increase its impact, include these following elements:

1) Eye contact.
2) Smiling.
3) Voice modulation.
4) Movement and gesturing.
5) Energy and enthusiasm.
6) Using whatever opportunities are available to allow your customer to be animated, too.

a) Holding one end of a tape measure (this is also a helpful device for showing lots).

b) Having a customer sit in a particular part of a room to get the impact of living there.

c) Having them "use" or "feel" certain features in the kitchen or other areas.

Attention to these types of details is as important as the details of your homes. After all, another of the unique opportunities of the model demonstration is a longer period of time for you to deepen your relationship with your customer. As much as you need to get to know about them, through asking, listening and qualifying, remember that it is just as important for them to get to know you. Not just you as a salesperson or counselor or expert, but you as a fellow human being.

While the customer may want to avoid you, don't assume that this is the case. Remember that they are a traffic light. Only a red light means stop. Yellow means proceed with caution.

As you and your customer get to know each other better, you can also get certain types of feedback during the model demonstration which you cannot get in any of the other selling arenas. You have opportunities to get them to more clearly articulate their needs. As we said earlier, this is often the time when you can "let them tell you how to sell them a home."

We talked two weeks ago about "rewarding their behavior." Remember that whenever a customer does give a response, be sure to follow up on their comments to encourage them to keep talking, and to show that you are concerned with meeting their needs. Showing enthusiasm for your customer is just as important as showing enthusiasm for your homes.

When the customer is uncommunicative, you must sometimes ask questions in order to generate responses. In the early stages of your demonstration, keep the questions as non-threatening as possible:
"How important is this room to you?"
"What plans do you have for your extra bedroom?"
These types of questions keep your presentation on track without causing the savvy customer to think, "Uh-oh, here come the closing questions. Don't get caught up in too many consecutive affirmative responses. You may accidently wind up buying one."
Always assume that your customers know what you're up to, and treat them as though you respect their intelligence.

Sometimes in order to create involvement you need to tell stories of how other customers have reacted to a particular feature, or benefitted from the feature. It is also appropriate to give your own reactions. This is one way you let them get closer to you.

Take advantage of opportunities to use the model demonstration to get them to talk more about their discontent with their current home. This can be especially effective when you are standing in a strong part of your home — an area which you know is better than where they live. If you have an outstanding master bedroom suite, you can ask, while you're standing in it, "How does your current master bedroom lay out? Do you like this better?"

The more you can get them to express discontent with their current home, the better you can learn their needs. These expressions of discontent also help you to establish an environment where your message to the customer can soon become this: "Before long, the problems of your current home will all be part of your past."

Sometimes it is appropriate during the model demonstration to try to get them to talk about other homes they have seen. Be careful if you try this. Since your goal is to get them to focus on your homes, it can be risky or cause you to lose momentum. If you're on a roll, then keep the focus on your home and don't distract them with thoughts about other options. But if you feel as though the whole process just isn't going anywhere, or you can't get it focused, or you're losing control, then you might make the judgment call that you've got nothing to lose. In this event, getting them to talk about other places that they have liked, or disliked, might help you to get a foothold.

During your model demonstration, spend enough time explaining construction techniques that you show your expertise, and your company's expertise, to the customer. Some customers care more about this kind of information than others. If they do care, spend enough time on this aspect of selling to satisfy their appetite. If the customer is not interested in construction information, spend a few minutes on it here or there anyway. They don't necessarily have to understand every word you're saying. Your expertise will still increase their confidence and their comfort level.

As we discussed with "Creating Value," people want to buy from experts. If you show that you know more than other salespeople, it implies to the customer that you work for a more conscientious company. They can translate this approach into better quality and customer service. Naturally, you do not want your display of expertise to become tedious. Pick a few of your home's strengths and focus on those.

One of the objectives of your demonstration is to reveal to your customers those benefits which they would not have discovered on their own. Some of these benefits may seem small: benefits of products that exist in your kitchen, bathrooms, fireplace or windows.

Most customers will have at least minor interest in any superiority that you can convey in your major systems:
• Heating and cooling system.
• Plumbing system.
• Flooring system.
• Energy efficiency.
• Various structural systems.

If you have more than one model, there are several other points you will want to remember.

1) Your models may not all have the same theme. In fact, it is likely that they will be different, because usually each model has been designed to appeal to a different set of needs and tastes within your market. The concept of your entire product line may be your overriding theme, but then each home can have a "subconcept" — a specific theme.

2) During your demonstration you're hoping to arrive at the conclusion that one home will meet their needs better than the others.

Be careful not to jump the gun on this. Until you have enough information from the customer, you must take the position that all of your models have unique strengths, and together your models create a balance. Don't tip the balance until the customer tells you which way to tip it. Once the customer expresses a particular set of needs, or a strong preference for a particular one of your models, then you can set about reinforcing the customer's feelings. Usually the only times you want to make one model sound better than the others are:

a) When you know that their preference is final and you are going for the final close.

b) When your customers seem unable to make up their minds and you are going for broke.

c) When you have one particular model you are trying to promote. (This could be the case if you have only one model available, or an excess of inventory).

Going back to the first week when we laid out our *Strategy to Achieve Momentum,* we have now reached the fifth stage — "Getting the customer to pick out a favorite model." It is important that throughout your demonstration you never lose sight of that goal. Getting them to like your product is certainly an important goal. But your higher goal — the goal which will keep your momentum going and boost you on into the next stage — is getting them to pick their favorite. Picking favorites — favorite community, favorite model, favorite homesites, favorite exterior, favorite options — is the key to creating urgency and fear of loss.

When your customers do reach the point where they have picked out their favorite model, it is extremely important that you take one more step immediately. Ask them to tell you *WHY* that model is their favorite. It is important to your momentum and your position of strength that they not only pick out a favorite, but express in their own words to you why it is their favorite.

When people express themselves verbally, it strengthens their convictions. This is the critical moment when customers can begin to close themselves. You can now begin to act as an "assistant buyer." You can also quote their own comments back to them later when necessary. (And you may have an opportunity to quote their comments later on to other customers as third-party endorsements.)

This principle of getting customers to express themselves is especially important because the spoken word has always had an almost "mystical" power about it. For example, two people may be in love for years without ever actually saying the words, "I love you." Then suddenly they say it, and the whole relationship seems to take on a new dimension, even though in one sense it seems that nothing has really changed. But something has changed. The emotion has taken on the power and conviction of the spoken word. So when customers pick out their favorite, make sure they know why, and say why.

Once they have picked out their favorite model, your next goal is the sixth stage of the *Strategy to Achieve Momentum* — "Get the customer to pick out a favorite homesite."

Your final objective in your model demonstration is therefore to set the stage for taking the customer to your homesites. You need to create enough of a sense of anticipation that they believe they can benefit by taking this next step. Rather than try to tackle this strategy today, we will pick up at this point in our next meeting on "Showing Homesites."

- - -

More and more companies are getting away from the notion that there is one right way to demonstrate models. Therefore we did not try to lay out one particular path or technique for demonstrating models. For example, the sequence in which salespeople show the various areas in each model can vary according to the strengths and weaknesses of that model, and according to personal needs which the customer has already revealed. Sometimes salepeople will choose to linger in a particular part of the home, while in the next model they might pass quickly through that same area. Sometimes salespeople decide that the customer should not even see all the models, and this has to be their shot to call.

We have taken the approach that there is much more value in studying principles and strategies for model demonstration, and then sharing experiences and techniques of your salespeople in order to give life to these principles and strategies. We are attempting to avoid creating an atmosphere which is directed only to rookies. We are assuming that your sales team is at various levels of experience, where your veterans can offer the benefits of real-life experiences to rookies, and rookies can offer testimony to the continuing importance of the basics to veterans.

You may consider some other uses of time in this session if there are particular areas of your team's expertise that you feel you need to strengthen. Two examples of topics you may wish to pursue are:
1) Reading blueprints.
2) Construction specifications.

You may wish to devote a short amount of time to such topics as these in your sales training sessions, or you might want to make them a subject of a separate meeting, with a member of your construction department helping you to lead the program.

SHOWING HOMESITES

To the Manager

This session is, in many respects, a continuation of Session Four. Many of the principles for showing homesites are similar to those for demonstrating models. As with the last session, you may need to adapt the principles of this session to your specific on-site situations.

The mechanics of showing homesites can vary, especially in two situations:

1) If your salespeople are unable to take customers to the sites because not enough land development has been done to make them accessible.

2) If your homesites are the least appealing element of your package, so that you must have the home virtually sold before you go to the sites.

When we use the term "homesites," we mean the specific "unit(s)" which the customer can buy. In the case of condominiums, for example, the "homesite" would be a location, not a yard. The approach we will take in this session will be the one which applies to the most frequent situation — taking the customer out to accessible homesites in order for them to select a particular one.

The theme which must continually remain at the forefront of this stage of the selling process is that the purpose of showing homesites is to set up the close. Showing sites must not be an end in itself. By the time salespeople reach this stage in the selling process they need to be thinking in terms of completing the sale — walking away from the site-showing stage as close as possible to a final resolution.

As with the model demonstration, you need to keep the meeting open to the wide variety of strategies which your salespeople have used successfully, especially those whose background includes a wider variety of product types and homesite types.

You might also want to use a portion of this meeting for honing certain technical skills which will help your salespeople to demonstrate their expertise: skills such as reading site plans or understanding principles of engineering and land development. As we suggested with construction details at the end of the last session, you might *even want to devote an entire separate session to these skills, with the help of an expert from another department.*

The Presentation

"Showing Homesites" is the last of the three major selling arenas that we have been discussing. As with the first two — the sales office and the model homes — we need to begin by asking the questions:
1) What opportunities will I gain if I show homesites?
2) What opportunities will I lose if I don't?

Perhaps more than the previous two arenas, there are a wide variety of factors which can influence your answer. Not only the seriousness and qualifications of your customer, but also your circumstances. What is the weather like that day? Are the homesites in that section easy to get to? Are the sites at your particular project more of an asset or a liability? If land development is not far enough along to allow you to get to the sites, then you must literally "take the customer to your homesites" on your site plan.

If your homesites are a major part of your value package, then showing those sites will usually be a major part of your momentum force. In this situation your sale will often reach its climax at the actual homesite which the customer decides is their favorite. Showing the sites will require a major commitment of your time and energy, and will be a major part of your planning in the preparation of your total selling strategy. In fact, your sale may not get very far along before you show your homesites, and it may not need to. If your homesites are your greatest asset, then they may be your primary selling arena.

On the other hand, if your sites are your weak link, then you will probably need to have the customer more committed to the idea of buying your home by the time they have finished seeing the models. In this situation your goal is not to sell the overall grandness of your homesites, but simply the fact that there is one site that is better than all the others.

When I say "homesite," I am referring to a specific unique unit.

In the case of a condominium or townhome, the homesite will, of course, be more the combination of individual features such as location, exposure, elevation and delivery date than actual acreage.

In any event, by the time you get to the stage of showing homesites, your own attention needs to stay focused on the close. You are coming down the home stretch, and when you are this far along in your momentum strategy, it is important that showing the sites not be an objective in itself, but the "beginning of the end." Just as your goal in demonstrating models was to get them to pick out their favorite, that same goal is even more important now. You are showing them home-sites for one primary purpose — to get them to pick out a favorite so that you can move into the final stages of your closing process.

In a "normal" situation, where your sites are away from the sales office and fairly easy to get to, the site-showing arena has three selling advantages over the other two arenas:

1) You have more control in this arena than in the other two.

You are away from the sales office — the phone, other cus-tomers, the whole array of distractions. You and the customer each have the other's undivided attention. They have also implied a cer-tain level of commitment in their interest by being willing to leave the sales office and models to accompany you on this journey. They know it will be harder for them to escape from you now.

2) You can create a sense of adventure.

You are out of the business environment and into the frontier. You can create an energy and involvement here which you may have been unable to create in the more formal environment of the model area.

3) You can begin to set the up the close.

You are now showing them individual pieces of "real" estate. You are speaking in reality and specifics, not in generalizations and hypothetical situations. They will have seen all that you have to show them, and they will have no choice but to make some sort of decision — even if their decision is to postpone their decision.

When we left off last week with demonstrating models, we fin-ished up by saying that our final goal in the demonstration was to get the customer to pick out a favorite model. This goal applies whether or not you did an actual "demonstration." If the customer toured the model homes alone and then comes back to the sales office, the principle is still the same.

To set up a sample scenario, it might go something like this:

Suppose they went through the models alone and are now returning to your sales office. As they walk in, you get up and ask, "How did you like them?"

Assuming that it's not a very talkative customer, but that they did like your homes, they might just answer, "We liked them."

"Did you have one that you liked better than the other two?" (This question may sound less threatening than, "Which one did you like best?")

"We liked the Brentwood."

"What did you like best about it?"

As we discussed before, their answer to this question will give you more insight into their needs, and it will give you information that you can use to reinforce your own position later. It will also cause them to "testify," which will help them to increase their own conviction. Be sure to give an enthusiastic, positive response to their statement in order to make them feel more confident in their decision, and in their relationship with you.

If exterior elevation is another critical choice in your product line, you would next go ahead and get a decision on that. Then you would begin to set up your homesites.

"We have two sites for that home. You might like Lot 34 better than Lot 38, but that's just a hunch. You're the better one to make that judgment."

You will need to make the decision of whether or not you want to go out on that particular limb. "Having a hunch" can backfire, but it is definitely an approach that you should consider. You don't have to be right. In fact, don't defend your position if they turn out to like another lot better than the one you had predicted. But in some cases you will feel that you have learned enough about their needs. Or you will know that one of your homesites is significantly better and you are almost certain that they will probably choose it anyway. Then this approach might help you to create some anticipation and excitement about seeing the homesites. This in turn can help you create urgency later on.

In any event you could conclude by saying, "Would you like to see them? We can get out for a few minutes, and that will give you a chance to learn a little more about our community."

Let's talk for a few minutes about going out on limbs to create interest. Do you think this approach of setting up a particular homesite is a valid one, or do you think a different approach would work better for you?

- - -

You want to take this opportunity to open up a discussion about set-ting up the site-showing stage. If the conversation then goes farther into an exchange of ideas on showing homesites, that is fine, too. Even more than with demonstrating models, you will probably hear different ideas on strategies for showing homesites, because your salespeople have different types of homes and different levels of desirability of their sites.

You can encourage a variety of approaches, but at this stage in the selling process you want to encourage those approaches which are boldest, and which are most focused on keeping the selling process moving toward the close.

- - -

Here's another question on planning your site-showing strategy. How do you determine what order to show your homesites in? Do you show you best site first, or last, or do you show your sites in geographic order, or does it matter?

- - -

There are several valid strategies here, and these strategies are made even more valid by the fact that salespeople believe in them. When they believe in their approach, they can execute it with enthusiasm and conviction. This is a good reason for being open to different methods rather than making a single method "mandatory" as your company's "official way of selling." A salesperson might believe in another method more, and therefore not be able to exe-cute the mandatory method with conviction or enthusiasm.

However, if you do take the "open-minded" approach, then you have every right to insist that your salespeople "play fair." They must be willing to admit when they're wrong, and be as open-minded to trying your methods as you are to accepting theirs. If their method isn't working, then they owe it to you and to the company to try another method to the best of their ability. This is a "fair deal" for all concerned, and you might want to articulate this "deal" to your salespeople if you think it is appropriate. This kind of approach can also help your company give birth to new ideas, as well as refining older ones.

Once you conclude your discussion of which lot to show first, there is one point which should be made in favor of showing your best homesite — or the one which you think will best meet the buyer's needs — first. That point is, once again, MOMENTUM.

- - -

When you decide which homesite to show first, it is important to realize that in this case the dynamics of new home sales are different from those of general brokerage.

Often brokerage agents will show homes in a particular order so that they can lead up to the best home at the end of their day. The strategy here is that they have control over the buyer for a certain agreed-upon period of time. They will show an agreed-upon number of properties which have been discussed in advance. At the end of this period of time they hope to close a sale.

So they may plan to show four properties, saving the best for last. The hope of this strategy is that the customer will get tired of looking as the best selection is about to be shown (or right after it has just been shown.)

Some agents show the best home next to last, using the last home to confirm the buyer's decision that there's no point in looking any further.

In new home sales, we don't always have the same degree of control. We never know when the customer's attention span will expire. In the meantime, our goal is to keep the momentum going. For this reason, in new home sales there is an argument in favor of taking your best shot first, and then showing your other sites in order to confirm or deny that choice. It can jeopardize your momentum, and possibly your credibility, if you plunge from the "high" of picking out the favorite model down to the low of show-ing a "dog lot" first.

If you choose to show a homesite first that you do not think will be their favorite, then at least let the customer know what you're doing. After all, you are trying to show them that you understand their needs and are trying to fulfill those needs.

Sometimes we allow our selling strategies to become too com-plex, and we wind up outsmarting ourselves. We can keep our approach honest, clean, simple and on-target by remembering one principle:

Sell to your customer the way you would sell to your best friend.

No matter how bad your sites are, there is always one which in some way can be described as "your best."

Some people will say, "You shouldn't try to sell off all your best homesites first. Then all you will have left is dogs." While this may be true, selling your dogs first while your better sites are also for sale is still an uphill battle, and is usually an unrealistic goal.

Usually the most effective strategy for getting rid of dog sites, aside from discounting them, is to limit your availability from time to time so that you force yourself to figure out a way to sell them. Even with this strategy, you are still trying to sustain momentum by selling the "best of the dogs" first.

One good strategy for dog sites is to use them with "bottom fish-ers." When a customer comes in determined to make a low offer, you can explain to him, "If you would like to make a low offer on one of our homes, let me try to help you out. I can't take in an offer this low on the lot you're looking at, because the builder knows it's one of our best homesites. It's worth more than the oth-ers — that's why you like it best. For exactly the reasons you like it, it will probably be the next one to sell. But if getting a big dis-count is your top priority, let me show you another site which I know the builder is a little more concerned about selling. He might be willing to deal on that one."

When you use this strategy, it is not necessarily to get the cus-tomer to really buy your worst site, although that's not entirely impossible. Your main goal is to try to neutralize the customer's feeling that he has superior bargaining power. You are putting his offer into a different perspective with the message, "You can't make your worst offer on our best homesite."

If you have enough information from the buyer to express an opinion of which homesite you think is best for them, you have to assume that you will be right most of the time. For those times when you are wrong, there is probably no harm done. And for those times you're right, you will often be able to create even more urgency when the buyer agrees with you that your first choice was best.

If you take the approach that you have a good selection and they're all about the same, your customers may not have the same level of conviction about their first choice, and therefore may not feel as much urgency.

If you are selling great homesites, then naturally that is a benefit you want to emphasize. You want to begin to pitch your homesites in the First Ten Minutes, and then get them to the sites as soon as possible after they've picked out a favorite model. In some cases the choice of homesite may even be more important than the choice of model.

If you have less desirable sites, it is important not to get discouraged. For many salespeople, their homesites become a growing source of anguish to them as time goes by, until they get to the point where they believe it is an insurmountable obstacle. The thing to keep in mind is this: Statistically, most people buy mediocre sites, even though most people start out demanding a good site as one of their criteria. Many, many people buy bad sites every day. The reason is that in the end the homesite is not always the top priority that it started out to be. Most people wind up buying the total package, making concessions somewhere in order to get the best total package. More times than not, the concession is in the homesite. They wind up putting the home and its price above the site.

While undesirable features about your sites may certainly close off a portion of the market to you, don't overestimate the size of that portion. And don't be ashamed of your homesites. As we discussed with Concept Selling, it is important to keep your focus on what you are, and not get bogged down in what you are not.

When you have poor homesites, you will have to get closer to the close before you show them. In these cases the model demonstration becomes even more important. The major part of your close will come after they have seen the models and before they have seen the sites, because in effect you are asking them to buy in spite of your sites. In this case the purpose of showing the sites is merely to help them decide which one to buy, and not whether to buy. If they are not sold on your home before they see the home-sites, then showing sites may do you more harm than good. In these types of situations the principles we discussed last week become even more important, as the models will often become your primary closing arena.

One last point on preparing your strategy for showing your homesites. Suppose you have an objection which you know every-one will raise, such as the example of backing up to a road which we discussed two weeks ago. In that situation it is often better to bring up the issue before you get to the sites. You are not necessari-ly bringing it up as an objection, but merely as a fact. You might do this at the site table. If the customer questions the item, and you realize that it could be an objection, you can begin to overcome it in the sales office by explaining why other buyers have found it desirable (or acceptable).

The reason for bringing the objection up before you get to the actual homesite is in order to protect your momentum when you get there. You want to make sure that momentum continues to be a top priority at every stage of the sale, and this is more important now than ever.

Arriving at the homesites if often one of the most critical moments in the momentum process. If you run into a brick wall at that moment — especially if the brick wall is a surprise — it could do far more damage than if the customer is prepared for it. The last thing you need is for your momentum to suddenly unravel just as you're getting within striking distance of the close.

Here we bring into play the same principle we discussed before with Concept Selling: getting the customer to see your product from your perspective at the very start. It is much easier to help them shape their perspective at the beginning than it is to change their perspective once it has been formed. To protect your momen-tum, you need to avoid situations which will cause you to backped-dle. You can help to avoid these situations by getting the customer to see your point of view at the start.

- - -

You have now completed the portion of the discussion which concerns preparing your strategy for showing homesites, and you will be moving into the specifics of what to do as you take the customer to the sites.

- - -

The trip to the homesites with the customer is as important as the time spent on the site.

If weather permits and the distance is reasonable, take the opportunity to walk with the customer to the sites. If this is not possible, take your time driving. Now that you are out of the sales office, you have the opportunity to create a more relaxed atmosphere with the customer. Your conversation can be more leisurely, less formal. As you go through the community, you are letting them "feel" that this is a nice place to live. Show whatever community amenities are already installed before you get to the homesites, and tell about future ones. By the time you get to the sites, you want the customer to already feel that the community is right for them.

As you pass by the homes of neighbors who have already moved in, tell your customer anything about these people which may be helpful to your sale, and which you're sure the existing homeowner (and the federal government) would not mind a neighbor knowing. Give similar information about people who have bought but not moved in.

The neighbors are the life of your community. They are also your third-party endorsements. Tell why your prospect would like the neighborhood, and also why the neighbors bought at your community. This information is especially helpful when a neighbor bought a home or site which is similar to the one you are trying to sell.

People often do not ask many questions about the neighborhood. This does not mean it is not important to them. Neighborhood is one of the top needs of most customers, whether they say so or not. Many people are more reluctant to ask questions about the neighborhood than about other topics. Others just don't have these questions as close to the front of their minds on the first visit as they have questions about price, homesite and product features.

When you arrive at the site, your approach will naturally vary to some extent on how far along the home is in construction. If the home and the site grading are completed, then of course you are selling reality. If the home is partially completed, then you have an opportunity to sell construction. Sometimes you may want to sell certain features of a home by going into a similar one which is under construction nearby. If you choose to demonstrate features in a home that is already sold, be sure that it is not on a better homesite than the one you are trying to sell.

Usually by the time a home is under construction you can give a fairly accurate representation of the final grading just by looking at it.

If you are showing a site where neither the home nor the grading has been started yet, then you are facing the real challenge. Many salespeople make the mistake of avoiding this type of situation. Actually, there are wonderful selling opportunities in this scenario. There is a pioneering aspect to this situation which can create tremendous excitement and involvement. This excitement begins, once again, with personal enthusiasm. Be prepared before you get to any lot to tell what the features, advantages and possibilities of that homesite will be. Be able to tell why you like that site. You don't have to build castles in the sky. You only have to show enthusiasm, and tell why the homesite is special.

If it is a corner site with a tiny back yard, then it is great because most people think the back yard is more important before they buy, and then decide that the front yard is actually more important after they buy.

If the homesite backs up to a school, then it is great because during the times when buyers are home — in the evenings and on weekends — the school is "open space."

If the lot slopes up in the back, then it is great for privacy and landscaping. If it slopes down then it has a great view overlooking what's behind it.

If the homesite is on a pipestem driveway, then it is great because it has more privacy from the street, and because other people who buy homes on pipestems generally make good neighbors, or they wouldn't buy a pipestem site.

Whatever the liability of any particular homesite is, be sure you are prepared before you get there to tell why other people like that type of site.

When you go to a homesite, take 3 things with you:
1) The site plan.
2) An engineer's ruler.
3) A 100-ft. tape.

The trip to the homesites needs to be a rich and exciting experience for the customer.

If the home has not been started, assume that the customer will be confused and disoriented. Part of the gratification of this experience for the buyer is figuring out what's going on, and experiencing the thrill of "envisioning."

At the same time that you are selling the facts of how the homesite scenario will develop, you are also selling your own expertise. In this experience, the customer's appreciation of your expertise can have a particularly strong impact upon his buying decision.

Many of your competitors will not be going to as much trouble as you are in this phase of the sale. It is important that you work with your construction department in the field to develop your comfort level with the details of this aspect of selling.

There are 3 reasons this expertise is so important:
1) The information must be conveyed correctly.
2) Showing superior knowledge in the areas of construction and engineering can help you establish superior credibility over your competitors.
3) Because this is the most adventurous aspect of the sale, a special sort of bonding can develop between you and the buyer during this experience which cannot always develop in the sales office or model homes.

If you are showing a vacant, ungraded homesite, try to create emotional involvement by getting the customer physically involved. If you are measuring distances, have the customer participate by holding one end of the tape, and then have him move with you from point to point.

If you are explaining the final grading, you can get the customer involved with that as well. If you know that you will have to give a complicated explanation of the grade at the site, take a ball of string with you along with your other three items. At the site, use the engineer's ruler and the site plan to determine how much the grade will drop. Let the customer look over your shoulder and show him exactly what you are doing with the site plan. A site plan can create a considerable amount of fascination to a customer who has never used one before.

If you determine that the grade will ultimately drop 4 feet in 45 feet when the grade is finished, ask the customer to stoop down and hold one end of your string at his feet with one hand. Have him hold the starting end of your tape in the other hand. Then walk 45 feet away from him. Raise your end of the string 4 feet up your body and hold it there. Then explain to the customer that the grade will drop at approximately the same angle as the string. (You may be able to use the tape itself to perform the function of the string.)

Explaining drainage is also very important, especially on homesites where part of the yard slopes downward toward the home. Show the customer all the grading lines, crowns, swales and arrows necessary to convey to him how the water will be carried past his home and into the storm drains.

All of these techniques can be used at your sales office or trailer if you are in a situation where you cannot get to the homesites. You simply do them directly from your site plan.

Another way of conveying the approximate slope of a site is to triangulate it with your engineer's ruler on a piece of paper. Use the horizontal line as the distance, the vertical line as the drop, and the connecting line as the grade.

Train yourself to take a pace which is exactly 2 feet or exactly 3 feet. This will enable you to pace off distances when your tape is unavailable, or when only an approximate distance is necessary.

You do not want your engineering explanations to become tedious or overworked. You are using them to convey correct information, demonstrate expertise in order to raise the buyer's comfort level, and create customer involvement. As with model demonstration, you have one ultimate goal in showing homesites and keeping your *Strategy to Achieve Momentum* moving forward: to "get them to pick out a favorite homesite" — one which your customer acknowledges is better for him than any other.

Again as in model demonstration, when they have picked out their favorite, be sure to get them to tell *why* it is their favorite. If you get this far, you are coming down the home stretch toward the close. This is where we will pick up next week.

- - -

In this session, as in the last one, we have tried to build in enough slack time for discussion of particular issues which your salespeople may be facing. We have also tried to anticipate enough types of situations to provide principles which can be applied to most of them.

Again it is important to make sure the tone of the meeting stays focused upon providing productive solutions to challenges as a group. Whenever possible, try to apply specific principles which you have discussed — whether they came from this program, from you, or from the experiences and insights of people in your group.

Solving a problem is always a triumph. But when you can extract a principle from the solution which can be applied again in the future, you have accomplished something even greater. Your highest goal in any training program is not to teach people how to act, but to teach them how to think. If people know how to think, they can figure out how to act.

The next session is the last one. It will begin with an overview of how the Strategy to Achieve Momentum has been leading up to the close. Then it will pick up where this session left off — setting up the close during the site-showing stage — and will continue through the final closing process.

CLOSING

To the Manager

In this session you will be tying together everything you have covered in the five previous sessions.

Closing is more than a single event. It is a total process. This will be an important theme in your final session. The days of closing "lines" and "gimmicks" are winding down.

How the close "develops" is more important than how it "happens."

The trend of this program has been to start out the first week with a format which is more presentation than participation, and evolve into a format which is more balanced. In closing there are a wide variety of effective approaches, and your group should now discuss as many of them as possible. As with previous topics, your goal is to provide your team with a "menu" of options for different situations. There are three reasons to invite as many different approaches as time permits:

1) Closing (both the process and the technique) varies from one salesperson to the next depending on many factors in their personality.

2) The closing process evolves in a slightly different way in every transaction.

3) Salespeople need to be able to approach the close in different ways, depending on the personality of their customer.

In this session you will be covering 3 major topics:

1) How the closing process develops through the Strategy to Achieve Momentum.

2) How to create urgency.

3) How to bring the closing process to a final "close."

The Presentation

Everything we have been talking about for the past 5 weeks has been about closing. The reason is that closing is really a process, not just a single climactic event. Closing is a *series of decisions.* Closing becomes awkward and difficult when you think of it as an action which is separate from the rest of the selling process. If you think of closing as a process, then the final "closing moment" can often be the easiest part of the sale.

In its most ideal form, selling is *raising the customer's comfort level until the sale becomes inevitable.* "Raising the customer's comfort level" is one of the goals of the *Strategy to Achieve Momentum.* This whole strategy is a way to put the selling process on a closing track from the minute the customer walks in the door, and then keep it there until you have gone as far as you can go with each transaction. It is a non-threatening approach, so the customer's comfort level can continue to rise as the process progresses.

We are still facing the reality that the strategy may "fail" at least 90% of the time. But a *Strategy to Achieve Momentum* will allow you to maximize every opportunity you have, no matter how great or small. The strategy we have been discussing is aggressive without being hard sell. You "continue through the buying process until the customer causes you do stop," but you don't back the customer into a corner. You allow them to have the "control" they want, while you have the control you need. You resolve this dilemma by focusing on need-fulfillment. Need-fulfillment involves 2 things:

1) Learning what needs they have.
2) Showing them what needs they should have which your product fulfills.

For the past 5 weeks we have been discussing stages 1 through 6 of the *Strategy to Achieve Momentum.* Today we will complete the last 2 stages.

We finished up last week talking about getting the customer to pick out a favorite homesite, and then telling us why it is their favorite. That brings us up to the point of asking for the order:

• How do we make it happen?
• How do we make it comfortable?
• What happens if we fail?

Some salespeople find "asking for the order" more comfortable if they have already explained the buying procedure once before they get to that final moment. There are two especially good times to do this:

1) As you are giving them financing information.

2) As you are showing homesites.

Either way, they should have gotten at least some basic financing information by the time you explain your buying procedure for the first time.

Let's say you've given the customer at least the amount of the down payment and the income needed to qualify before you showed the homesites. Now, while you are at the site, or walking back from it, you can say to the customer:

"When we were talking earlier about financing, I mentioned that the typical down payment is about $14,000. Actually what people do when they buy here [talking about 'what other people do' can be less threatening than saying, 'if you buy here'] is they put $3000 down when they sign a contract, and then the rest is due at settlement."

- - -

If standard procedure at your company is to take "deposits" or "lot holds" a few days before doing a contract, then the salesperson can take the explanation a step further:

"Sometimes folks will say, 'We're pretty sure we want to buy that one, but we just have a couple more things we want to think about. Is there any way you can take the home off the market for us?' And we do have a policy for that where we just take a refundable check for $100."

Whatever your procedure for closing is, discuss this strategy of "presenting the buying procedure once in advance" in terms of that procedure. If your salespeople have the leeway to use whatever procedure will work for a particular customer, then you can discuss several different approaches.

- - -

The principle here is that if you go through the procedure once before the final moment arrives, then the customer will be expecting it, and will be familiar with it when it does arrive. If it is familiar, then it will be more comfortable — there will be no shock factor.

This type of approach is not for everyone. Some people who do use it do it only when they're sitting down doing financing. This technique should not be considered a "trial close," although observing the customer's response to this information can be useful. But its purpose is only designed to increase the customer's comfort level with the buying process.

Trial closing can be sort of a strange topic, because it means different things to different people. The purpose of a "trial close" should be to do a "climate check" on your momentum and to determine if you have a green light, a yellow light or a red light.

Some salespeople don't even like to use the word "trial close." They would rather simply say that there are certain questions throughout the selling process which help them to test their customer's "buying temperature," as they learn the customers's circumstances, qualifications and needs. Examples of these questions would include:

1) Qualifying questions.
    a) "Do you have a particular time frame for moving?"
    b) "Will you be selling the place where you live now?"
    c) "Is this the price range you were hoping to stay in?"

2) Questions designed to elicit reactions to your home (presumably favorable ones).
    a) "How do you like this master bedroom?"
    b) "How does this kitchen compare with where you're living now?"
    c) "How do these wooded homesites compare with other sites you've seen in this price range?"

3) Questions designed to elicit opinions or preferences.
    a) "Would you rather have a walkout or an inground basement?"
    b) "Which elevation do you like better, the one with the porch or the one without?"
    c) "Which room is more important to you, the living room or the family room?"

These types of questions can be considered "preliminary" closing questions because they tell you if you still have a green light. Yet they are not threatening. They are service-oriented — not selfish. They don't sound like you're trying to jump the gun. They don't sound like you're asking, "Look, do I have a chance of selling you a home today or not?"

A "trial close" should be a climate check, not a premature close.

A "premature close" is "attempting to close before you have prepared the customer to be closed." It is trying to close before you have given the customer the information that you would require before you would buy. "Premature closes" come across as selfish and lazy, and they can be far more threatening than motivating. They can produce several problems in your overall selling strategy:

1) They can cause the customer to lose confidence in you as a counselor, a caring person, or a professional salesperson.

2) They can cause the buyer to become defensive.

3) They can bring your selling momentum to an abrupt halt.

It's like the kind of flower that closes up at night, and then opens in the morning sunlight. You may have gotten the customer to the point where you (the sunlight) have caused the buyer (the flower) to open up. An unexpected premature close can suddenly be like a total eclipse in the middle of the day which causes the flower to immediately close back up again.

Several examples of premature closes are:

1) Asking the customer what day of the month they would like to settle before they have told you they intended to buy.

2) Asking the customer what color carpeting they want, and then starting to write out the contract as though the carpeting decision implied that the buyer was ready to buy.

3) Asking the customer within two minutes of meeting them, "If I could give you everything you're looking for in a new home, would you buy today?"

Having said all of this about premature closes, the fact is that some people are very good at it. They have honed their techniques and have repeated them so many times that they can use them very comfortably. Just like some salespeople are very successful with a hard sell approach. If you are successful with hard sell, don't stop.

Hard selling is a gift, and if you have it then make the most of it.

But the truth is that most people in new home sales today cannot succeed at hard sell.

Hard sell typically works better on small-ticket items. Hard sell works on many customers in this situation because they will buy the inexpensive item in order to end the anxiety of the confrontation. Giving in and getting it over with is easier for many customers than saying "no." It is harder for this approach to work in new home sales because:

* Homes are too expensive.
* There is too much time for buyer's remorse to kick in after the contract is signed.

Now you might be thinking at this point, "But you can't always be non-threatening. I wish it were that easy, but in real life it's not, unless you're just an order-taker." And you're absolutely right. A non-threatening demeanor is how you get to the close, but not necessarily how you execute it.

Ideally the selling process should lead to a non-threatening close. Yet there are times when the close must be threatening in order to generate a significant response. You obviously cannot rely on the customer to initiate the close, so what should you do? And when should you do it?

Let's say you have gone through all the stages of the selling process up to the close, but you know the close will be threatening. Now you're faced with the question, "Do I close even though it may be threatening and could blow everything, or do I wait for a better time?"

The answer is, "You should close."

Once you have gone through all the stages of your *Strategy to Achieve Momentum*, you should *always* close, even if the close must be threatening. That is the only way you will have any chance to resolve the issue.

One of the reasons you've worked so hard developing a counselor relationship, establishing rapport and gaining credibility is so that when the time comes when you have to be threatening, it is acceptable because you are a professional salesperson.

Even when you cannot close the customer successfully, you have not "blown everything." You have simply achieved the best possible resolution for that day.

Although you may have very little chance of succeeding with your close, one of 2 things will happen:
1) You may be pleasantly surprised, or
2) You will at least know what to do next.

Remember, the customer really does expect us to close. They've known all along what we do for a living. The important thing is that we close as a service, and not as an act of aggression. You have performed a series of other services leading up to this point. You are their "assistant buyer," helping them to buy their new home.

Since we've been saying that a variety of closing approaches really do work, let's stop for a minute and talk about closing techniques. Then we'll come back to "Creating Urgency," and drawing the close to an end.

But for right now, I would like to throw out a three-part question and see what your thoughts are:
1) On a scale of 1 to 10, how do you rank yourself as a closer?
2) Why do you prefer your method of closing?
3) What kind of "trial closes" — or "preliminary closes" — if any, do you use in order to lead you toward your final close?

- - -

This discussion could go all over the board, and it's good if it does. Don't worry about disagreements. The more disagreements there are on this topic, the more exposure your salespeople will get to new techniques.

You may also find differences in interpretation of particular terms such as "assumptive close" or "premature close." That's okay, too, but it will help if you get people to define their terms when you think it's beginning to get fuzzy. One thing you will have to do as discussion leader is to wind up with a consensus of how you want to define your terms, so you will not have people thinking they're disagreeing when they're really not.

Once you have finished this discussion you are ready to move into the nuts and bolts of the final close. The next section is one you may want to modify, or leave out altogether, depending upon your local market conditions at the time you administer this program.

- - -

The concept of creating urgency has changed over the last few years. Through the 1970's and 1980's everyone accepted the principle that "if you don't buy it today, it will cost you more tomorrow." With this principle now playing a much smaller role in the marketplace, we have to search for other ways to create urgency.

Creating urgency can sometimes become a crutch. By that I mean we can rely on it too much, and wind up believing we can't sell without it.

Sometimes you are in a marketplace, or situation, where it's easy to create urgency because of your circumstances. We all know examples of those situations:

1) "This is the last one like this."
2) "The price of the next one will be higher."
3) "This is the only one in your time frame."
4) "For a limited time only, we can guarantee your interest rate."

In real life we are not usually lucky enough to have this type of situation.

"Creating urgency" is sort of an odd phrase, because it implies that urgency is something which is contrived. Then when we are unable to contrive it, we think to ourselves, "I can't make any sales because I can't create any urgency."

We need to think for a few minutes about what it's like for people who sell other kinds of products. They might think we've had it easy all these years because we always had two things going for us which most salespeople don't have:

1) Our product almost always goes up in value.
2) Every piece of real estate is unique.

People selling clothing off a rack, or new cars off a lot — how do they create urgency when the item is not unique and does not appeciate in value?

Basically, they have a strategy for getting you involved with their product, and getting you to want their product enough that you don't want to be without it any longer. The customer reaches the decision that their life will be better with the item than without it, and there's simply no reason for them to postpone improving their lives.

In car sales the most crucial part of the involvement strategy is the test drive. In clothing it's trying on the item. This is why in new home sales the model demonstration and trip to the homesites can be such valuable opportunities.

Urgency does not usually grow out of a clever gimmick. It grows out of a momentum-oriented selling process which focuses on creating customer involvement and fulfilling the customer's needs.

Sometimes we try to contrive an "urgency strategy" to help us sell. When we're lucky enough to have the tools available to create such a strategy, that's great. If we're down to the last of our wooded lots, and those are the only wooded lots in our market, then by all means, we should create an urgency strategy out of that.

But we still must keep our focus on the bigger picture. The fact is that regardless of your urgency strategy, customers will not buy your home unless:

1) They believe your home is better for them than where they live now.

2) They believe that your home is better for them than any other alternative out there.

3) They really, really want your home.

So what does it take to create urgency?

There are six elements of urgency in new home sales which you need to stay focused on throughout your selling strategy.

1) The customer must be excited about the home. This is the *emotional* element.

2) They must believe that you are the best available alternative in the market (and better than where they live now). This is the *rational* element.

3) They must believe that there is one home in your selection which is best for them.

4) If they believe that one is the best, then it is logical to assume that the next customer who walks in the door will feel the same way. There is a good chance their favorite home will be the next one to sell. Now we are adding the *fear of loss* element.

This approach to creating fear of loss is purely reasonable. It does not sound like you're trying to bully them. Most customers don't like to hear things like, "If you don't buy it someone else will," or "I have someone else who's chomping at the bit for that home." Sometimes this approach may be appropriate, but most of the time it will be perceived as antagonistic, manipulative and confrontational. Yet sometimes the point still needs to be made. The alternative approach we're talking about here is softer and sounds more credible.

In addition to being one of the 6 elements of urgency, fear of loss enters into our *Strategy to Achieve Momentum* as Stage 7: *Create* fear of loss. This is the one stage in the strategy which may be optional. If you don't need to "create" fear of loss in order to close, then don't. You could run the risk of overkill. Sometimes buyers pick out their favorite lot and then are ready to buy. They may sense a fear of loss all by themselves, or they may be motivated to buy just to get it over with. If you don't sense that you need to create fear of loss in order to close, then skip that stage and ask directly for the order. You will have to make this judgment call on the spot.

5) They believe they are in the right place at the right time.

It will help you to create urgency if customers believe that your particular selling situation is offering them some sort of unique opportunity — that this is "their lucky day." While this is not always possible, it is still something to think about. As you are approaching your final close, is there anything about your customer's situation that allows you to say, "You are really fortunate to be here today"?

Perhaps the home they are interested in will soon pass beyond the point where certain options can be ordered. Maybe the home next door just sold to someone who could be the perfect neighbor for your current customer. Perhaps your customer service department has just implemented a beneficial new policy. Maybe they are the first customers to have a chance to see a particular home since it was drywalled, or since the final grading was completed.

None of these examples are really anything so special. They're just small benefits which may help the customer to think of today as offering an opportunity to them. The point is: Is there anything about your situation that can possibly begin to make the customer believe, "Maybe this was meant to be."

The belief that something "was meant to be" can be a very powerful motivator. You want to plant these seeds without necessarily using those exact words.

6) They realize there is no reason to postpone improving their lives.

Customers don't need a cataclysmic event to force them to buy. Most buyers just get to the point where they would rather buy than not buy. That is where your goal ultimately lies in creating urgency — getting them to the point where they realize that as soon as they make a commitment to buy your home, their quality of life will start down a better road than the one they're now traveling.

This is a very obvious point in selling, but it's still one that is easy to lose sight of as we get bogged down in the small stuff, and begin to lose sight of the forest because there are too many trees in the way.

- - -

At this point it could be helpful to bring these principles to life with a discussion. To see how these principles can apply to real situations, ask the following question, and then see which of the above six categories the answers fall into, or if new categories need to be created.

- - -

Think of all the sales you've made in the past month, and see if you can remember any times when there was urgency, whether you created it or not. What were some of the factors that created urgency for your buyers?

- - -

There should be a fairly broad range of answers to this question. Together these answers can come together to help the group gain insight into the real nature of urgency. If anyone says they made sales without urgency, that can also a valuable message — that creating urgency isn't everything in closing.

Once this discussion is concluded, you are ready to move on into a discussion of specific closing techniques. This also will be largely a discussion-oriented topic. Closing is real life, not theories and gimmicks. The more real-life success stories you can bring into a discussion on closing, the more dynamic your session will be.

- - -

I want to spend the rest of our last meeting brainstorming 2 final issues:
1) How does the actual "closing moment" work?
2) What do you do when your close "fails"?

I want to ask several questions concerning how the closing moment works. Please use this chance to bring up any questions you have about closing that you think we can brainstorm as a group.

As we have done before, the goal here is to create a menu of as many possibilities for effective closing techniques as we can. If you hear one that you've never tried but you might want to experiment with, write it down and try it the next time you feel the opportunity is right. Then you can let the rest of us know how it worked for you.

1) Do you have a particular closing technique, question, or pattern that you use frequently, or do you vary it every time?

It is important to have at least one closing question (or statement) that you know you will feel comfortable using when you arrive at the closing moment and the customer is not taking any initiative on their end. You know you have gotten through the sale, and you know the customer is expecting you to close. Now you just need to get the words out. Here is a sample of the types of questions that many salespeople ask in this type of situation. Each example is in the form of a question, but most of them can be converted into a statement format.

* "When someone decides to buy a home here, what they do is...[Explain your contract and earnest money process]...Would you like to go ahead and do that?"

* "Would you like me to take it off the market for you?"
* "Would you like to see how this looks on paper?" ("Would you like to start going over some of the forms?") ("Would you like to go ahead and start the paperwork?")
* "Are you ready to go ahead with the next step?"
* "Would you like to have it?" ("Does this look like the one for you?") ("Would you like this one?") ("Would you like to put your name on it?")
* "Do you feel you want to discuss it a little further, or would you like to move forward?"
* "Are there any other issues you need to resolve in order to make a decision you'll feel good about?"

2) Do you have a particular place where you like to be when you ask for the order — the lot, the model home, the sales office?

3) Do you close for a contract or a lot hold?

- - -

In answering the third question, some salespeople may answer, "I do both. It depends on the situation." In this case, the followup question would be, "How do you decide?"

This is a hotly-debated strategic issue. Some salespeople (and companies) are adamantly opposed to lot holds on four grounds:
1) It puts the customer in the position of power. The builder is bound to the customer, but the customer is not bound to the builder.
2) It diminishes the urgency (or fear of loss) factor, instead of increasing it.
3) It allows the customer who is ready to buy an opportunity to have second thoughts and get cold feet.
4) It allows the customer to tie up homes all over town while they continue to shop for the best deal.

The opposing school of thought supports the use of lot holds for six basic reasons:
1) Although some of your deposits will kick out, you will ultimately gain more sales than you lose because you have a strategy to deal with those buyers who are more than 60% certain, but less than 100%. The lot hold system will ultimately net more sales because it

will allow those buyers who are 60% sure to have the opportunity to grow to 100%.

2) It allows the customer to become more comfortable with you and with the buying situation by showing them that you are not trying to "hustle" them or "pressure" them into a purchase.

3) You can show a greater amount of immediate activity of your sales board, thereby creating more momentum.

4) You will have fewer cancellations after contract because most of the "buyer's remorse market" will cancel during the lot hold period.

5) The lot hold strategy seeks to dominate the "almost" buyer's consciousness after they walk out of your sales office, so that you have more control over this customer than you would have if they walked out empty-handed. You are at least assured of one more significant contact with them.

6) You can schedule contracts more conveniently. You don't spend an entire weekend afternoon missing traffic in order work on a contract with a customer who then bails out at the last minute.

The "lot hold" strategy has its greatest value when it is supported by two assumptions:

1) Getting the contract must always be the first priority. Taking a lot hold is a back-up position.

2) You are offering the lot hold as a service to those customers who are almost certain they want to buy, but just need a few more days to put their mind at rest. Or you might offer to take a lot hold because you want to do the contract later on when it's quieter. In both of these situations you are still maintaining your dignity and protecting your position of strength.

You never want to get the customer to give you a lot hold just because "they have nothing to lose." These are the lot holds which, in the long run, do more harm than good.

Once you complete your discussion of closing for contacts vs. lot holds, another possible question for your group could be:

- - -

4) Can you remember any closes that you were especially proud of — any sales that you believe you made because your close was special?

- - -

We could have taken a flashier approach to this final seminar on closing: something more along the lines of "25 Closes That Are Guaranteed to Double Your Sales!" But since this training program will be part of your long-term relationship with your salespeople, our approach is designed to protect your credibility as their manager. Most salespeople today just don't buy the "magic close" approaches that seem to drop out of the sky. They want to know what is really working today for salespeople like them. It is important that your salespeople not walk out of this final session feeling cynical. They need to feel that the issue of closing has been covered realistically, open-mindedly, intelligently and productively. The approach we are using here is the one which has generated the best feedback in the training sessions which we have conducted for a variety of builders.

The next topic is how to recover when the attempt to close fails to produce a sale. This topic has something of a "Mission: Impossible" aspect to it, so in this discussion your group may be more likely to look to you for solutions. We have structured this portion of the session to include some discussion, but we have also suggested techniques which have been used successfully by other salespeople throughout the country.

- - -

Now let's say you've gotten to the point where you've successfully gotten through the first seven stages of the *Strategy to Achieve Momentum.* You've done your best to confirm the customer's decision that there is, in fact, a number one choice. Since that is the customer's first choice, it's logical to assume that it will be the next one to sell.

You've done all you can, and you have not yet hit a red light, so you know you're ready to ask the closing question. Whatever your closing question is, you go ahead and ask it. Let's suppose your question is, "Would you like to have that home?"

Their answer is, "It's a nice home. We just weren't expecting to buy a home today. We need to go home and talk about it for awhile."

This sort of thing happens often enough that you need a strategy for dealing with it. Does anyone have a way that you would normally handle this type of situation?

- - -

You can see which way this discussion goes, and then as the opportunity arises you can offer several suggestions for them to respond to. We will offer these suggestions below and then you can weave them into your discussion as you feel it is appropriate.

- - -

When the customer rejects your attempt to close them, you have to make the judgment call at that moment whether your next goal is to:
1) Continue to try to sell them a home that day. (Keep closing.)
or
2) Simply try to find out what's really going on with them. (Switch gears from closing to gathering more information.)

Your goal in the latter case is no longer primarily to sell to them, but to regain your footing. You close again only if there is an obvious opening.

Let's take a closer look at this second scenario first, and then work our way back to the first one.

If your main goal after the rejection is to gain feedback, there are several approaches you could take.

1) Ask them point blank why they didn't buy.
"I know there are a lot of things about the home that you love. [You might then want to list the items from their comments of why they chose that particular model and lot.] Is there anything you don't like?"

This is an approach that you want to use cautiously, because you don't want to start off down a negative road. It's a good one to use if you don't know exactly why you're losing steam, and feel that if you can't resolve this issue you might never see the customer again.

2) Reinforce the fact that buying will be the positive step which can lead them to a better life.

"We talked before about how great it will be when you finally do get a new place, and it seems from what you said that life really will be a lot better for you here. If you have the power to take the step that will improve your life, what is it that's holding you back?"

Whether you can use an approach like this depends on the type of relationship you have with your customer. If it is a frank and open one, then this approach might get them to face their situation head on and tell you where they really stand. If your relationship with them has developed along more cautious lines, then this approach could seem offensive.

3) Respond as though you had really expected them to buy, because people buy from you all the time.

"Most people who get as far as you have gotten do wind up buying here, and I just want to make sure I haven't left any stones unturned. Do you mind if I ask you a few questions?"

This approach may seem a little more casual than the last two. It is intended to position you as confident and successful. It also makes the statement that other people reach the buying point by this stage, and live to tell about it.

If you would feel more comfortable offering something of an apology for your forwardness, then that approach might be okay, as long as you don't move yourself into a position of weakness in the process. The more comfortable this moment is for you, the easier it will be for you to make it comfortable for your customer. Lieutenant Columbo used the "apologetic" approach very successfully when he questioned his suspects.

If you think there are times when this approach might work for you, you could say, "I hope you don't mind my asking you these things, but I'd really love to sell you a home. For one thing it's my job, but also I've really enjoyed working with you, and I'd love to have you as a permanent customer and a member of the neighborhood."

This approach takes the "cat-and-mouse" element out of your questioning, but does it in a kind, credible and likeable way.

4) Another approach would be to ask them directly how close they are to buying. That's what you really want to know anyway, and you're certainly not out of line asking the question that they know it's your job to ask.

"On a scale of one to ten, with ten meaning you'd buy the home, how much do you like it?

If the customer's response is below "5", then your question becomes, "What is it that's sitting between you and 5? Is it anything I can can help you address, or is it something I haven't covered yet?"

Again your motive at this point is not necessarily to sell them a home today, but to find out what you have to do to sell them a home at all, or even if it will ever be within your power.

If the answer is 5 or higher, then you can begin thinking about a way to get some sort of commitment from them today. This gets us back to the first approach which we mentioned earlier for when a customer rejects your attempt to close: "Continue to try to sell them a home today."

If the customer gives you an answer of 5 or higher, then you need to ask yourself whether you want to take the risk of that customer walking away empty-handed and turning into less than a 5. For this type of situation, would a refundable deposit or a full contract with a kickout clause help you to gain more sales than you lose over the long haul?

5) Sometimes the customer seems to feel that there is really no reason for them to buy today, even though they like what you are selling better than anything else they've seen, and they've picked out a favorite model and lot. You are looking for a way to create fear of loss without making them feel as though you're trying to bully them.

Once they have convinced you that they are not going to buy your home today, you could say to them: "I can certainly understand not wanting to move too fast. You don't want to make a decision you'll regret. While you're here, as long as you've picked out your favorite, which one is your second choice?"

They may go ahead and pick out their second favorite, or they may seem puzzled by the question. In either event you could follow up by saying, " Most people I've talked to recently seem to feel the same way you do about the one that's your favorite, and we sell an average of about one home every ten days here. What I can do is if your first choice sells before you get back, I can give you a call and see if you want to go for the other one."

Like some of the other approaches we've discussed, there are times when this one will be too risky. For some of your customers you may feel that this approach is too much "all-or-nothing." But for others you might be looking for some way of making them stop and think about the fact that if they wait, there really is a good chance their favorite will be gone. It happens all the time, and there's nothing wrong with telling them that.

6) In your role as counselor, you can tell them anecdotes of other customers who waited and were heartbroken, losing their favorite home to someone who came in after them, but who was more "decisive" or "impulsive."

With this type of approach you are not dealing with threats, only with probabilities.

As we said before, when the customer rejects your attempt to close, it does not mean that you failed, or that you "lost a sale." You simply brought it to the best resolution you could, and you left no stones unturned.

If you are able to execute a strategy which will take you as far with every customer as they can possibly go, and the transaction only stops when the customer says they can't go any farther, then you have truly maximized every opportunity, and you will get more than your share of the market that you are targeting.

- - -

By this time in your presentation there has probably been enough group discussion that you don't have much time remaining in this final session. You can now ask if there are any other points about closing which anyone would like to discuss.

This completes our sample training program. Once the group has become comfortable with this type of interaction format, you can then continue your training meetings on a regular basis to cover new topics (or review old ones) as the need arises.

Recommended Reading For Professional Growth And Development

101 Ways to Reward Employees. Bob Nelson, Workman Publishing Company, Inc.

A Motivational Approach to Selling. James F. Evered. American Management.

Becoming A Manager. Linda A. Hill. Harvard Business School Press, Boston, Massachusetts.

Coaching For Improved Work Performance. Ferdinand F. Fournies. Liberty Hill Press.

Developing High-Performance People. Mink/Owen/Mink. Addison-Wesley Publishing Company, Inc.

First Things First. Stephen R. Covey/A. Roger Merrill/Rebecca R. Merrill. Simon & Schuster.

Get Ready To Manage (video). Dave Stone & Tom Richey.

Get The Best. How To Recruit The People You Want. Catherine Fyock. Business One Irwin.

Hiring Winners. Richard J. Pinsker. ISBN 0-8144-5051-2.

How to Master the Art of Selling. Tom Hopkins.

How To Win Friends & Influence People. Dale Carnegie. Simon & Schuster.

How To Read A Person Like A Book. Gerald Nierenberg and Henry A. Calaro.

How To Talk So People Listen. Sonya Hamlin. Harper & Row.

How To Run a Successful Meeting In Half the Time. Milo O. Frank. Simon and Schuster.

I Hear You. Eastwood Atwater. Walker and Company.

Iacocca, An Autobiography. Lee Iacocca.

If It Ain't Broke, Break It. Robert J. Kreigel. ISBN 0-446-51539-6.

In Search Of Excellence. Thomas J. Peters and Robert H. Waterman, Jr.

It Doesn't Take A Hero. Norman Schwarzkopf.

Leadership In Action. Helmut Maucher. McGraw-Hill, Inc.

Leadership Secrets of Attila The Hun. Wess Roberts. ISBN 0-446-51516-7.

Leadership When the Heat's On. Danny Cox/John Hoover. McGraw-Hill, Inc.

Management by Objectives and Results. George I. Morrisey, Addison-Westley Publishing Company.

Management. Tasks. Responsibilities. Practices. Peter F. Drucker. Harper & Row.

Managerial Communication. Paul R. Timm. Prentice-Hall.

Managing Assertively. Madelyn Burley-Allen. John Wiley & Sons, Inc.

Managing By Influence. Kenneth Schatz and Linda Schatz. Windy Enterprises.

Managing Effectively. Joseph & Susan Berk. Sterling Publishing Co., Inc.

Managing the Problem Employee. Edward Roseman. American Management Associations.

Managing With Integrity. Charles E. Watson. Praeger.

Marketing New Homes. Charles R. Clark and David F. Parker. NAHB. Washington, DC.

Megatrends. John Naisbitt. Warner Books.

Motivation In The Real World. Saul W. Gellerman. A. Dutton Book.

New Home Sales. David Stone. The Stone Institute. Los Gatos, CA.

Nido Qubein's Professional Selling Techniques. Nido Qubein, Rockville Center, NY. Farnsworth.

No Bull Sales Management. Trishler. Business & Finance Publications.

Over The Top. Zig Ziglar.

Peak Performers. Charles Garfield. William Morrow and Company, Inc.

Sam Walton—Made In America. Sam Walton with John Huey.

Secrets Of The Superstars; Excellence in Selling New Homes. Bonnie C. Alfriend, 2984 Cormorant Rd., Pebble Beach, CA 93953.

See You At The Top. Zig Ziglar.

Seeds of Greatness. F. Denis Waitley, Ph.D., Old Tappan, NJF: Fleming H. Revell.

Selling In the 90's ... The Official Handbook For New Home Salespeople. Bob Schultz, Boca Raton, FL.

Selling Is Simple—Not Easy, But Simple. Fred Herman. New York Vantage Press, 1970.

Selling Personality: Persuasion Strategy. Walter Gorman. Random House.

Seven Habits of Highly Effective People. Stephen Covey.

Straight Talk For Monday Morning. Allan Cox. John Wiley & Sons, Inc.

Success In New Home Sales. Richard Tiller. Tiller Marketing Services, Herndon, VA.

Swim With The Sharks Without Being Eaten Alive. Harvey MacKay. William Marrow and Company.

The Managerial Woman. Margaret Hennig/Anne Jardim. Pocket Books.

The 5 Minute Professional (audio cassette tapes). Bob Schultz. New Home Specialist, Boca Raton, FL.

The Domino Effect. Donald J. Vlcek, Jr. Business One Irwin.

The Effective Executive. Peter F. Drucker. Harper & Row, Publishers.

The Official New Home Sales Development System (video). Bob Schultz.

The Organized Executive. Stephanie Winston, WW. Norton & Company, New York, NY.

The Practice of Management. Peter F. Drucker. Harper & Row Publishers, Inc.

The Practice of Management. Peter F. Drucker. Harper & Row Publishers, Inc.

The Secrets of Power Negotiating. Roger Damson. Nightingale Connate Corporation.

The Selling Power of a Woman. Dotty Walters. Prentice-Hall.

The Seven Habits of Highly Effective People. Stephen R. Covey. Simon & Schuster.

The Time Trap. Alec Mackenzie. American Management Association.

The Unnatural Act of Management. Everett T. Suters. ISBN 0-88730-551-2.

The Working Leader. Leonard R. Sayles. The Free Press.

They Shoot Managers Don't They? Terry L. Paulson. Ten Speed Press.

Think And Grow Rich. Napoleon Hill.

Tough Times Never Last, but Tough People Do. Robert H. Schuller, Nashville: Thomas Nelson.

Who Stole The Professionals. Richard Flint. Pendelton Lane Publishing.

Winning Images. Robert Shook. Macmillan.

Books on new home sales and management
by Bonnie Alfriend and Richard Tiller

Qty	Title	Price	Total
____	**NEW HOME SALES MANAGEMENT:** *How To Build and Lead a Winning Team* by Bonnie Alfriend & Richard Tiller	$29.95	_____
____	**SECRETS OF THE SUPERSTARS:** *Excellence in Selling New Homes* by Bonnie Alfriend	$24.95	_____

"In SECRETS OF THE SUPERSTARS, Bonnie Alfriend has distilled the quintessential information that today's new home salesperson must know to be successful. This book should be required reading for sales associates, sales managers, marketing directors, builders, marketing support personnel, plus lenders, insurers and title officers. In short, anyone and everyone involved in the building industry. Hats off to an insightful chronicle of our nation's most important sales discipline! The writing style is creative, witty, and above all, pertinent." — Tom Richey, Richey Resources Co.

Qty	Title	Price	Total
____	**SUCCESS IN NEW HOME SALES:** *Developing the Right Mentality and Techniques* by Richard Tiller	$19.95	_____

Total of Items Ordered _____

California residents please add 7.25% _____

Shipping and Handling — $3.50 for the first item, $1.75 for each additional item _____

TOTAL AMOUNT DUE _____

Make Check Payable to:
Alfriend and Associates, Inc.
2984 Cormorant Road
Pebble Beach, CA 93953

Charge to: ☐ VISA ☐ MasterCard #_____ Exp. _____

Signature _____ Date _____

You can also place your order by phone (1-800-710-8827) or Fax (408-648-1773).